GLOBAL SOCIAL
PROBLEMS

D1464724

GLOBAL SOCIAL PROBLEMS

EDITED BY VIC GEORGE
AND ROBERT M. PAGE

Polity

First published in 2004 by Polity Press Ltd.

Polity Press
65 Bridge Street
Combridge CB2 1UR, UK

Polity Press
350 Main Street
Malden, MA 02148, USA

ISBN: 0-7456 2951-2
ISBN: 0-7456 2952-0 (pb)

A catalogue record for this book is available from the British Library and has been applied for from the Library of Congress.

Typeset in 10.5 on 12 pt Sabon
by SNP Best-set Typesetter Ltd., Hong Kong
Printed and bound in Great Britain by MPG Books Bodmin Cornwall

For further information on Polity, visit our website: www.polity.co.uk

Contents

Acknowledgements

Our thanks to all our contributors and to Louise Knight, Andrea Drugan and Caroline Richmond for all their hard work in connection with this volume.

Thanks are due to the publisher Taylor and Francis for permission to include material in the first section chapter 6, which first appeared as part of an article by Kam Yi-Mak and Larry Harrison on 'Globalisation, cultural change and the modern drug epidemics: the case of Hong Kong', in the journal *Health, Risk and Society*, 3 (2001), 39–57. Details of this international journal, which is concerned with the social processes influencing the taking, communicating, assessing and managing of health risks, can be found on the publisher's website, <http://www.tandf.co.uk>. Thanks are also due to Kam Yi-Mak, who commented on an earlier version of this chapter.

Vic George and Robert M. Page

Contributors

Kathy Attawell is a freelance health and development consultant who has worked in the field of HIV/AIDS since 1987. She has undertaken assignments for clients that include the UK Department for International Development, European Commission, WHO, UNAIDS and USAID.

Stephen Castles is Professor of Migration and Refugees Studies, and Director of the Refugee Studies Centre at the University of Oxford. He has carried out research on migration, ethnic relations and citizenship in Europe, Australia and Asia, and is the author of many books and articles on these topics.

Andrew Dobson is Professor of Politics at the Open University, UK. He works in the field of environmental political theory, and among his publications in this area are *Green Political Thought* (3rd edition) (Routledge, 2000), *Justice and the Environment* (Oxford University Press, 1998), and *Citizenship and the Environment* (Oxford University Press, 2003). He has also edited *The Green Reader* (André Deutsch, 1997), *The Politics of Nature* (with Paul Lucardie) (Routledge, 1993), and the forthcoming *Political Theory and the Ecological Challenge* (with Robyn Eckersley) (Cambridge University Press, 2005).

Mark Findlay is a Professor in the Faculty of Law at the University of Sydney, and Deputy Director of the Institute of Criminology at that University. He also holds a research chair at the Nottingham Law School. Professor Findlay's current research interests relate to international criminal justice, and he has recently published *The Globalisation of Crime* (Cambridge University Press, 1999).

Vic George is Emeritus Professor of Social Policy at the University of Kent, UK. He has written extensively on various issues of social policy, particularly poverty and inequality, at both the national and the international level. He has adopted a political economy approach in his work – one that stresses economic, political and cultural forces. His latest book, co-authored with Professor Paul Wilding, is *Globalization and Human Welfare* (Palgrave, 2002).

Norman Ginsburg has been Professor of Social Policy at London Metropolitan University since 1996. He has published extensively in the social policy field, including *Divisions of Welfare: A Critical Introduction to Comparative Social Policy* (Sage, 1992) and recent articles on globalization and social policy, British housing policy in the twentieth century, urban regeneration policy, and a framework for critically comparing welfare states.

Claudia Hasanbegovic was born in Argentina, where she practised law and was an active advocate for women and human rights. She has recently submitted her PhD in social policy at the University of Kent. She is the author of *Violencia marital en Cuba*.

Larry Harrison was, until his retirement in 2001, Reader in Addiction Studies at the University of Hull. He is currently an Honorary Research Fellow at the University of Kent at Canterbury, where he is conducting research into social support and the risk of substance dependence. Co-editor of *Risk, Health and Welfare: Policies, Strategies and Practice* (with Alaszewski and Manthorpe, Open University Press, 1998), his recent research papers have been published in *Addiction and Substance Use and Misuse*.

Sean Loughna is a Research Officer at the Refugee Studies Centre at the University of Oxford and is Content Coordinator of Forced Migration Online. Much of his published work has focused on Latin America and civil society.

Robert Page is Reader in Democratic Socialism and Social Policy at the University of Birmingham. He has published on a wide range of topics in the field of social policy. His publications include *Stigma* (Routledge & Kegan Paul, 1984), *Altruism and the British Welfare State* (Ashgate, 1996), *Modern Thinkers on Welfare* (edited with Vic George, Prentice-Hall, 1995), *British Social Welfare in the Twentieth Century* (edited with Richard Silburn, Palgrave, 1999) and

Understanding Social Problems (edited with Margaret May and Edward Brunsdon, Blackwell, 2001).

Jan Pahl is Professor Emeritus of Social Policy at the University of Kent. Among her research interests are domestic violence, the control of money within the family, health and social care, and ethics in research. She has published widely in all these fields: her books include *Private Violence and Public Policy* (Routledge, 1985) and *Money and Marriage* (Macmillan, 1989).

Mei-Kuei Yu is Vice-Secretary General in the Taiwan Association of Social Workers, specializing in issues concerned with domestic violence and service delivery systems. She was formerly employed at Taipei City government and was a social worker there. In 2003 she was awarded a PhD in social work at the University of Kent, UK.

Introduction

This book focuses on two major themes: the influence of globalization on a series of global social problems, and the policy response at the global level.

It is impossible to measure the effects of globalization on any of the social problems covered in the book for several reasons: there is no agreement on the meaning of globalization; the available data are neither adequate nor reliable; and globalization is only one of several possible influences on the various social problems addressed. All that can be attempted is to indicate the various ways in which globalization influences the depth and spread of a particular social problem.

The initial challenge in a book of this kind is to define what we understand by the term globalization and the constituent elements of a global social problem. Given that social scientists are acutely aware of the way in which definitions can influence perceptions of the nature, extent and appropriate response to various phenomena, it is not surprising to find that this is a considerable challenge.

The definition of globalization defies universal agreement. Like all other major concepts in the social sciences it includes theoretical as well as ideological elements. In chapter 1, an attempt is made to simplify this discussion by identifying four different approaches to globalization: the neo-liberal, the Marxisant, the pluralist and the sceptical. Each approach is allied with an ideological view of the world. The neo-liberal stresses the value of the market as opposed to the state for the promotion of human welfare; the Marxisant does the exact opposite; the pluralist believes that both the market and state can contribute to the improvement of human welfare; while the sceptical approach questions the very existence of such a process as globalization.

This chapter also makes the case for understanding globalization in pluralist terms (i.e. a long-standing process of global interconnectedness with economic, political, social and cultural effects). Emphasis is given to the way in which globalization has been, and will continue to be, fuelled by political, economic, technological and cultural forces. Its effects on local communities, population groups and nations can be both positive and negative. Opinion is often divided on how to assess its effects; for example, is the spread of Western culture to other parts of the world desirable or not? How beneficial is the 'export' of high technology to developing countries? Although the spread of globalization to different parts of the world has been uneven, no country has totally escaped its impact – benign or malign. Affluent countries have been driving the globalization process as a result of their relative economic, political and social power. Developing countries have, on the whole, been on the receiving end.

In turning to our second theme, it can be argued that a 'global' social problem should satisfy four criteria:

1   The cause of the problem should be found in global rather than national processes.
2   Such problems can spread across national borders despite the efforts of sovereign states.
3   The problem is increasingly difficult to resolve at a national level.
4   Supranational bodies have emerged in order to assist nation-states in dealing with the social problem concerned.

Clearly, though, some social problems are more 'global' than others. It is, for example, more difficult for a nation-state to respond effectively in isolation to problems such as global warming or drug dealing than to family violence. Even different aspects of the same social problem may vary in their 'global content'. It is, for example, easier for the nation-state to deal independently with crimes such as burglary than with drug trafficking or a localized environmental hazard such as a landfill site as opposed to atmospheric pollution.

In a volume of this size it is possible to cover only a selection of global social problems. Inevitably this involves a subjective selection process. The inclusion of problems such as poverty and substance abuse may prove uncontroversial; others such as family violence perhaps less so. We hope, however, that our choice is broad enough to capture the diversity of issues involved in understanding the two major themes of the book mentioned above.

The response of the international community to the problems created by globalization has lacked impetus, direction and coherence. National interests, as well as sectional interests within countries, have dominated the agenda. The successive failures of the World Trade Organization to agree on the reduction of subsidies to farmers in the rich countries so as to create a fairer world trading system is a constant reminder of the dominance of national over international interests. Yet, it would be mistaken to conclude that no progress has been made in the creation of global institutions to combat social problems, as is noted in chapter 2. The various United Nations bodies such as the ILO, the WHO, UNICEF and UNHCR may not have delivered as much as they promised, but the beneficial impact of their work should not be underestimated. The positive role played by various non-governmental organizations (NGOs), not least in terms of their educative role in raising public awareness of global social problems, also needs to be highlighted. Progress has been slow and erratic, but it is difficult to conceive of a viable alternative to national and international collaboration in dealing with the global social problems discussed in this volume. Problems that affect rich as well as developing countries are more likely to attract the attention of the global community than those that are primarily the concern of the latter. Self-interest has always been a stronger force in public policy than altruism at both national and international level. The current global network of institutions needs strengthening if it is to deal more effectively with the undesirable effects of globalization, though there appears to be no significant movement in this direction at present.

Dobson's chapter on the environment reinforces several of the points made in the first two chapters. Globalization is an asymmetrical rather than a symmetrical process, with the rich countries doing most of the globalizing and the developing countries being passive 'recipients'. The effects of globalization are 'lumpy' rather than smooth, with the poorer countries feeling the effects more than the rich. Environmental issues that can be responded to without adverse effects on the economy of the affluent world, particularly of the USA, are more likely to be dealt with by international bodies than other environmental problems. Moreover, there is no international body with the authority or the legitimacy to impose solutions to generally accepted environmental problems, and, on current evidence, the situation is unlikely to change for the better in the near future. Yet progress has been made in improving some aspects of the environment partly as a result of international conventions and government decisions at the national level.

Poverty has long been recognized as a social problem at both the national and the international level. It is also readily acknowledged that poverty often lies at the heart of many other social problems – as many contributors to this volume note. In chapter 4, George argues that globalization has contributed to the rise of poverty in some countries but has had the opposite effect in others. Countries that previously formed part of the Soviet bloc, as well as sub-Saharan countries, have experienced sharp rises in poverty in recent years. Other countries in Asia, however, have seen standards of living rise and poverty rates reduced. Globalization is one of the many factors that have contributed to this uneven picture. This chapter also highlights the problems involved in defining and measuring poverty at both the national and the international level as well as making historical comparisons. Most of the data for both the historical and the comparative estimates compiled by the World Bank are indicative rather than definitive. According to the World Bank's definition of poverty (income below $1 per person per day), the level of such deprivation in developing countries increased in absolute terms but declined in proportional terms during the past decade or so, though with significant country variations. In the sub-Saharan countries, poverty increased both numerically and as a proportion of the total population. Present anti-poverty policies are unlikely to make any significant impact on the reduction of world poverty. Writing off the debt of developing countries and creating a fairer trading system are the two major changes needed for poverty reduction.

Globalization is related to crime in a variety of ways, as Findlay shows in chapter 5. First, the truncation of time and space brought about by globalization has meant that people, goods, money and images can traverse the globe at record speeds. This applies equally to criminal activities. Second, the real and perceived widening economic gap between the rich countries and many of the poor countries acts as a stimulus to further crime. Third, the increased social marginalization of many groups in advanced industrial societies serves to encourage criminal activity. Fourth, the attempts by some of the rich countries to impose their culture and to dominate some of the developing countries can foster violent reactions, as the recent rise in anti-Americanism demonstrates. Globalization, however, has encouraged the growth of global as well as regional bodies charged with the responsibility of combating crime, albeit with limited success.

In chapter 6, Harrison examines globalization and the drug market from a historical perspective. He illustrates how the emergence of a world market changed the nature of both the production and the consumption of commodities, including drug substances, ranging from coffee to cocaine. The economic interests of both national bodies and private companies drove this process forward despite the evidence of the harmful effects of drug taking. The acceleration of the globalization process during the past fifty years has been accompanied by an exponential growth in the numbers of people taking drugs. Although there are national variations in drug taking, it is now, according to the United Nations Office for Drug Control and Crime Prevention, a 'global phenomenon' affecting all countries. Side by side with this growth in drug taking, globalization has helped to bring about an increased global effort to reduce drug production and drug consumption. As in other areas, however, the global UN policy is not based solely on a set of scientific, rational criteria. It is also a bargaining process shaped by compromises reflecting profit, self-interest and ideology.

Attawell's contribution deals with what has been described as a global disaster – the HIV/AIDS epidemic. Around 50 million people worldwide are affected today, the vast majority of whom live in developing countries. This reflects not simply the world population balance but also the higher vulnerability of developing countries to AIDS. Sub-Saharan countries have the highest incidence of AIDS in the same way that they also have the highest poverty rates. Poverty and AIDS are causally related in a variety of ways. It is, for example, the case that poor people are more likely to contract AIDS. Conversely, AIDS can slow down economic development at the national level and reduce incomes at the individual level. In as much as globalization has increased poverty, it has also helped to increase vulnerability to AIDS; and population mobility as well as labour migration, boosted by globalization, are associated with AIDS.

A central issue in the globalization debate is the significance of the nation-state. Neo-liberal writers have argued that the nation-state has lost influence in the face of multinational companies and technological innovation. Marxisant writers tend to support this view, even though they decry it. Pluralist writers maintain that, while the nation-state has lost some of its powers, it still has a supreme role to play in promoting the welfare of its people. The chapter on AIDS highlights this by illustrating how governments in some sub-Saharan countries, most notably Uganda, have managed to control the spread of AIDS in co-operation with UN bodies. The policy response of the international community to AIDS has been, however, rather weak despite the strong anti-AIDS rhetoric. Developing countries cannot afford to increase expenditure on AIDS prevention; they urgently need the assistance of the rich world. Yet, official international assistance to the twenty-eight countries most affected by AIDS declined between 1992 and 2000.

It can be argued that family violence, the theme of Pahl, Hasanbegovic and Yu's chapter, does not conform to the description of a global social problem on the grounds that it satisfies only three of the four criteria outlined earlier. Yet globalization has had an effect on both the incidence and the recognition of the problem in a variety of ways. Where globalization led to unemployment and poverty, it has contributed to the incidence of family violence. Globalization has helped to focus attention on the problem of family violence in a number of countries by the dissemination of information. The growth of a global debate on family violence has also led to demands for an improved policy response in this sphere in various nations. Moreover, if family violence is defined more broadly in order to encompass sexual exploitation, then globalization becomes far more central to the problem. Pahl and her colleagues provide statistical evidence that shows that about one-quarter of women in the world suffer violence at the hands of their husbands. There are variations between countries, and it is almost certain that these figures underestimate the extent of the problem. The response of the United Nations in condemning family violence has been forthright but, as in other areas, its effectiveness has been less impressive. These authors also refer to evidence from interviews with women in three countries – England, Taiwan and Cuba – which indicates both commonality and difference in the way the problem is perceived and dealt with by the state.

In turning to the issue of racism, globalization is a composite process of various strands, some of which give support to this phenomenon while others tend to weaken it. The economic domination which rich countries exert over poorer countries (particularly under colonialism), as well as class and caste divisions, served to reinforce the notion that some ethnic groups are biologically or socially inferior to others. However, the tendency for globalization to emphasize the universal nature of human experience, the global over the local, and the general against the particular has helped to bolster a belief in the equality of human beings. In chapter 9, Ginsburg shows how both these complex processes have been at work even though the first seems to be of more central concern.

Racism at both the individual and the structural level has been endemic in all societies. The ancient Greeks referred to non-Greeks as 'barbarians' and justified slavery on the grounds of the biological inferiority of the slave. The vocabulary has changed but racism persists, and it is often institutionalized in the practices of state institutions. Yet, some progress has been made. Discrimination has been made a legal offence in most countries; the United Nations has long campaigned against racist practices; the European Union has condemned racism; the European Court of Human Rights has on several occasions taken governments to task over their treatment of individual immigrants; and several NGOs have emerged to champion the cause of racial tolerance. At the same time, the nature of immigration policies pursued by rich countries is fundamentally racist as its principal aim is to exclude black people. So long as globalization is dominated by its current neo-liberal ideology, it will continue to bolster racism, hence the need for a more reformist ideology.

Migration and globalization have co-existed over the centuries, reinforcing each other. Population movements, both economic and enforced, have been a feature of everyday life since the early days of civilization and have contributed to the improvement of human welfare. Indeed, the high living standards currently enjoyed in the West have been built on migrant labour that was recruited by governments during the post-1945 period. The present concern with migration derives from the fact that it has accelerated in recent decades; it is directed mainly towards the rich countries, and it is mostly unsolicited. There are, of course, many causes of migration, of which globalization is just one. Castles and Loughna examine how globalization has impacted on migration through improved transport systems, closer social network systems between immigrant communities and their countries of origin, better transmission of cultural images contrasting life in the affluent world with that of the impoverished countries, and the growth in the disparities in living standards between the North and the South.

This rise in the volume of migration (legal and illegal, economic and political) has created a social panic in the West. It has led governments to introduce various measures, either independently or jointly, to contain such movement. These include more restrictive immigration laws, tighter border controls, less generous state allowances for migrants, and pressurizing developing countries to stem the flow at source. Such measures have been adopted despite the fact that the 'ageing' demographic profile of many rich countries would seem to suggest that a growth in the number of young immigrants would be beneficial. The various attempts to stem the level of migration have so far proved relatively unsuccessful. Globalization pressures appear to be stronger than government containment measures.

Perceived as a process, globalization will continue to expand its reach and deepen its grip on the global level. On the other hand, it is doubtful whether the neo-liberal influence on global agencies charged with the responsibility of combating the undesirable effects of globalization will change substantially in the short term. In the absence of a competing progressive ideology, the social problems discussed in this book will continue unabated.

I

Globalization, Risk and Social Problems

Vic George

The Chinese prophet's wish cum curse 'May you live in interesting times' aptly describes the current era ushered in by the accelerated process of globalization of recent years. The increasing speed and rate at which news, images, music, capital, goods and people incessantly traverse the globe make for a more exciting and interesting life, but they also make for greater insecurity and risk – more crime, disease, drugs, terrorism, insatiable consumerism and environmental destruction. Globalization has always been Janus-faced, with a positive and a negative side as well as with differential distributional effects.

This chapter seeks to explore some of the central issues in the debates on globalization and to relate these to the themes of risk and of global social problems that are the concerns of this book.

Globalization: a contested issue

The numerous approaches to globalization have been grouped under four headings by Held et al. – hyperglobalists, sceptics, transformationalists and deterritorializationists (Held et al. 1999, 11–16); under five headings by Scholte – internationalization, liberalization, universalization, modernization and supraterritoriality (Scholte 2000, 15–16); into four categories by Fitzpatrick – the sponsors, the sceptics, the doubters and the hecklers (Fitzpatrick 2001, 164–5); and into four groupings by George and Wilding – the technological enthusiasts, the Marxisant pessimists, the pluralist pragmatists and the sceptic internationalists (George and Wilding 2002, chap. 1). It is this last fourfold categorization that is used in this chapter, for it attempts to cover both the theoretical and the ideological strands of each approach.

Definitions are both dangerous and necessary. They are dangerous for they are simplifications of far more complex realities; they are necessary because they encapsulate the various authors' perception of reality and enhance the usefulness of scientific, political and policy debates. Above all, however, definitions are ideological because they 'fundamentally shape descriptions, explanations, evaluations, prescriptions and actions' (Scholte 2000, 42). It is for this reason that definitions of important concepts, including globalization, are contested, with the result that disagreement is the norm rather than the exception.

Neo-liberal enthusiasts

Many in this group see globalization as a condition rather than as a process – it has arrived rather than being still in the making. It describes the contemporary world in which finance, trade, investment, news and images travel at record speed. Globalization refers to the 'borderless world' that we live in today where nation-states have become redundant (Ohmae 1990). Similarly, Masakazu claims that, in today's globalized world, 'states have ceased to be the main agents. For example, in the economic sphere it is not states but rather the invisible forces of the market that are playing the biggest role both in creating various problems for the world and in solving them' (Masakazu 2001, 59). Indeed, states have not only been overtaken but they 'have become unnatural – even dysfunctional – as actors in a global economy because they are incapable of putting global logic first in their decisions' (Ohmae 1995, 120).

By and large, this group tends to support a neo-liberal ideology. Hence, they view globalization as the victory of capitalism over socialism and of small government over universal welfare states; and they see globalized capitalism as the 'end of history' (Fukuyama 1992). Globalization is a most welcome development; it benefits everyone and it is also irreversible, according to this group.

The globalization of finance, trade and investment is the result of technological changes in the last quarter of the twentieth century and the consequent decisions taken by business people. Changes in information technology, telecommunications and transport made it possible for entrepreneurs and the market to move capital, business and investment wherever they willed. Governments and politicians could do very little to stop this, though many did a great deal to facilitate it. Technology and the market rather than politics and the politicians have been the driving forces behind globalization.

Marxisant pessimists

Marxisant pessimists view globalization as the process that has led to the latest stage in the long development of capitalism. They have departed from Marx's optimistic view that eventually capitalism will dig its own grave to the pessimistic view that capitalism seems at present to have triumphed: 'If imperialism is the latest stage of capitalism, globalism is the latest stage of imperialism' (Sivanandan 1999, 5).

As an economic system, capitalism has always had to find ways and means to deal with its internal contradictions in order to survive. In historical terms, colonialism was the first way that capitalism used in order to survive the increasing pressures from the rising working class of industrial countries in Europe. This was followed by imperialism and is now succeeded by globalism – the condition brought about by the process of globalization. Though they accept that technology played a part in the globalization process, Marxisant pessimists view technology as a tool used by capitalist institutions to maintain and increase profitability. Technology and politics, mediated by a pro-capitalist ideology, have been the driving forces behind the globalization process.

The world capitalist system operates as a whole unit through the operations of multinational companies to the benefit of a world capitalist class. In Sklair's words, 'the transnational corporation is the major locus of transnational economic practices; the transnational capitalist class is the major locus of transnational political practices; and the major locus of transnational cultural-ideological practices is to be found in the culture-ideology of consumerism' (Sklair 1995, 6). Marxists have always seen the nation-state as a tool serving the interests of the capitalist class – globalization has merely internationalized this relationship. Not unexpectedly, they view globalization with total hostility, for it serves the interests of the stronger groups and nations in the world. Above all, many consider the possibilities of socialist egalitarian reform to be as remote as ever. Globalization has strengthened the powers of capital and weakened those of the labour movement. It may have encouraged the growth of social movements, but these are not a strong and coherent force to overthrow capitalism. The future is bleak, with increased inequality and alienation.

Pluralist pragmatists

It is the work of pluralist writers that provides the most comprehensive analysis of globalization (Giddens 1990; Robertson 1992; Held et al. 1999). They view globalization as a complex, multifaceted process that affects all aspects of life – economic, political, cultural and social. Moreover, it affects not only how nations and institutions behave but also how individuals see themselves in a global setting. It is a long-term process that has been propelled by technology, economics, politics and knowledge to create a 'global cosmopolitan society' which 'is shaking up our existing ways of life, no matter where we happen to be' (Giddens 1999, 19).

The two essential features of this broad gobalization process are the demise of time and space and the rising public consciousness that the world is getting smaller and becoming more compacted. This is brought out in the definition offered by Robertson, one of the early influential writers in this group: 'Globalization as a concept refers both to the compression of the world and the intensification of consciousness of the world as whole' (Robertson 1992, 8).

The notion of the compression of time and space is not unique to this group. It appears in the writings of all three groups but it is explained differently – as the result of technology pure and simple by the first group; as the outcome of capitalism's way to rescue itself from its own internal problems by the second group; and as the result of technology, economics, politics and knowledge by this group. The increasing perception by ordinary citizens that the world is being globalized has both its positive and negative aspects. It encourages, for example, the formation of anti-poverty movements as well as terrorist groups that span the globe; it bolsters more egalitarian gender relationships as well as wider use of drugs; and so on.

The sceptics

A small group of social scientists have been sceptical about the usefulness of the notion of gobalization. They accept that the world has become more international but not transnational and global where national boundaries have lost their meaning. They raise two fundamental and related objections to the idea of globalization as put forth by the neo-liberal enthusiasts. To begin with, historical evidence shows that the flows of capital, investment and trade as proportions of GDP are no higher today than they were at the end of the nineteenth century. Moreover, migration movements were free then compared to the draconian restrictive measures that exist today in a world that is supposed to be 'borderless'. Secondly, the dominant economic literature surrounding globalization today is nothing more than right-wing ideology dressed up as impartial economic science. The claims that small government, free movements of financial capital, maximum competitiveness and such like are an integral part of economic development in a globalized world are simply tenets of right-wing ideology designed to stifle opposition to the inequalities created by governments, international bodies and multinational companies. The sceptics accept that national economies and large firms have become more international today than they were before, but this is different from claiming that they have become transnational, that is, global. Multinational firms are not 'footloose' with the ability to move across the globe as they please. National governments are still sovereign, though less so than before – a view shared by the pluralist pragmatists: 'For the political right in the advanced industrial countries the rhetoric of globalization is a godsend. It provides a new lease of life after the disastrous failure of their monetarist and radical individualistic policy experiments in the 1980s' (Hirst and Thompson 1999, 262).

An assessment

What then is globalization? The approach used here is similar to that of the pluralist pragmatists: a political economy approach where economics, politics and culture separately and jointly extend both the spread and the depth of globalization (George and Wilding 2002, chap. 1). What can one conclude from this very contested debate? Any conclusions, including those listed below, are a mixture of ideology and evidence, and readers have to make up their own minds.

- First, globalization is process and not a condition. As such, it is more fully developed in some parts of the world than in others. There are still millions of people without a telephone or a television set, and only a tiny minority of the population in the industrially developing countries is connected to the internet. As a United Nations report points out, in mid-1998, 'industrial countries – home to less than 15% of people – had 88% of Internet users' (UNDP 1999, 62), and most of them lived in the United States. Globalization is thus a very uneven process – high in the rich countries and low in the poor.

- Second, globalization is a multifaceted process covering all aspects of life – economic, political, cultural and social. These are interrelated processes, but concentrating on the economic, as some groups do, can overestimate both the extent and the depth of globalization in the world. Financial capital can move around the globe faster than, say, good labour standard practices. Globalization is uneven not only geographically but also sectorally.
- Third, globalization is not just an external force but a very personal one too, affecting the way people behave. It influences the work of governments and multinational companies as well as the behaviour of people in relation to, say, work, marriage, music and sport. It is far easier, quicker and cheaper, for example, for football fans to accompany their team on away games abroad than it was twenty years ago; similarly, music spreads worldwide in record time today compared to the past; and so on.
- Fourth, globalization is a long-term process rather than the result of the very recent advances in information technology. The compression of space and time that is at the heart of globalization dates back to the beginnings of civilization. It was fast during some periods, slow during others and non-existent during unusual periods of social stagnation. It has drawn its strength from changes in all countries over the centuries and it is not just a Western process.
- Fifth, various forces – economic, technological, political and scientific – have propelled the process of globalization over the years. Monocausal explanations of complex processes, such as globalization, oversimplify and mislead. The truth is always messier than that. Technology, for example, has facilitated the globalization of finance but it has not done this on its own. Political decisions at the national and international level have reinforced the push given by technology. Similarly, the pursuit of profit by capital has been one of the driving forces, but again it operated through the medium of the nation-state and was simply one of many factors. The various forces behind the globalization process – technology, capital, politics and knowledge – interact in a variety of complex ways so that it is impossible to stratify them.

- Sixth, globalization has co-existed with different ideologies over the centuries. During the second half of the twentieth century, for example, globalization was accompanied first by a Keynesian, pro-universal welfare-state ideology and then by the current neo-liberal ideology. The nature of the ideology co-existing alongside globalization at any one period is not an inherent part of it – it is always up for grabs, politically speaking.
- Seventh, enough has been said so far to suggest that the effects of globalization on human welfare are neither totally benign nor totally malign and that they also vary between both countries and groups within countries. Globalization creates wealth as well as poverty; improves health standards as well as breeds new diseases; protects and destroys the environment; and so on. It is this issue that the next section of the chapter examines.
- Eighth, globalization has somewhat undermined the powers of the nation-state, but it is a serious error to claim that it has super-seded them. The nation-state retains a great deal of its powers and reacts and shapes the pressures of globalization. Different states react differently depending on the nature of their economy, political systems and national institutions.

The effects of globalization

We divide the effects of globalization on societies and on individuals into the economic, the political, the social and the cultural, fully recognizing that they overlap and are interrelated.

Economic effects

The economic effects of globalization cover financial flows, trade, foreign direct investment, the work of the multinational companies and economic growth.

The speed, the volume and the complexity of financial flows have increased considerably in recent years due to technological inventions as well as government policies that did away with controls of capital flows. As a result, huge sums of money can now be transferred across the world in minutes at any time of the day and night. The recent sharp increase in volume is due not only to the greater activity of financial institutions but also to the incorporation into the global system of the ex-Soviet countries.

The complexity of financial flows has also increased to include government aid, foreign direct investment by multinationals and bank finance of various types. These three different types of financial flow have different effects on the economic growth of the recipient country. Government aid, usually from the advanced industrial to the industrially developing countries, can have positive as well as neutral effects. When it is given in the form of 'tied aid' the recipient country has to use it to buy goods and services from the donor country, and this may not always be conducive to economic growth. Other forms of aid can contribute to improvements in economic growth and poverty reduction, depending on the terms attached to aid and on a number of internal political and institutional factors – the nature of government policies, the stability of the political system and the efficiency of the government machinery. The volume of aid, however, depends on political factors rather than the degree of globalization. Thus the amount of aid given as a proportion of the gross domestic product (GDP) of the advanced industrial countries has declined over the years – 0.48 per cent in 1965, 0.35 per cent in 1985, and 0.23 per cent in 1998 (Randel et al. 2000, 3).

Foreign direct investment (FDI) is obviously directed to those countries that will yield the most profit in a secure way. Whether this benefits the country is a secondary and derivative consideration. FDI that involves the establishment of factories and businesses is far more likely to benefit the country than FDI used to take over existing enterprises or employed for the quick extraction of mineral resources. In 1997, 59 per cent of total FDI was for 'cross border mergers and acquisitions' (UNDP 1999, 31). As with trade, most of FDI – about 70 per cent in 1997 – went to the advanced industrial countries, while the greater part of the remainder went to a small number of industrially developing countries – China, Brazil, Mexico and Indonesia. The poorest countries receive very little FDI.

Private bank financial flows can have different effects on economic growth depending on their nature. Certainly, speculative short-term capital flows may prove detrimental if they are withdrawn abruptly without due consideration to the effects this may have on the country's banking system and its economy. The economic crisis of the late 1990s in Asia was sparked off by such outflows of speculative capital. Though there is now considerable concern as to how to prevent such speculative and volatile flows, 'few economies can insulate themselves from the daily operations of world financial markets' (Held et al. 1999, 234).

Trade and globalization are connected in a dual causal relationship. The movement of goods and services from one country to another enhances the globalization process; vice versa, globalization facilitates foreign trade. Most of the substantial rise in foreign trade in the last quarter of the twentieth century was among the advanced industrial countries. The proportion of world exports going to these countries was almost identical in 1985 and 1999 – 68.1 versus 68.3 per cent. Similarly, the proportion of exports from the advanced industrial countries to other such countries was 72.7 per cent in 1985 and 73.0 per cent in 1999 (United Nations 2000d, 260–3). The major change during this period was the emergence of South and East Asia as an important trading region, particularly as the source of exports to other developing countries. While exports from this region to other developing countries was 35.9 per cent of the total of the region's exports in 1985, the corresponding proportion in 1999 was 42.4 per cent. Sub-Saharan Africa remains a stagnant trading region – it accounted for 1.1 per cent of world exports in 1985 and 0.6 per cent in 1999 (ibid.).

Though globalization has boosted trade, it has not changed the unequal terms of trade that militate against the poor countries because of their reliance on primary products for the bulk of their exports. The political institutions set up by the world community to oversee fair play in trade have proved vulnerable to the power and pressure of the wealthy nations so that they have not counteracted the inequalities of the market, and have sometimes even reinforced them.

Multinational companies (MNCs) have benefited a great deal from increased globalization and they, in turn, have boosted globalization further. They have increased in number and in financial power in recent years. The financial worth of many MNCs exceeds the GDP of many countries, including some of the affluent countries. In 1997, the total value of sales in US dollars by General Motors exceeded the GDP of Norway, Poland, Greece, Israel, Saudi Arabia, South Africa, the Philippines and many others (UNDP 1999, 32). The debate as to whether MNCs benefit the countries where they operate is rather vacuous because what matters is the kind of terms under which they are allowed by the government to operate. Clearly their operations are designed to increase their profitability, but this need not exclude the possibility of benefits to the country if the terms are right. Governments, however, that set stiff conditions in terms of labour standards, minimum wages, occupational benefits and taxation levels may find that the MNCs will move to more lenient regimes. The activities of MNCs have obvious political implications, but they also have less obvious cultural implications. A primary aim of an MNC is to encourage a consumer culture, and particularly a preference for its own products through advertising, sponsorship of sporting events and even charitable activities.

There are many internal and external factors that affect the rate of economic growth in a country – globalization is just one of these. There is no evidence to support the view that deepening globalization necessarily improves rates of economic growth. The world economy grew at an annual average of 3.2 per cent during 1980–90 but by only 2.5 per cent during 1990–9. During these two periods, the GDP of the developing countries as a group grew by 3.4 per cent and 3.3 per cent per annum respectively; the GDP of the advanced industrial countries grew at a slower rate – 3.1 and 2.4 per cent respectively. The evidence also shows that increased globalization has benefited some countries but harmed others. Thus the GDP of East Asia in the 1990s grew by 7.4 per cent, while the GDP of the ex-Soviet countries in Europe and Central Asia that became the focus of rapid globalization declined by 2.7 per cent per annum (World Bank 2000a, 294–6).

Population growth in the developing countries during these two decades was higher than in the advanced industrial countries, with the result that inequalities in incomes per capita between the two remained pretty constant. For some countries, such as the sub-Saharan states, incomes per capita rose at a lower rate, with the result that inequalities between them and the rich countries widened. We will return to this theme in chapter 3.

To sum up this section: globalization has increased the volume, speed and intensity of financial flows, trade and the operations of MNCs, and these have had variable effects on rates of economic growth. Moreover, these effects have benefited some countries more than others, with the result that globalization pressures 'have further marginalized many developing countries' (UNDP 1999, 31).

Political effects

We have already pointed out that the nation-state has been one of the major actors behind the evolution and the recent strengthening of the globalization process. Now we need to see whether, first, supranational political bodies, second, global market forces and, third, global social problems have come back to haunt the nation-state and to impinge on its autonomy to manage its affairs as it thinks best.

As far as supranational bodies are concerned, the evidence shows that they have acted as checks or partners of the nation-state in at least four ways. First, there are the instances where the nation-state agreed to share its power with a supranational body on specific issues. For example, the police forces of many nations have agreed to co-operate with the activities of Interpol in the fight against crime.

Second, when countries become members of a supranational body, they agree to abide by its regulations in specific areas. Member countries of the European Union, for example, have to abide by certain rules and regulations enacted by the European Parliament even though they may not be in agreement with some of them. UK governments in the 1990s, for example, had to amend their labour legislation so that it did not discriminate against women in relation to pensions and other social benefits. At the international level, decisions by the World Trade Organization are binding and sanctions can be imposed against recalcitrant governments.

Third, there are situations where the nation-state is at the mercy of a supranational body because it is in financial or other difficulties. The imposition of structural adjustment programmes by the IMF and the World Bank on many industrially developing countries was, as we shall see later, controversial and contrary to the wishes of many governments.

Fourth, governments may be signatories to certain international conventions and may be legally bound to act accordingly, as in the case of several protocols on the protection of the environment. Sometimes the obligation to obey protocols may not be legal, but ethical, as in the case of several of the International Labour Organization's codes on labour practices. Often, too, protocols are open to more than one interpretation so that response to them varies from one nation-state to another.

There is general agreement among the four groups of writers discussed earlier that global market forces and MNCs have constrained the freedom of the nation-state to act as it thinks fit in its economic and social policies. There is disagreement, however, on how severe this restriction has been. The neo-liberal enthusiasts stand out as the only group that argues that this is so severe and irreversible that the nation-state has become an anachronism. All the others maintain that this restriction applies more to some areas of government activity than to others, that the picture varies from one country to another depending on a host of institutional factors and that the nation-state still possesses substantial powers. Thus governments remain supreme in such areas as education and health but not where taxation and social security benefits are concerned.

The third major force behind the nation-state's loss of exclusive power within its borders has been the globalization of risk and of social problems. Problems such as environmental destruction, drug addiction, terrorism, AIDS and certain types of crime cannot be dealt with adequately at the national level only. International action is needed, too, and this means co-operation between nation-states and the creation of international bodies to plan and to oversee what is needed to cope with the problems. Global social problems necessitate global social action, and this means a partnership between the national and the supranational bodies.

In brief, the nation-state has had to share power with bodies above it, below it and alongside it, sometimes enhancing and sometimes restricting its potential for satisfying the welfare needs of its citizens. It 'has lost its previous claims to supreme, comprehensive, absolute and exclusive rule' and has become 'part . . . of a wider, multilayered complex of regulation in which private as well as public agencies play key roles' (Scholte 2000, 157). But this should not be seen as an unmitigated disaster because it involves a window of opportunity for collaborative action between states on issues that are international or global in character. It also begins to lay the foundations for forms of citizenship that go beyond the national. European citizenship for member countries of the European Union is an obvious example; the recognition by United Nations bodies of the notion of basic rights for all – including prisoners, refugees, asylum seekers and others – is a first small step in the gradual evolution of a more fully fledged conception of rights at the international level.

Social welfare effects

Social democratic governments have been caught on the horns of a difficult dilemma: how to satisfy the rising demands of their citizens for better social welfare provision and how to resist the pressures of the global market for a reduction in the costs of their welfare states – how 'to square the welfare circle' and how to create an 'affordable welfare state'. So far, attempts to deal with the dilemma have relied heavily on reducing welfare costs. Globalization has played a major role in this.

Experience from the 'welfare restructuring' reforms in Europe during the 1990s suggests that governments have used several restrictive ways to find solutions to this dilemma. They have privatized certain public utilities; they have transferred part of the state welfare burden to the private sector; they have increased charges for some services; they have made eligibility criteria more difficult; they have reduced the generosity of benefits; they have made employment in the public sector less advantageous; they have introduced new management techniques designed to reduce expenditure; and they have encouraged communities to take more responsibility for the everyday running of services (George 1996, 20–2).

Similar attempts were made to control public expenditure in industrially developing countries through the imposition of structural adjustment programmes by the IMF and the World Bank in the 1980s and 1990s. Food subsidies were lowered, expenditures on social security, education and health were reduced, public utilities were privatized and labour market protection was diluted in an effort to reduce the size of government activity and expenditure (Stewart and Berry 1999). As in the case of the advanced industrial countries, the result was a rise in poverty and income inequality in many countries.

Both 'welfare restructuring' and 'structural adjustment programmes' were based on the neo-liberal premise that small government, low welfare expenditure and lean and mean management are essential ingredients for improved rates of economic growth. Experience has proved otherwise, and the World Bank acknowledges it now: 'Some countries followed policies of liberalization and privatization, but failed to grow as expected. Other countries intervened to a relatively large extent in markets and enjoyed rapid growth' (World Bank 1999, 16).

Cultural effects

The notion of culture refers to the values, attitudes, customs and norms that shape behaviour in order to create a national identity. The globalization process inevitably transmits the cultural traits of one country to another in a variety of ways – through trade, tourism, sport, literature, music, fashion, the press, radio, television, films, the internet and so on. In theory all cultures can appear on the world's cultural stage and transmit their traits across the globe. In practice, it is mainly Western culture in general and American culture in particular that is beamed across the globe today because it reflects the dominant world societies.

The central question is whether this process is leading towards a homogenization of global culture or whether national cultures act as filters, accepting in modified forms some elements of Western culture and rejecting others, thus maintaining their identity, if not their distinctiveness. Four main positions have emerged on this issue.

First, globalizing enthusiasts see the spread of American consumerist values as strong enough to create a homogenized world culture. As a result, 'everywhere everything gets more and more like everything else as the world's preference structure is relentlessly homogenised' (Levitt 1983, 93). The homogenization of cultures is natural and to be welcomed, according to this perspective.

Second, there are many on the left who see the homogenization pressures as the result of the pursuit of profit by the large MNCs (Sklair 1995); it is a process to be deplored and resisted, for it is nothing more than 'cultural imperialism'. Despite their opposition, they find it difficult to suggest realistic ways of resisting the homogenization of national cultures. To do this successfully one has to resist the operations of MNCs, and this is no easy task.

Third, there are those who believe that the crude onslaught of American culture through films, fashion, music and consumption has created enough hostility in many traditional cultures to lead to a rejection of Americanism and a strengthening of national cultures. They reject the notion implicit in the previous two approaches which sees individuals and local cultures as passive recipients of foreign cultural images. Islamic fundamentalism is the best manifestation of this position.

Fourth, there are the pragmatists who share the view that national cultures and people do not absorb the essence of Western culture that easily. They may eat McDonald's food and wear Reebok shoes, but that does not mean that they accept the family values and gender relationships of the West. National cultures absorb bits and pieces of Western culture and may modify even these to suit local conditions, but that does not signify the eclipse of national cultures. As Axford puts it: 'the choice faced by local subjects and local cultures is neither cultural annihilation nor a forlorn and romantic quest for cultural autarky . . . but a more complex and messy "organization of diversity"' (Axford 1995, 167).

In conclusion, it seems that, so long as there are different languages, religions and national experiences, national cultures will survive even though their distinctiveness will be blurred to incorporate and reflect aspects of a more cosmopolitan culture that is in the making. National cultures will continue to be central to the definition, causation and amelioration of social problems.

Global risks and global social problems

Debates on social problems are long-standing and largely unconnected to the debates on globalization. Debates on social risk are of more recent origin and they hone into debates on globalization quite well. This is partly because the literature on social problems has been primarily prescriptive – what should be done to deal with the various social problems. The opposite seems to be the case with the literature on risk – it has been primarily analytic, concerned with explaining how risk in a globalizing world is generated, how it spreads and how it affects our lives.

Risk

This section concentrates on the work of Giddens and Beck, for their work has been the most influential. In pre-modern societies, i.e. during the pre-industrial era, the major risks were the result of natural disasters – floods, droughts, earthquakes – which were attributed to supernatural forces beyond the control of human beings. In early modern societies, i.e. during the early period of industrialization, it came to be accepted that the nature and causation of risks was social – sickness and unemployment, for example, were the result of human factors and solutions to them were possible. In late modernity, i.e. during the advanced period of industrialization, risks have become the result of our success – of our increased knowledge and affluence. Risk in modern society is created 'by the very impact of our developing knowledge upon the world' (Giddens 1999, 26). Thus the type of risk that exists today differs from that of previous societies in several respects.

First, contemporary risks are inevitable, for they are the direct result of technology and industrialization rather than of human action. Environmental pollution is the outcome of industrialization and not the result of the actions of individuals.

Second, they are invisible, at least in the early stages. It is impossible to detect the ill effects of intensive industrialized agriculture on human health until late in the food chain; it is impossible to foresee the unintended consequences of many new drugs until there are the first victims.

Third, contemporary risks are the result of affluence rather than of scarcity. It is not so much our wish to abolish undernutrition but our quest for ever-increasing consumerism that is the problem in affluent societies. The more industrialized and affluent the world becomes, the greater the number of global risks. Advanced technology is inherently polluting.

Fourth, unlike risks in pre-modern and early modern societies that were local or national, risks in late modernity are global in their spread and effect. Hence, they affect the very people who manufactured them – what Beck calls the 'boomerang curve'. As he puts it, 'perpetrator and victim sooner or later become identical' (Beck 1992, 38). Social class or living in an affluent society is no protection against such risks. As a result, modern risks are egalitarian in their effects.

Fifth, it is impossible to calculate the costs and consequences of such risks, with the result that it is not possible to devise insurance schemes that protect individuals against them. Acid rain from one country can destroy forests in another, with undesirable effects on the local community now and in the future. As Beck puts it: 'the injured of Chernobyl are today, years after the catastrophe, not even born yet' (Beck 1996, 15). Traditional insurance schemes with their concept of individual liability are not a practical possibility.

Sixth, risks are on one hand the result of increased globalization, but on the other they act as agents for further globalization to create a global risk society. The unintended ill effects of modern drugs, for example, are felt the world over, since a few pharmaceutical companies dominate the world market: 'The multiplication of risks causes the world society to contract into a community of danger' (Beck 1992, 44).

Seventh, societies in late modernity are characterized by a spirit of individualization and reflexivity. Tradition becomes less important as a motive for individual or institutional action. Rather, 'social practices are constantly examined and reformed in the light of incoming information about those practices, thus constitutively changing their character' (Giddens 1990, 38). People do not accept risks as given or beyond their control. This creates new possibilities for individual action but also greater individual insecurity. Traditional family patterns, gender roles, work practices are crumbling, allowing for more self-expression but also creating more stress for the individuals involved. The spirit of individualization may enhance self-expression but it is also fraught with risk. In brief, risk can have positive and negative effects on both the individual and society.

A number of criticisms have been levied against the risk thesis, correct though it may be in its essentials. First, Beck 'confusingly sees risk as simultaneously reinforcing positions of inequity and as democratising, creating a global citizenship' (Lupton 1999, 68). While he stresses the fact that poverty 'attracts an unfortunate abundance of risks', he also argues that 'poverty is hierarchic, smog is democratic' (Beck 1992, 35, 36). While it is true that environmental pollution can affect us all in some ways, it is also true that those who live in the congested urban slums or in the shadows of electric pylons – usually the low-paid – will suffer more.

Second, the claim that modern risks are global, for they travel fast across the world, while risks in pre-modern societies were local is not always the case. The Black Death decimated Europe very quickly despite the lower level of globalization that prevailed in the fourteenth century, when transport and travel were rudimentary. While this is true, it is equally true that the spread of diseases from one end of the globe – from China to Europe – is much more likely today than in earlier periods in history for obvious reasons.

Third, the risk thesis tends to overstress the force of technology and to underemphasize the importance of private profit in the creation of risk. It is not simply technology that pollutes but the type of technology used by firms in the pursuit of profit maximization. There is after all a great deal of clean technology that could be used were it not for the remorseless pursuit of maximum possible profitability.

Fourth, the thesis concentrates on economic and environmental risk and tends to give less attention to the social. There is no serious discussion, for example, of racism, of gender discrimination, and so on. Social risks are brought into the picture through the discussion on individualization but they are not centre stage. Giddens attempts to cover this rather briefly by arguing that globalization has changed such institutions as the family and work to the extent that they have become 'shell institutions'. They have changed considerably even though the 'outer shell remains' (Giddens 1999, 18–19).

Fifth, the risk thesis tends to highlight the malign effects of globalization and to neglect its benign effects. Any attempt to assess the effects of globalization in the area of risks and social problems must take into account both its positive and its negative effects. Globalization has, for example, encouraged the growth of multinationals, whose work can have both positive and negative effects on the living conditions of a country.

It is a political issue as to whether the nation-state and the international community together have the power and the will to rope in the risks created by globalization. Such risks are not always completely beyond the control of political action at the national and international level. As Turner puts it: 'the growth of globalization creates both an environment of risk and a set of opportunities for the expansion of social rights. Without an expansion of citizenship, the globalization of risk will have wholly negative consequences for health and well-being' (Turner 2001, 17).

Global social problems

Debates on social problems precede those on globalization and risk by a long way. Clarke usefully divides the various approaches to social problems into the naturalistic and the constructionist perspective (Clarke 2001). The first accepts the existence of certain social problems in society, discusses how they developed and puts forward solutions. It is a prescriptive, social action approach. A common thread going through this approach to social problems is that there is a public issue troubling society that needs societal rather than individual action: 'The defining of any phenomenon as a social problem implies that this is an occurrence that requires some form of collective response rather than an individual solution' (Page 2001, 17).

The constructionist perspective 'starts from asking how some conditions come to be defined or construed as social problems' before discussing any solutions (Clarke 2001, 3). It is primarily a sociological rather than a social policy approach – why and how some social situations are labelled social problems and others not. While the first approach runs the risk of lacking a sound theoretical base, the second is prone to the criticism that it concentrates on theory to the point that it neglects the policy implications.

Whatever their differences, both approaches are concerned with social problems at the national level. So far, no connections have been established with the literature on globalization. In today's world, however, social problems are global rather than national in character in varying degrees. What then distinguishes global social problems as distinct from social problems that are to be found in many countries? These two categories overlap but they are different. An 'ideal' global social problem satisfies the following four criteria.

First, its causes are to be found in global social processes. Environmental pollution, for example, stems from industrial methods of production, from transport systems and so on that are global and not simply national in character.

Second, these problems spread across national borders despite any efforts by the nation-state to the contrary. AIDS has spread across the world despite national efforts to contain it because of travel and tourism.

Third, it is increasingly difficult to solve these problems on a national level alone. Whatever national governments may do, drug addiction will continue because the supply of drugs does not necessarily come from home production. Global solutions are needed for global social problems.

Fourth, supranational bodies have emerged in an effort to assist nation-states to deal with social problems. Interpol has for many years now worked in conjunction with national police forces to combat crime; Oxfam and other non-governmental organizations have been striving to reduce poverty on a global scale; the United Nations has held many conferences over the years to find ways of reducing gender inequalities and violence against women; and so on.

Of the social problems covered in this book, environmental pollution is the global problem par excellence – it meets the four criteria to the full. Crime does this in a less clear way. It is possible, for example, for the nation-state to deal with many forms of crime within its borders even though it will find it impossible to deal with those forms of crime that are international in nature – drug trafficking, for example. The same can be said of violence against women, where national efforts can be – and are – effective.

Conclusion

This chapter uses a political economy approach to globalization where economic, political and cultural factors are important, even though economic forces play a greater role than the other two. Globalization is a fact of life today despite its uneven coverage of the world. It brings both risks and benefits and it affects countries and groups differently. Its malign effects stem primarily from its neo-liberal ideology, and this needs to change if the global social problems to which it gives rise are to be ameliorated.

A multidisciplinary approach is best suited in understanding contemporary global risks and social problems – one that takes account of the economic, the political and the cultural. The distinction between risks and social problems may be sound in the academic literature but, since the fundamental purpose of the social sciences is to improve human welfare, the term social problems is preferred to that of risk, for it is broader and also connotes a more social action approach.

A partnership between national and international agencies is best suited for the amelioration of global social problems. Working together, the nation-state and the international community can achieve far better results than ploughing their own individual furrows.

Since globalization is here to stay, the need for globalization with a human face – one that promotes both economic growth and human welfare – is urgently needed. This necessitates the abandonment of the current neo-liberal ideology and the creation of robust global institutions to partner the nation-state in a joint effort to curtail the undesirable effects of globalization and to find solutions to the global social problems discussed in this book.

Further reading

George, V., and Wilding, P. (2002). *Globalization and Human Welfare*. Basingstoke: Palgrave.
Lupton, D. (1999). *Risk*. London: Routledge.
May, M., Page, R., and Brunsdon, E. (eds) (2001). *Understanding Social Problems*. Oxford: Blackwell.
Scholte, J. A. (2000). *Globalization: A Critical Introduction*. London: Macmillan.

2

Globalization and Social Welfare

Robert M. Page

This chapter will explore the relationship between globalization and social welfare. What impact has globalization had upon welfare developments in advanced industrial societies as well as in developing nations? Has it led to a growth in supranational governance or influence and a corresponding decline in the ability of nation-states to determine their own welfare policy?

In the first part of this chapter the impact of globalization on the traditional welfare state will be explored, while the second part will examine the global dimensions of social policy.

Globalization and the welfare state

The notion of globalization

As with many social science concepts, the term globalization has an elusive quality. While there is general agreement that the term relates to an increased level of economic, political and cultural interconnectedness, there is considerable disagreement over both the extent and the impact of globalization (see Hirst and Thompson 1996; Held et al. 1999). There is continuous debate over such matters as the emergence, or otherwise, of a global economy (Hay 1999; Pierson 2001), the degree to which Westernized forms of culture have taken hold across the world (Hertz 2002; LaFeber 2002) and whether the 'authority and capacity of the interventionist state' (Pierson 1996,

124; see also Weiss 1998) has been undermined. Moreover, as George's earlier (chapter 1) categorizations indicate, differing 'value' positions relating to globalization have emerged. For example, neo-liberal enthusiasts contend that globalization is an 'impersonal' force driven by economic and technological developments that governments can respond to, but not shape. In contrast, the Marxisant pessimists believe that the interest of capital has been highly influential in determining the direction of globalization.

The impact of globalization on the welfare state

There is a divergence of opinion concerning the impact of globalization on the welfare state. According to some commentators it is misleading to suggest that it inevitably leads to welfare retrenchment (Norberg 2001). As Legrain contends, globalization is 'not an all-or-nothing, take-it-or-leave-it package; it comes with a wide menu of options. You can have all-American small government or Swedish style high taxes with cradle-to-grave welfare. You can have free trade in software but not in films. You can allow in long-term foreign investment but keep out hot money. You can choose to welcome more immigrants, or fewer' (Legrain 2002, 203). Critics contend, however, that it is extremely difficult for nation-states to pick and mix those aspects of globalization which it regards as desirable while resisting those it deems less attractive in the way that Legrain suggests (Mishra 1999). This is particularly so if one considers the impact of globalization on traditional social democratic welfare states (see Taylor-Gooby 2001).

Globalization and the social democratic welfare state

Given that much contemporary discourse surrounding globalization is underpinned by neo-liberal or conservative ideas (see Hutton 2002, chap. 6), it is not surprising to find that the social democratic welfare arrangements which flourished in Western Europe between 1945 and 1975 have now come to be portrayed in some quarters as outmoded and as a barrier to future prosperity. In the new global economy it is argued that those countries which persist in providing their citizens with extensive welfare benefits, job security and minimum wage guarantees, funded by high rates of corporate and personal taxation, will find it increasingly difficult to compete with those nations which operate on the basis of residual forms of welfare and lightly regulated labour markets. As Pierson explains,

> In the new and open trading order, they can [only] compete and sustain standards of living by moving from a 'passive' (or rights-based) to a more 'active' (and employment-oriented) welfare state, by 'flexibilizing' labour markets and allowing for greater wage dispersal (while seeking to foster a skills economy), by reforming their tax systems (to make them less progressive and to redistribute costs away from capital and the employment of labour), and 'rationalizing' public sector services (to increase their 'efficiency'). (Pierson 2001, 70)

The assertion that social democratic welfare regimes must adapt or wither in the face of economic globalization has been contested. The fact that most transnational trade remains hemispheric rather than global, and that many services need to be locally sourced casts doubt on overly deterministic accounts of economic globalism and its consequences for state welfare. While some companies might be attracted by the promise of low corporate taxes and light regulatory frameworks, others see greater long-term benefits in locating in high tax countries that provide better communications, high quality public services, a clean environment and safe neighbourhoods (Legrain 2002). Moreover, Rieger and Liebfried (1998) have argued that the advantages of economic globalization are unlikely to be realized unless compensatory welfare arrangements offering citizens a degree of security are in place. They contend that the growth in free trade, brought about by dismantling protectionist economic measures, required the development of state welfare provision, which protected the victims of change. Indeed, it could be argued that the economic advantages of globalization are only likely to be realized in those developed countries opting for the extensive forms of social protection which encourage citizens to accept the increased insecurity of more flexible labour markets (Bonoli et al. 2000, 65–6).

While it is difficult to assess the precise impact of globalization on social democratic welfare systems, many such regimes have sought to refashion their welfare arrangements. While this process has taken varying forms, a number of key trends can be identified. There has been a move away from universal forms of state protection towards means-testing, tighter eligibility requirements, increased private-sector involvement and greater decentralization. This can be illustrated by reference to the nation that is often cited as an exemplar of social democracy – Sweden. Sweden experienced a severe recession in the early 1990s. Negative growth rates were recorded from 1991 to 1993 and unemployment rose from 1.7 per cent in 1990 to 8.2 per cent by 1993. Although these adverse economic indicators have been linked to ineffective and ill-timed economic policies (Palme 2002), it is clear that some of the features of economic globalization, such as deregulated financial markets, prevented central government from using some traditional policy options (devaluation, deficit financing) to deal with this crisis. As a result, expenditure cuts and tax variations were used to counter growing budget deficits. It is quite plausible to portray these changes as pragmatic responses to short-term economic difficulties rather than a fundamental challenge to the social democratic underpinning of the Swedish welfare state (see Timonen 2001; Gould 2001). However, the growth of private-sector welfare (Moller 2002), more individualized state pension arrangements and a less generous unemployment benefit scheme are all indicative of a greater willingness to adopt some of the policy options which organizations such as the SNS Economic Policy Group (Jakobsson et al. 1998, 1999) have been promoting in an effort to boost Sweden's position in the globalized economy. It seems unlikely that future economic downturns in Sweden will lead to the increased levels of social protection which were commonplace in the past. As Kosonen sums up, 'deregulated capital markets, internationalization of enterprises and Europeanization set tighter limitations upon economic and social policies, so that the pressures of globalization are likely to push the Nordic countries to re-evaluate their welfare policies' (2001, 171).

Globalization and developing nations

There is considerable debate concerning the impact of growth-driven 'free trade' on the economies and poverty levels in developing nations (George and Wilding 2002, 86–8; Torres 2001; UNDP 2002). In part this reflects the precise mix of policies pursued by a particular country. As Stiglitz notes, 'Some policies promote growth but have little effect on poverty; some promote growth but actually increase poverty; and some promote growth and reduce poverty at the same time' (2002, 82). Disentangling the precise relationship has been complicated by anti-democratic and corrupt forms of governance in a number of developing countries, such as the Congo Republic and Nigeria, which have led to the squandering of scarce resources on conspicuous forms of consumption by wealthy elites. Of course, more democratic forms of governance will not of themselves eradicate such corruption, but they are usually a step forward. As Birdsall and Haggard point out, 'all governments are vulnerable to the misappropriation of public funds, no more or less in the area of social policy than in other areas such as spending on infrastructure and defense. But democracy has the advantage of providing opposition groups with incentives to ferret out such abuses in the process of political competition' (2002, 95).

In turning to the impact of economic globalization on state welfare arrangements in developing nations, there does appear to be a common trend at least in the case of those appearing in the low to medium categories of the UN *Human Development Report* (UNDP 2002). Although there are significant differences in life expectancy, adult literacy and GDP per capita among the 120 counties categorized in this way (see Kennedy 2002), their approach to welfare has been heavily influenced by what has come to be known as the 'Washington consensus' or 'global conservatism' (Hutton 2002). According to the 'Washington consensus', economic growth is seen as the best means of increasing living standards in developing countries even though it might lead to greater disparities in the distribution of rewards. Extensive publicly financed and delivered welfare programmes are seen as an impediment to growth. Accordingly, those nations that have sought financial assistance from transnational organizations such as the International Monetary Fund (IMF) or the World Bank have been expected to undertake extensive forms of economic and social restructuring along neo-liberal lines. Typically, this has involved reductions in public expenditure, the phasing out of subsidies and tariffs, increased selectivity in welfare provision, user charges, privatization and lower levels of personal taxation. The IMF and the World Bank acknowledge that measures of this kind will give rise to short-term pain in the form of higher unemployment, reduced access to health and education services, and higher charges for water and other utilities. However, they contend that the economic benefits accruing from such restructuring will prove worthwhile in the medium term. In practice, though, the predicted gains often failed to materialize. For example, the structural adjustment programmes introduced in sub-Saharan Africa in the early 1980s did not lead to predicted improvements in living standards and employment levels or reduce the extent of indebtedness. Negative trends of this kind have also occurred in parts of Latin America and Eastern Europe (Kapstein and Milanovic 2002). Indeed, in the latter part of 2002, Argentina responded to its rapidly deteriorating economic situation by defaulting on a substantial debt repayment to the World Bank.

The unwillingness of both the IMF and the World Bank to prescribe policies that more accurately take account of the diverse circumstances of recipient nations has only served to intensify underlying economic problems.

The growing influence of these organizations in determining the pattern of social policy has led many commentators to highlight the importance of studying social policy from a global rather than solely from a national or regional perspective. As Deacon states, 'the era of global social policy has arrived' (1998, 129).

Towards global social policy?

There are good grounds for studying social policy from a global perspective. There has been a growing recognition that social issues such as crime, asylum seeking or HIV/AIDS have global dimensions, which necessitate a far greater level of cross-national collaboration than in the past. This could lead to demands for increased levels of supranational regulation and provision. According to George and Wilding, global social policy will differ markedly from national social policy as it will need to be 'flexible enough to accommodate states at very different levels of economic and social development, more focussed on regulation than on social provision, more concerned with minimum standards and safety net type provision than with the pursuit of equality' (2002, 167–8).

The key question to consider is whether a global social policy of this kind is likely to emerge given the diversity of interests and perspectives. For example, neo-liberals are likely to resist any attempts to introduce forms of global governance designed to promote social justice or sustainability if this constrains free market activity.

Those who favour increased transnational regulation or control believe that such measures are necessary in order to protect the rights of citizens and workers and to counter the worst excesses of global capitalism.

Protection of the rights of citizens and workers

In terms of human rights, reformers want to build on various post-1945 initiatives such as the United Nations (UN) Declaration on Human Rights (1948), the covenants on Civil and Political Rights

(1966) and Economic, Social and Cultural Rights (1966) and the conventions on the Elimination of Discrimination against Women (1979) and the Rights of the Child (1989). While these developments have proved useful, reformists believe that more is required at a global level to ensure that a greater proportion of citizens can obtain effective forms of redress when they adjudge their human rights have been violated (Brysk 2002).

The greater mobility of capital has also led to demands for increased worker protection. Minimum enforceable labour standards have been called for to prevent firms from moving production to those countries with lower labour standards, thereby providing an unwarranted boost in profitability. The reformers believe that the International Labour Organization (ILO) can play a key role in this sphere. Founded in 1919, the ILO has attempted to secure international agreement over such issues as basic labour standards, trade union rights, the minimum working age and the prohibition of forced labour. In seeking to prevent a so-called race to the bottom in terms of labour standards, the ILO has, however, been accused of acting in ways that reinforce the competitive advantages of developed nations. For example, apparently benevolent forms of regulation such as the prohibition of child labour can have adverse consequences on developing nations. As Munck points out, if children in such countries are prevented from 'working on carpets or footballs', they may 'be driven into prostitution or destitution' (2002, 130) (see also OECD 1996).

Controls on global capital

The reformists also seek increased global regulation of the activities of multinational corporations (MNCs), as well as greater control over direct foreign investment and transnational capital movements.

It is contended that national governments are no longer able to control the activities of MNCs. The latter have proved highly effective in minimizing their tax liabilities, not least by internal pricing mechanisms that allow them to declare profits in nations that levy lower corporate taxes. They have also proved adroit in moving production to nations with less regulated labour markets, thereby providing opportunities to increase profit margins. MNCs have been successful in resisting calls to open up their own 'captive' markets to greater competition and in exploiting legal loopholes which allow them to operate in environmentally destructive ways.

Concern has also been expressed about the negative impact that Foreign Direct Investment (FDI) can have in developing countries. Although it is acknowledged that the degree of such investment should not be overstated (FDI tends to be concentrated in OECD countries – see Held et al. 1999, 247–51), it is clear that this process can prove problematic for developing nations (Lind 2003). The arrival of prominent foreign companies can lead to the closure of indigenous enterprises which find themselves unable to compete with their more powerful rivals. While such a development can lead to lower prices for consumers in the short term, this advantage quickly evaporates as MNCs exploit their monopoly position by increasing prices in the medium term. In addition, while an increase in the number of foreign banks may serve to give financial stability to a developing nation, their unwillingness to lend to small and medium-sized firms can undermine the prospects for economic growth (Stiglitz 2002). Finally, direct foreign investors are often able to secure contracts on very favourable terms, safe in the knowledge that they can rely on their national government to exert pressure on any developing nation that subsequently threatens to default on an 'exploitative' agreement.

Further criticisms have been directed at the destabilizing effects of transnational capital movements. The combination of technological change and deregulation means that capital can now be moved across the world at devastating speed. While this development has helped to foster cross-national trade and investment, reformers point out that it has provided opportunities for speculative currency trading, which can have serious impacts on national or regional economies (Lee 1998). In order to counter currency speculations, reformers have campaigned for the introduction of a so-called Tobin tax. As Dieter explains, 'James Tobin proposed a tax on all transactions involving foreign exchange as a means of throwing some "sand" into the overly fast gears of international capital flows' (2002, 88). It has been estimated that a 0.1 per cent automatic tax on all financial transactions could raise funds of around $400 billion annually, which could be used to ease the plight of the world's poor (Townsend 2002).

One of the key issues is whether it would be politically acceptable to set this tax at a level that would prevent large-scale speculations against a particular currency. As Dieter continues, 'A tax rate of 0.1–0.25 per cent, as proposed by most proponents of a Tobin tax, would hinder only small-scale speculation, but not the massive, large-scale speculation recently experienced in East Asia' (2002, 89).

Let us now turn to the prospects for progressive forms of global social policy.

Prospects for progressive global social policy

What are the prospects for a more progressive form of global social policy? Can key transnational organizations such as the IMF, the World Bank and the WTO be persuaded to pursue policies that improve the economic and social well-being of disadvantaged peoples and nations? What role might non-governmental agencies play in the pursuit of social justice? Might the anti-globalization movement have to be relied on to develop more imaginative ways of tackling inequality and injustice? Let us examine each of these aspects in turn.

Transnational organizations

Undoubtedly, some of the more 'progressive' transnational organizations such as the UN, the World Health Organization and the ILO will continue to promote social justice by pressurizing those countries with poor human rights records and corrupt forms of governance to operate in more socially just ways. Such bodies can also encourage richer nations to increase their aid budgets and adopt fairer trading arrangements. In addition, they can help to persuade developed nations to refrain from offloading subsidized goods on poorer countries or prioritizing their intellectual property rights where it causes untold harm, such as the refusal to allow cheaper antiretroviral drugs to be provided to African states with high rates of HIV/AIDS.

However, it needs to be recognized that these bodies are not as influential as the IMF, the World Bank or the World Trade Organization. Unless there is a significant change of direction on the part of these organizations there is little prospect of securing significant change. It is pertinent, therefore, to focus on these particular organizations.

The IMF and the World Bank were established following the Bretton Woods conference in 1944, to replace what Hutton describes as the 'beggar-my-neighbour trade and competitive devaluations of the interwar period' with 'a framework of universal rules that favoured economic openness and internationally agreed responses to individual economies' difficulties' (2002, 185). The role of the IMF was to provide transitional loans to those countries who were prepared to implement export-led economic reforms in order to overcome their trading deficits. The mission of the World Bank was to provide support with both reconstruction and development, particularly in what was then termed the 'Third World'. The subsequent collapse of this global world order in the 1970s, following US efforts to pursue more self-interested forms of domestic economic policy, led to a greater degree of economic volatility which undermined the more collective ethos of the IMF and the World Bank. By the 1980s the lending policies of the IMF were firmly based on the neo-liberal economic principles which had become pre-eminent in Washington. Whereas previously the IMF had been at pains not to challenge the broader political objectives of indebted governments, it was now prepared to demand ever more stringent forms of 'adjustment'. In consequence, during the 1980s, Mexico and other Latin American countries 'had to accept swingeing cuts in public expenditure and structural adjustment programmes imposed with increasingly ideological fervour: basic programmes of health, education and poverty relief were regarded as wasteful and extravagant – and thus were savaged' (Hutton 2002, 195). The World Bank also embraced this neo-liberal perspective in the 1980s. Countries applying for loans had to demonstrate a willingness to follow prescribed forms of economic management.

The Bretton Woods conference had also led to the establishment of a General Agreement on Tariffs and Trade (GATT), in 1947 which aimed to remove trade barriers and stimulate international commerce. Under GATT, for example, a series of multilateral agreements led to a reduction in 'average import duties on manufactures from over 40 per cent to . . . 3 per cent' between 1948 and 1994 (Scholte 2000, 104). Increasing concern about GATT's ability to settle trade disputes or impose sanctions on member nations led to the establishment of the World Trade Organization (WTO) following the Uruguay round of negotiations between 1986 and 1994. As O'Brien et al. point out, 'The WTO not only extends the mandate of the GATT into new areas but also redefines the relationship between national governments and the world trading system through the creation of an effective dispute settlement mechanism, the provision of a trade policy review mechanism (TPRM) and the development of a set of mandatory codes' (2000, 136). Although the WTO is an intergovernmental rather than a supranational organization (its remit is to reflect the collective interests of member nations, all of whom can veto any proposed rule change), it has come to be regarded as a highly influential promoter of neo-liberal trading arrangements. By asserting that trade should take precedence over social or environmental concerns the WTO has, it is argued, forced all nation-states to act in ways which bolster the economic position of powerful trading nations such as the United States. In essence, it is contended that the vast difference in power between WTO members has led to a situation in which its rules and operations have been developed in ways which protect the advantages of developed industrial countries in the North at the expense of their poorer neighbours in the South. As Scholte points out, 'the GATT/WTO regime has over the half century of its existence generally proved quickest to liberalize in areas like (most) manufactures and intellectual property where North-based interests hope to exploit opportunities in the South. Progress has tended to be slower in areas like agriculture and textiles where trade liberalization would give South-based interests greater opportunities in the North' (2000, 246). Although the WTO has made some concessions to developing countries, such as giving them greater time to implement agreements and providing advice on how to utilize dispute procedures, it remains the case that many of these poorer nations are often unable or unwilling to challenge the interests of more powerful states.

One of the major criticisms directed at the WTO is the way in which it undermines democracy (Monbiot 2000, chap. 10). For example, electors might choose a government on the basis of its commitment to full employment and the public provision of welfare services, only to find that these promises are subsequently bartered away in secretive WTO meetings. Although nation-states are able, in theory, to prevent free-trade principles being extended to sensitive spheres such as public services, this may prove illusory in practice. For instance, the WTO is keen to ensure that public services are opened up to international trade and foreign control if it can be proved that existing services operate in part on commercial lines. This could lead, for example, to NHS hospitals built under the Private Finance Initiative in the UK being purchased by a foreign private-sector company. Moreover, concerns have been voiced that future WTO agreements may include 'binding arrangements' which prevent the return of a designated service such as the railway system to the public sector (Monbiot 2002).

What possibilities exist, then, to transform powerful neo-liberal institutions such as the IMF, the World Bank and the WTO along 'welfarist' lines? There is some evidence that these institutions have begun to recognize some of the limitations of neo-liberalism. The World Bank and, to a lesser extent, the IMF have become more sensitive to social policy concerns in recent years, not least because of the negative impact of neo-liberal initiatives in East and Central Europe and in parts of Asia (George and Wilding 2002; Deacon 2001). For example, in its *World Development Report* for 2000/2001, the World Bank acknowledged that better economic and social outcomes could be achieved in developing countries if free market activity was combined with debt relief and appropriate forms of government intervention in areas such as education, training and health (World Bank 2000b). However, it is questionable whether this represents a fundamental change in the outlook of such organizations. According to Stiglitz (2002), unless the internal structures of the IMF are radically overhauled it is unlikely to change its neo-liberal orientation, despite the occasional rhetorical flourish to the contrary. Hutton shares this scepticism, arguing that the IMF is little more than an agent of the US Treasury devoted to sustaining 'American financial hegemony and policy prescriptions irrespective of the consequent contradictions and strains' (2002, 192–3).

Given that these organizations are unlikely to adopt more socially responsive policies in the near future, might the impetus for change come from the activities of non-governmental organizations and the anti-globalization movement?

Non-governmental organizations (NGOs)

Unquestionably, NGOs have become highly significant players in the broad sphere of global social policy. There are currently around 40,000 international NGOs, compared to just 6000 in 1990. Some of these have extremely large levels of support (the World Wide Fund for Nature has around 5 million regular supporters; Legrain 2002). The resources that such organizations are able to command are also impressive. According to Scholte, 'The mid-1990s budgets of the giants in this field included $586 million for CARE International, $419 million for World Vision International, $350 million each for Oxfam and Save the Children, and $252 million for Médecins sans Frontières' (2000, 152). Many of these organizations have been able to exert considerable pressure on both national governments and international governmental organizations (IGOs) to give greater attention to social and environmental issues. Such has been their influence that they have frequently been called upon by IGOs such as the UN to advise on such issues as human rights, gender equality, poverty and social development. Indeed, NGOs are often represented on official committees of these international bodies and take an active part in the drafting of policy documents. They have also played a key role in various international poverty relief schemes. Given their first-hand knowledge of prevailing conditions in poorer countries, many NGOs have been asked to implement IGO-funded social development programmes. As Yeates points out, 'This is partly a response to the poor performance of government development plans but it is also a result of a belief in the democratizing forces of civil society, the potential of NGOs to forge pro-poor political coalitions, and their greater efficiency and effectiveness more generally in delivering welfare services' (2001, 155). For example, since the early 1980s, the World Bank has come to recognize the valuable role that NGOs can perform in relation to its own social development strategy. Over time the NGOs have come to be seen as playing an important part in implementing World Bank projects (during the 1990s NGOs were involved in over 30 per cent of World Bank projects) and in policy formation (O'Brien et al. 2000).

While the activities of NGOs have undoubtedly helped to advance the interests of many disadvantaged and neglected groups across the globe, not least in areas which lack effective forms of national governance (Messner and Nuscheler 2002, 145–7), there are a number of reservations about their work (Lewis 1999). For example, many of these organizations have not adopted transparent procedures. It is often difficult to obtain information about their precise objectives, how they are funded (some donors prefer to remain anonymous) and how they formulate policy. Moreover, members of such organizations may have limited opportunities for participation and may play little part in the election or appointment of officials. NGOs also tend to be concentrated in the northern hemisphere rather than the South. These northern organizations already tend to be well represented on intergovernmental bodies. As Scholte notes, 'Fewer than 15 per cent of the NGOs accredited to engage with the United Nations (as of the mid-1990s) were based in the South' (2000, 279). It is often difficult for such organizations to take root in the South because of a lack of funds and limited organizational capacity. Even when an NGO is established, it tends to be the preserve of elite groups in such societies rather than more broadly representative.

While many NGOs have worked with IGOs in order to ensure that the positive aspects of globalization come to the fore, the emerging anti-globalization movement has taken a more sceptical stance.

The anti-globalization movement

A wide range of groups have been established with a view to challenging globalization because of the threat it poses to democracy, human rights and social justice. Such organizations have come together to protest at the meetings of bodies such as the WTO (Seattle 1999), the European Union (Gothenburg 2001) and the G8 (Genoa 2001). According to McGiffen, 'Most of the groups which have built the anti-globalization movement are small. Memberships are fluid and overlap, and many identifiable . . . bodies reject traditional forms of organization and are better perceived as 'rallying points' than as permanent structures' (2002, 62). Given such diversity, it is more difficult to identify what the anti-globalization movement stands for rather than what it opposes. While anti-globalizers may lack a coherent alternative to globalization (many would, in any event, be opposed to constructing an alternative blueprint), they would appear to be united in their preference for participatory rather than representative democracy, in their rejection of state solutions and in their belief of the need to develop increased interconnectedness between groups working at local, national and transnational levels.

Although the anti-globalization movement lacks a formal structure, a number of co-ordinating 'networks' have emerged. These include the World Social Forum and Via Campesina (McGiffen 2002).

The World Social Forum (WSF), which was established in Brazil in 2001, holds an annual gathering at around the same time as the meeting of the World Economic Forum (which business leaders and politicians attend). The WSF attracts a diverse range of delegates who exchange information, attend workshops and take part in rallies. For example, at the 2003 conference the topics discussed included 'neighbourhood councils, participatory budgets, stronger city governments, land reform and cooperative farming' (Klein 2003).

Established in 1992, Via Campesina aims to 'develop solidarity between different small farmers' organizations in pursuit of what it defines as just and equitable economic and social relations, environmental values including land conservation, sustainable farming methods and "food sovereignty"' (McGiffen 2002, 70). By building a broad-based movement in both the developed and developing world, Via Campesina seeks to ensure that farmers will be in a better position to challenge the introduction of questionable technologies such as genetically modified food or the proliferation of potentially harmful pesticides and fertilizers.

While the anti-globalization movement has undoubtedly helped to highlight the negative aspects of globalization, the diverse nature of this movement makes it difficult to see how it might advance the case of a more progressive global social policy. By eschewing formal political organizations and dismissing conventional collective action, the anti-globalization movement may succeed in creating a more diverse and participatory form of political discourse (Klein 2002), but it is unlikely to arrive at a position where it can challenge dominant transnational economic and social institutions or nations.

It seems unlikely, therefore, that we will see the emergence of what might be described as global social policy institutions in the foreseeable future. What seems much more likely is that nation-states will pursue distinctive welfare arrangements, although their choices will be constrained by global economic factors. Even those nations which have sought to establish closer economic ties with neighbouring countries, such as the member states of the European Union, have been reluctant to pursue common social arrangements beyond those deemed necessary for economic harmonization (Kleinman 2002). Although the demands for more equitable forms of global regulation may increase, the prospects for redressing historic patterns of inequality and injustice through global social policy are arguably less bright than they have been for half a century.

Concluding comments

There remains a vigorous debate about whether globalization represents an opportunity or a threat to social welfare (Mishra 1999; Deacon 2001; Palier and Sykes 2001; Yeates 2001, 2002). Those who contend that it provides an opportunity to 'promote human welfare on a global level and scale' (George and Wilding 2002, 211) believe that the emergence of diverse local, national and international networks can play a significant role in combating world poverty and breaking down the North–South divide.

Although NGOs and the anti-globalization movement have served to galvanize public support for a more progressive world order, the question remains whether this will prove sufficient to secure 'global justice'. While some worthwhile reforms are likely to be achieved by transnational organizations and global pressure groups, the idea that powerful nations such as the United States will willingly sacrifice their own economic interests in pursuit of a one-world agenda is highly optimistic. When the interests of these nations are threatened, experience suggests they will tend to ignore or violate any international treaties that they deem unworkable or outmoded.

Political parties of the centre-left are, according to sceptics, reluctant to challenge the neo-liberal underpinning of economic globalization. Indeed, they have tended to acquiesce in this process by adopting a more fluid set of values and policies that reflect 'new times' (Finlayson 2003). If accommodation of this kind gives rise to growing levels of political disengagement (such as lower electoral turnouts, especially among the young – see Butler and Kavanagh 2002), the possibility of constructing progressive global alternatives will become increasingly difficult. While there is still a possibility of countering the neo-liberal version of globalization, it is vital that those seeking a more socially just alternative do not underestimate the enormity of the task ahead.

Further reading

Deacon, B., with Hulse, M., and Stubbs, P. (1997). *Global Social Policy*. London: Sage.

Held, D., and McGrew, A. (2002). *Globalization/Anti-Globalization*. Cambridge: Polity.

Sykes, R., Palier, B., and Prior, P. (eds) (2001). *Globalization and European Welfare States*. Basingstoke: Palgrave.

Yeates, N. (2001). *Globalisation and Social Policy*. London: Sage.

3

Globalization and the Environment

Andrew Dobson

The extent and distribution of the problem worldwide

Globalization and the environment are related in reciprocal ways. Global environmental issues are an example of globalization at work, and they have contributed to the development of the modern environmental movement.

Environmental problems have been around for a long time, but in their earliest guises they were local, or at most regional. In part this was because even the biggest empires of the past had neither the reach nor the range required to make environmental impacts much beyond the territory they actually occupied. The Roman Empire, for example, was one of the largest ever seen at that time, but it had no impact on what we now know as Latin America, for instance. Global environmental problems are only 'possible', therefore, in the context of globalization. They are both created by globalization and an exemplar of it. Strictly speaking, relatively few environmental problems have a global character. It is much more common to come across environmental issues with an international range, such as the deposition of acid rain. Acid rain is caused by the emission of sulphur when it combines with water in the upper atmosphere. So, for example, industrial activity in Britain, combined with a westerly wind, takes the chemicals that contribute to acid rain towards Scandinavia. This is not pleasant for Scandinavians, but by no stretch of the imagination could this be called a global environmental problem.

The difference between 'global' and 'international', therefore, must always be borne in mind. Examples commonly offered of truly global environmental problems are climate change and depletion of the ozone layer. But even the latter might not count as global, since the greatest depletion occurs (or occurred) at a quite specific point – above the Antarctic ice sheets. The various health problems associated with ozone depletion, then, are more keenly felt in regions most proximate to the ozone hole itself – the tip of Latin America Australia and New Zealand, for example. Ozone depletion in the northern hemisphere is (or was) of a much smaller order, in the region of 3 per cent (Carter 2001, 229), with correspondingly less damaging effects. One can see how the question of whether ozone depletion counts as a 'global' environmental problem is moot.

At the same time, the growing awareness during the 1970s that the world existed as a (potential) political space in its own right had perhaps its most particular and dramatic instantiation in the environmental context. The now famous photographic images of the earth taken by astronauts on Apollo 8 in 1968 – the first people to leave the earth's gravitational pull and take whole earth pictures through a single porthole – lent at least metaphorical weight to a descriptive and prescriptive view of an interdependence that crossed national and regional boundaries. These photographs were also fundamentally nature images, with the green and blue earth wreathed in white cloud. This image of the earth as an interconnected natural system was bolstered by the publication, in 1972, of *The Limits to Growth* report (Meadows et al. 1974). The report sought to demonstrate scientifically what the Apollo 8 photographs suggested intuitively: that a planet of finite size cannot sustainably support economic and social systems that grow without regard for the context in which that growth takes place. Using computer modelling, Meadows et al. (1974) suggested that the limits to growth were dictated by the planet itself, and by the finitude of its non-human natural resources. At this point, the entire globe became the stage on which one particular aspect of the political drama was being played out – the environmental aspect. Ever since then, the globe has been indissolubly related in people's minds with the politics of the environment – more so, perhaps, than any of the other issues dealt with in this book. So powerful has been this connection, indeed, that, as I suggested above, the global nature of environmental problems and politics has probably been overstated. There are in fact very few environmental problems of a truly global nature.

So the relationship between globalization and the environment can usefully be viewed in two ways: first, environmental issues (or some of them anyway) can be regarded as examples of globalization and, second, much of the impetus behind the modern environmental movement is due, precisely, to the dramatically global nature of these issues.

In this section I wanted to say something about the distribution of environmental problems, but it turns out that the issue of distribution is intimately bound up with the theme of the next section, i.e. the ways in which globalization has influenced the causation and incidence of such problems. Let me leave my comments on distribution until the next section, then, but some further preliminary words are in order here. Determining the distribution of environmental problems in the global context will inevitably entail making judgements about what constitutes an environmental problem, and just what 'global' means. We have already seen that few problems are of a truly global nature, in the strict sense that they affect 'every inch and every hour of the globe', as Bill McKibben evocatively puts it (McKibben 1999, 46). Probably the only problem that is a genuine candidate for this description is global warming, or climate change – the subject of McKibben's book. There are some local or regional issues that have an impact on climate change and which might therefore be regarded as global problems in their potential impact. Examples of such issues are deforestation in the tropics and fossil fuel consumption in wealthy countries. There are also, from the opposite point of view, local and regional problems that are caused by global ones. Thus sea-level rises and desertification (in some cases) have their proximate or near-proximate cause in global climate change. I shall say more about this in the context of my remarks about the global distribution of problems, below.

You will often find the distinction between 'common-pool' and 'common-sink' environmental resources in the literature. Common-pool resources are items, objects, or collections of items or objects to which it is difficult or undesirable to assign property rights. An example might be stocks of fish in the North Sea. So nations are assigned fishing rights in certain geographically delimited waters, but particular fish or shoals of fish 'belong' to no one. Common-pool resource problems abound – we are regularly reminded how fish stocks are being depleted around the world, possibly below the rate of regeneration in some cases. But common-pool problems are not usually global problems; they are generally local or regional. I shall say some more about the significance of this in the chapter's third section on dealing with global regional problems.

If common-pool problems refer to the extraction end of the process of production, then 'common-sink' issues relate to the disposal of the unwanted by-products of the process. A common-sink problem arises where these by-products are disposed of in media that are unowned and where the disposal has damaging effects of one sort or another. Disposal can of course take place in many media – in the ground, in the sea, or in the air. In some cases common-sink problems are local and regional, as in the acid rain example to which I referred earlier. But common-sink problems are more likely to have a global character than common-pool ones, simply because one of the media – the atmosphere – is of global reach and range. 'It is inconceivable that any one can effectively own the atmosphere', writes David Goldblatt, 'and no one can be effectively excluded from its usage, yet the consequences of any single action can have impacts of a highly unpredictable and volatile nature all over the planet' (Goldblatt 1997, 79). One rule of thumb, then, for determining whether an environmental problem is global or not is to ask whether it is a common-pool or a common-sink problem. The latter are more likely to be global than the former. So I do not offer a definition of 'global' here, but I do want to signal caution before claiming that this or that environmental issue is a global one – and this is clearly important in the context of this book, the intention of which is to examine the effects of globalization on specifically global social problems.

We also need some guidance in respect of what constitutes an *environmental* problem. Some commentators argue that, since our environment is anything that surrounds us and provides us with the context for our life, all problems are in some sense environmental problems. Thus we are accustomed to hearing of the 'built environment', for example, and the extrapolation that cities are really no different from the countryside in that both are 'managed' and 'created' by human beings. There is obviously some truth in this, especially in a country like Britain whose countryside cannot be said to be 'natural' in the sense that is largely untouched by human hands. Much of the countryside that environmental organizations are determined to conserve or preserve in Britain is the product of hundreds of years of human activity, so their campaigns can be regarded as aimed as much at the preservation of culture as at the preservation of nature.

At the same time, though, it would be perverse to argue that we cannot at all distinguish between 'natural' and 'human-made' environments. The house in which I am writing this chapter is a different kind of thing to the tree outside the window, even though both have the imprint of the human – the house was built by humans, and I planted the tree. I believe that we can talk sensibly, then, of 'non-human nature', and I take environmental problems to be about that kind of nature and the problems that arise from our relationship with it. Bearing all this in mind, I propose to use global warming as the paradigm case of a global environmental problem, although I shall refer at times to other issues, such as ozone layer depletion, that are plausible candidates for the dubious accolade of a 'global' environmental problem.

The ways in which globalization has influenced the causation and incidence of the problem

We are now in a position to say something about the distribution of global environmental problems. There is an observable tendency in globalization literature to think of it as if it (globalization) behaved in the same way as a drop of ink on a piece of blotting paper: its spread is gradual, eventually all-pervading, and of broadly equal influence around the world. This view is couched in terms of the *interdependence* of states in the post-Westphalian, globalizing world. The language of 'interdependence' implies that states make their way through a globalizing world, 'negotiating' for advantage where possible, but with such negotiations undergirded by the recognition that no state can expect to isolate itself from the effects of other states. Here is an example of this understanding of globalization:

> First, it involves a stretching of social, political and economic activities across political frontiers, regions and continents . . . second, globalization is marked by the growing magnitude of networks and flows of trade, investment, finance, culture and so on. Third, globalization can be linked to a speeding up of global interactions and processes, as the evolution of world-wide systems of transport and communication increases the velocity of the diffusion of ideas, goods, information, capital and people. And, fourth, it involves the deepening impact of global interactions and processes such that the effects of distant events can be highly significant and even the most local developments can come to have enormous global consequences. In this particular sense, the boundaries between domestic matters and global affairs become fuzzy. In short, globalization can be thought of as the widening, intensifying, speeding up and growing impact of world-wide interconnectedness. (Held 2002, 60–1)

In the environmental context this view takes the form of assertions that we are all subject to the effects of global warming (for instance). At a very high level of generality this may be true: it is after all a condition of our definition of 'global' that everyone and everything be included under the spatial umbrella. But this level of generality tells us nothing interesting about the incidence of global warming as experienced by real people in real places. This experience is 'lumpy' rather than even, and in this regard global warming is a reminder to us to regard 'ink blot' descriptions of globalization with some suspicion.

It may be no coincidence that one of the most outspoken critics of these descriptions is an environmentalist – moreover, an environmentalist from one of the poorer regions of the world. Vandana Shiva writes that:

> The 'global' in the dominant discourse is the political space in which a particular dominant local seeks global control, and frees itself of local, national and international restraints. The global does not represent the universal human interest, it represents a particular local and parochial interest which has been globalized through the scope of its reach. (Shiva 1998, 231)

Shiva's point is that some countries globalize, while others are globalized: 'Through its global reach, the North exists in the South, but the South exists only within itself, since it has no global reach. Thus the South can *only* exist locally, while only the North exists globally (ibid., 233). Globalization is, on this reading, a constitutively asymmetrical process in which not only are its fruits divided up unequally, but also the very possibility of 'being global' is unbalanced.

Global warming is an archetypal example of asymmetrical globalization at work. Some countries produce global warming and others suffer its consequences. (Although, given the way in which climatic systems transcend national boundaries, 'country' can be regarded as only an approximate unit of analysis, and the so-called strange weather that afflicts every country – including wealthy ones – in the guise of floods, storms and droughts can be regarded as a kind of climate change boomerang effect.) Thus two islands that were part of the Pacific nation of Kiribati have disappeared (Environmental News Network 1999) as sea levels have risen – yet these islands had no impact themselves on climate change, the engine of their destruction. It is also important to see that the effects of environmental problems are always mediated by social and economic conditions. This is true even of non-anthropogenic problems, i.e. ones not caused by human beings. Earthquakes in California produce many fewer deaths than earthquakes in Turkey, not because Turkish earthquakes are intrinsically more damaging than Californian ones, but because median levels of wealth in California permit infrastructure construction that is relatively earthquake proof. The same rule applies – and will apply in a globally warmed future – in the context of anthropogenic environmental problems. Sea-level rise will be experienced differently in different places. Kiribati (average per capita income: $468 per annum; United Nations 2003a) will find it hard to take effective preventative measures while the Netherlands (average per capita income: $23,785 per annum; ibid.) will be able to construct sophisticated defences. Thus a full account of the distribution of environmental problems around the globe needs to include reference to the social and economic conditions through which they are experienced. In this sense the material in this chapter needs to be read alongside material in the next one ('Globalization and Poverty').

Let me conclude this section by saying that 'causation', 'incidence' and 'distribution' (the three headline themes of this section and the previous one) are indissolubly bound together in the environmental context. Global warming (as the paradigm global environmental problem) is *caused* by wealthy countries and, while its *incidence* and *distribution* might be regarded as formally isomorphic, the actual experience and effect of impact are mediated by differential social and economic conditions.

The ways in which global and regional bodies have tried to deal with the problem and with what success

All international difficulties are dogged by the problem that there is no international body (at the global level anyway) with the authority or legitimacy to impose solutions, and the environment is no exception to this rule. Environmental problems are therefore usually addressed through bilateral or multilateral agreements, sometimes within frameworks laid down by the one international body that does have some legitimacy and authority, the United Nations. Indeed the United Nations has raised the profile of the global environment in unprecedented fashion through a series of major conferences (Stockholm in 1972, Rio de Janeiro – the famous 'Earth Summit' – in 1992, and Johannesburg in 2002).

In what follows I propose to take two environmental problems as case studies of attempts to deal with transboundary environmental issues, and to draw some conclusions about the conditions for success and failure from them. The issues are ozone depletion and global warming – with the caveat that I expressed and explained earlier that the former might not be regarded as a 'global' environmental problem at all. Let me take this example first, nevertheless.

The function of the ozone layer (as far as human beings are concerned anyway) is to absorb some of the ultraviolet (UV) radiation that arrives from the sun and to prevent it reaching the earth's surface. High UV levels can produce skin cancer and cataracts and may even adversely affect human immune systems. It is believed that ozone levels in the mid-ranges of the stratosphere (20 to 35 km above the earth's surface) have fluctuated in the past but always within a range that has made UV absorption tolerable.

In the mid-1920s, however, Du Pont and General Motors began to look for more stable chemicals than those used to date in some industrial processes, especially in refrigeration. Carbon-based molecules containing chlorine and fluorine called chlorofluorocarbons (better known in the environmentalists' lexicon of infamy as CFCs) seemed to be the answer. They are stable, relatively non-toxic and cheap to produce in industrial quantities. Production of CFCs grew apace until by the end of the 1970s they were being used in many industrial processes and products, including refrigeration and aerosols. However, one of the qualities of CFCs turned out to be one of its problems – at least as far as the ozone layer is concerned. CFCs are long-living molecules, and it was recognized that at certain points in the process of production–consumption–waste (e.g. when refrigerators are disposed of) they must eventually find their way up into the stratosphere, where the chlorine and fluorine components would break down ozone. This could then result in a higher incidence of the UV-induced problems referred to above.

A key feature of what happened thereafter was the battle for scientific corroboration that the ozone layer was indeed thinning, and this issue of scientific consensus is often one that dogs attempts to deal with global environmental problems. In this particular case the United Nations Environment Programme (UNEP) funded a study in 1975 by the World Meteorological Society to examine the scientific basis of the problem, but it was not until the British Antarctic Survey based at Halley Bay released the results of years of ozone observation in 1985 that showed an unequivocal 'hole' in the ozone layer over the Antarctic that a scientific consensus finally emerged. During the preceding ten-year period countries had stacked up against each other, with the US, Canada, Norway, Sweden and Finland arguing for remedial action, opposed by a group including Britain, Italy, Germany, France and Japan. The consensus among opponents of a ban began to break down as Germany broke ranks under considerable domestic pressure, and an agreement was finally reached in 1987

– the Montreal Protocol – to reduce CFC production to 50 per cent of 1986 levels by 1999 (Carter 2001, 231). As further scientific confirmation of the problem emerged, more radical steps were taken, and in the 1990 London Amendments a total ban on ozone-depleting chemicals by 2000 was agreed.

The ozone story is still regarded as a major high water mark in resolving global environmental problems. Whether it can provide a model for dealing with such problems across the board is less sure. A number of factors came together to make the final agreements possible, and we should not assume that they can be reproduced in all cases. First, the issue of scientific consensus was crucial. As I indicated above, the major political players in the ozone game (and I include corporations like Du Pont in this mixed bag) were persuaded in a relatively short space of time that the causes and effects of ozone depletion were scientifically demonstrable, and that the thinning of the ozone layer constituted a threat to human and non-human welfare. But it would be a mistake to assume that science was somehow sufficient in itself to do the job of persuading initially reluctant governments and companies to rein back on, and eventually ban, ozone-depleting chemicals. Science is itself a social activity, and scientific conclusions are processed through the interests that make up the social, political and economic landscape. If those interests had been badly served by the scientific conclusions reached by the Halley Bay scientists and others, it is pretty certain that the consensus that emerged would have been much longer coming – if it had been reached at all. Du Pont, and its political sponsors the United States government, were well aware that CFC use in China, India and other southern states was growing, and that indigenous producers were jockeying for position in this growing market. They realized that a ban on CFCs would create a lucrative market for CFC substitutes, and that they were well placed to take advantage of this change because of their ability to sink large amounts of research and development money into the search for substitutes. It is no coincidence that by 1988 – just one year after the initial Montreal Protocol – Du Pont had invested $40 million in the development of CFC substitutes (Goldblatt 1997, 85). If such substitutes had been impossible to find it is very much an open question as to whether the Montreal Protocol and the London Amendments would have been possible at all. So it would be naïve to think that science 'on its own' can turn the environmental tables. It has a much better chance of doing so if the political and economic wind is blowing in the right direction.

In part, of course, the direction of the political wind is dictated by those countries and corporations that blow hardest. In this case ozone diplomacy was massively assisted by the fact that the United States was in favour of a change of direction. Indeed US administrations only blinked when it was realized, as the process of ratification of the Montreal Protocol got under way in individual countries, that it was going to be hard to get developing countries on board. The three most significant of these countries in this context – Brazil, China and India – refused to ratify it (Carter 2001, 231), arguing that they hadn't caused the problem so they should either be allowed to continue using CFCs or receive 'clean' technology transfer or financial assistance to use and develop substitutes. In the face of US resistance a multilateral fund for developing countries was agreed in London in 1990 and China and India finally came on board. We might regard this as the 'ethical' or 'justice-based' dimension of global environmental politics. Agreement on dealing with the causes and effects of global environmental problems is unlikely unless solutions are regarded as just, especially by those countries which – usually quite rightly – regard these problems as caused by the development paths taken by wealthy countries. These countries have reaped material rewards from such development paths, and the developing world asks why it should pick up the bill for mitigating the – admittedly largely unanticipated and unintended – consequences of such asymmetrical wealth accumulation.

In sum, we might conclude that a number of not necessarily repeatable factors contributed to the successful way the ozone depletion problem was dealt with. Scientific consensus was forthcoming, and the importance of the political acceptance of this consensus must be recognized. This acceptance was in turn produced by and mediated through the anticipated profits generated by the possibility of CFC substitutes. Far from being an obstacle to 'business as usual', then, the Montreal Protocol and subsequent London Amendments turned out to be a precondition for doing more and better business. This anticipatory approach was part of a third important factor – the energetic lobbying and diplomacy on behalf of restricting ozone-depleting chemicals by the major international power, the United States of America. And, finally, the importance of equity in arriving at successful and legitimate solutions to global environmental problems was eventually – if belatedly – realized.

None of these factors is so obviously and productively present in the second case study to which I want to refer: climate change, or what is more commonly referred to as 'global warming' or the 'greenhouse effect'. The more neutral 'climate change' is probably the most accurate term for the phenomenon, since it incorporates the possibility of the systematic drops in temperature that seem to be part and parcel of the 'strange weather' of recent years. All too often one hears the assertion that global warming can't be occurring because some places seem to get colder. But the phrase 'global warming' does accurately capture an important feature of what was until recently an entirely natural (that is to say, non-anthropogenic) phenomenon. It is the process by which some gases trap the sun's heat near the earth's surface. Without this effect, temperatures on the surface of the earth would be much lower than they are at present and 'life as we know it' would be impossible.

Climate change only became a global political issue once it was suggested that the processes of production and consumption of some states, peoples and communities on the planet were altering the climate beyond the 'natural' oscillations experienced up until the Industrial Revolution. In brief, the Industrial Revolution utterly altered the development paths of those who promoted it and benefited – and sometimes suffered – from its consequences. Up until the late eighteenth century humankind had operated what we now refer to as a solar economy. Energy, with a very few exceptions, was entirely derived from the sun in one form or another – wind for windmills, for example. The Industrial Revolution unlocked vast stores of energy in the earth's crust – coal, for example, and later oil. This has come to be known as the 'carbon economy'. Burning these fuels releases carbon dioxide and other gases into the atmosphere, and as these gases build up they exaggerate the impact of the greenhouse effect. The overall rise in temperature that ensues influences the climate in unpredictable ways. Those who argue for a mitigation of these consequences believe that they adversely affect human well-being, particularly in those parts of the world where people cannot afford the infrastructural and other responses that are required.

One of the factors involved in successful ozone diplomacy, it will be remembered, was the scientific consensus that surrounded the issue. Such consensus has been harder to generate in the context of climate change. The most respected scientific body in this case is the Intergovernmental Panel on Climate Change (IPCC). The IPCC has struggled for over a decade to convince major political players that global warming is actually occurring, and that this warming is caused by human activities rather than by natural fluctuations. It is almost certainly fair to say that there is a general consensus among scientists on these two issues now, but the lack of another feature of the successful ozone story has simply become more marked and obvious as a result. I pointed out there that the *political acceptance* of the consensus established by scientists was essential, particularly by those countries best placed to make a difference. This acceptance has not been forthcoming, particularly from the United States of America. I shall come back to this point shortly, but a brief account of the process of climate change diplomacy is in order first.

The very first World Climate Conference was held as long ago as 1979, where it was agreed that anthropogenic climate change might well be a reality. In 1988 participants in the Toronto conference recommended a 20 per cent cut in climate change emissions by 2005, and it was in this year that the IPCC was set up (Carter 2001, 233). These recommendations were not binding on participants, and although some took unilateral action to reduce emissions, most did not. The next key moment was at the Rio Summit in 1992 when the Framework Convention on Climate Change was signed, leading to the Kyoto Protocol in 1997 where legally binding targets on participants were established and agreed. This protocol committed developed countries to reducing their greenhouse emissions, collectively, by about 5 per cent below 1990 levels in the period between 2008 and 2012. The Kyoto Protocol was received with a mixture of jubilation and despair: jubilation, because for nearly a decade it had appeared impossible to get countries to sign up to legally binding targets, and despair, because those targets came nowhere near to satisfying the demands of the environmental movement – or, indeed, of the IPCC itself, which recommends a 60 per cent cut in 1990 greenhouse gas emissions by 2012. The Kyoto Protocol, even if fully adhered to, will produce only a 5.2 per cent cut, delaying warming that would have occurred in 2094 to 2100 – just a six-year respite.

I say 'even if fully adhered to' because it is at this point that the importance of political acceptance of the scientific consensus on climate change and the political will to do something about it snaps most clearly into focus. It will be remembered that the USA played a key lead role in moving ozone diplomacy ahead and obliging other 'developed' countries to ban the chemicals responsible for ozone depletion. In this context it was what is called, in the language of 'regime formation', a 'lead state'. The opposite of a lead state is a 'veto state', and this is the role the USA has come to play in the climate change context, with potentially devastating consequences for mitigating the effects of climate change. The important thing to remember is that the USA is responsible for 25 per cent of greenhouse emissions, so its refusal to ratify the Kyoto Protocol is of fundamental importance. At the time of writing (March 2003), the most recent stage of the Kyoto Protocol on climate change was negotiated in Marrakesh, Morocco. Despite the relatively feeble nature of the protocol, of the thirty-nine countries that started out on the long road from Kyoto in 1997, only thirty-eight reached Marrakesh in 2001. The one that dropped out was the United States of America. Despite the fact that the USA, with just 5 per cent of the world's population, produces a quarter of the world's greenhouse gases, eleven times as much per head of population as China, twenty times more than India, and 300 times more than Mozambique – despite all this, the USA claims that the Kyoto Protocol is 'unfair', since it exempts developing countries and is against the USA's best economic interests.

These two reasons for the USA parking itself outside the agreement highlight the differences between the climate change and ozone cases. In the latter case, the economic interests of the major players were in fact best served, as I pointed out above, by moving to a ban on ozone-depleting chemicals. There was money to be made by developing and selling substitutes, and doing so was scientifically and industrially relatively easy. No such easy option exists in the case of climate change. In this instance we are talking about the very energy base of one of the most momentous revolutions in human history – the Industrial Revolution. Thinking 'substitutes' here means thinking in terms of shifting paths of development adopted by the most influential countries in the world for the past 200 years. It means moving back from a carbon to a hydrogen economy. No doubt there is money to be made there too, but not in a sufficiently short space of time to satisfy corporate accountants' immediate bottom lines.

Similarly, the issue of developing countries has dogged climate change negotiations. Developing countries are not enjoined by the Kyoto Protocol to do anything to mitigate the effects of climate change, on the grounds that they have not contributed to the problem. Moreover, developed countries are expected to transfer technological and financial resources to the developing countries to enable them to pursue 'cleaner' development paths. Finally, developing countries are generally in favour of firm targets and binding commitments, while the pull from developed countries (and even some developing countries – especially the oil-producing ones) is in the direction of more vague agreements on co-operation. Each of these problems between 'North' and 'South' has its origins in disputes over equity. The United States, in particular and at the time of writing, has its own rather special view of what equity means and what it entails, and this has proved a major stumbling block to achieving the kind of success we saw in the ozone case.

It is instructive, indeed, to compare the two cases for a moment, since this makes clearer the kinds of precondition required for dealing effectively with global environmental problems, and points us towards the chapter's final section, on trends in the incidence and resolution of such problems. The ozone success story, it will be remembered, had four 'pillars'. First, a scientific consensus regarding the nature, cause and importance of the problem was quite quickly established. This has been less easy in the climate change case. Second, the major political and economic players accepted the scientific evidence as definitive, and 'lead' states were powerful and influential enough to persuade 'veto' states to come on board. Once again, this political commitment has been singularly lacking in the context of global warming, with especially damaging effects given that the world's biggest contributor to global warming has stayed outside the agreement. Third, producers of CFCs realized that large profits could be made quite quickly from the production, marketing and sale of substitutes. The shifts required to mitigate global warming are much bigger and wide-ranging, and the financial incentives for doing so are less apparent and certainly less immediate. The political economy of ozone depletion, in other words, is more propitious for 'business as usual' than that of climate change. Finally, the principle and practice of equity has been harder to establish in the case of global warming than for ozone depletion.

Further trends in the incidence and resolution of global environmental problems

I began this chapter by saying that global environmental problems are an example of globalization at work (that's what makes them global), and are in this sense 'made possible' by globalization. This assertion might be read in two ways. First, that globalization is the condition for the *possibility* of global environmental problems, and second that globalization will *necessarily* produce environmental problems. Which of these one chooses will largely determine one's view of 'trends in the incidence and resolution of global environmental problems' – the subject of this final section of the chapter.

The less contentious of the two options, I take it, is the first one. I pointed out at the beginning of the chapter that even the most massive of empires of yesteryear had only regional effects. Now, though, increased economic interpenetration has reached a stage at which the world's most powerful economic players have a potentially global impact. Global warming is perhaps the most stunning example of this phenomenon at work. As we saw at the beginning, Bill McKibben has argued that 'every inch and every hour of the globe' has come under the sway of human influence. Under these conditions, global environmental problems are always possible, and maybe even likely, but not necessary. Globalization here is regarded as a largely neutral phenomenon, a backdrop against which things happen – some good and some bad. When bad things happen – when a global environmental problem arises, for example – international institutions and the machinery of international agreement crank into action and efforts are made, with greater or lesser success (compare, once again, the ozone and climate change cases), to deal with them. Within this context we are now clearer about the kinds of factor that will influence such success and failure: scientific consensus, political acceptance of the science, comparative economic advantage and the costs associated with change, and issues of global equity. These seem to be the determining characteristics of the success or failure of attempts at dealing with global environmental problems within a broadly 'neutral' view of globalization. In this context contingent events will always have an important role to play. The United Nations, for example, has performed a key role in both ozone and climate change diplomacy, and will be important in most imaginable future global environmental problem resolutions. At the time of writing, however (March 2003), the United States and Britain have dealt a blow to UN credibility by embarking on a war with Iraq without UN sanction. It would be odd if this had no knock-on consequence for the effectiveness of the UN as an honest broker in future global environmental problem negotiations. On this reading, the future of the 'incidence and resolution' of global environmental problems is hard to predict, subject as it is to the push and pull of contingent circumstances.

The alternative view is that the particular type of globalization we might currently be said to be undergoing will *necessarily* bring global environmental problems in its train. In part this is because, it will be argued, globalization is driven by the logic of capital accumulation. The processes of production and consumption that this entails, coupled with the short time horizons associated with calculations of profit and loss, put inevitable strain on the ecological context within which the relentless drive for accumulation takes place. In the language used earlier in the chapter, the 'sources' and 'sinks' on which human and other life depend are continually driven towards their thresholds of tolerance. We may occasionally find ways of getting more from less, as the optimists say we will, but the logic of accumulation will never allow us to get less from less. So if getting less from less is a condition for reducing the incidence of global environmental problems, then this particular reading of globalization suggests that we will be unable to reduce them – given current practices.

At present we seem to be somewhere between these two options, where a particular version of globalization, driven and sponsored by the most powerful economies and polities, is taking on the appearance of inevitability associated with the 'necessitarian' school of globalization, while sharing some of the contingency of the ink blot school – precisely because particular and historically specific regimes are driving it. Let me try to explain.

I drew a contrast earlier in the chapter between the 'ink blot' and 'asymmetrical' views of globalization. The former has it that the effects of globalization are gradual, eventually all-pervading, and of broadly equal influence around the world, and the latter argues that inequalities of power are constitutive of globalization and its effects. If the asymmetrical view – or some version of it – is correct, then a massive burden of responsibility lies with 'globalizing' countries. It is clear that globalization offers huge temptations for globalizing countries too: the temptation to impose their 'local' view of the world on the rest of it. And this will be particularly tempting for those who regard their way of life as a global model for others. It might be argued that 'the environment' is an excellent medium through which to carry out this particular globalizing project. This works as follows.

The guiding thread of the asymmetrical view of globalization is that the capacity to act globally is unequally distributed. Both inference and observation lead us to the conclusion that those who can and do act globally are in effect projecting their local as everyone else's global. Now think, for a moment, of the ideal structure for a medium or a phenomenon through which to turn local language into global grammar. There must be a local 'view' of it, of course, but equally evidently this local view must be translatable into global effects. It must, in other words, be 'globalizable'. Even more ideally, enacting the local view locally should have immediate and constant global effects, such that every enactment of the local view is always simultaneously an act of globalization. Can there possibly be a medium and a phenomenon that live up to such exacting standards? Indeed there can: the environment is the medium and global warming is the phenomenon.

We have already seen how the current US administration has set its face against the Kyoto Protocol. Instead of standing shoulder to shoulder with the rest of the world over global warming, as it demanded the rest of the world did after the Twin Towers attack on 11 September 2001, the USA has embarked on a fossil fuel bonanza that will increase its greenhouse emissions by an estimated 35 per cent (Retallack 2001, 21). George W. Bush's national energy policy calls for between 1300 and 1900 electricity plants, the easing of regulations on the siting of power plants and refineries, the opening up of parts of the Arctic National Wildlife Refuge for oil and gas exploration, a cut in resources for renewable fuels of some 27 per cent, and a cut in federal investment in energy efficiency measures.

It is commonly argued that Bush is returning favours accrued during his 2000 election campaign, to which various oil, coal, gas and utility companies contributed some $50 million. These connections and favours surely are linked to America's withdrawal from the Kyoto Protocol negotiations. But they also represent a way of life, a way of life it is impossible to pursue without affecting people in other parts of the planet. In explaining his rejection of the Kyoto Protocol, George W. Bush said that 'a growing population requires more energy to heat and cool our homes, more gas to drive our cars' (Bush 2001). Bush would like to present this as a statement of fact, but it might be read, rather, as a prospectus for a way of life. 'Heat our homes' (rather than put on an extra layer of clothing); 'cool our homes' (rather than open the window); 'more gas' (rather than reduce fuel consumption); 'to drive our cars' (rather than get about less, or in a different way). This local prospectus, in turn, has immediate global effects in its contribution to global warming.

When the engine of globalization is in the hands of regimes, then, that are willing and able to use it to reproduce their view of 'the good' throughout the world, and when that view of the good entails an increasing incidence of environmental problems, current battles over global warming are a sign of things to come. That seems to be the position in which we currently find ourselves.

Further reading

Laferrière, E. (1999). *International Relations Theory and Ecological Thought: Towards a Synthesis*. London and New York: Routledge.

Martinez-Alier, J. (2002). *The Environmentalism of the Poor*. Cheltenham, and Northampton, MA: Edward Elgar.

Paterson, M. (2000). *Understanding Global Environmental Politics: Domination, Accumulation, Resistance*. Basingstoke: Macmillan; New York: St Martin's Press.

Thomas, C. (1992). *The Environment in International Relations*. London: Royal Institute of International Affairs.

4

Globalization and Poverty

Vic George

No other social issue has been under such intense academic and political scrutiny as poverty. Yet, agreement on its definition, measurement, extent, causes and solutions remains as elusive as ever because poverty is a complex political, economic, social and moral issue. A recent UN study identified six 'basic poverty definitions' (UNDP 1998, 16); another study came up with 'eleven different classes of definitions' (Spicker 2001, 154), with a number of sub-divisions in each class. It may be true that the core of all these definitions of poverty consists of 'unacceptable hardships' that are 'intolerably painful or shameful' as well as 'unnecessary', and hence in need of amelioration through collective action (Donnison 2001, 89), but this only shifts the debate to what constitutes 'unacceptable hardships'. Personal judgements are inevitable, and some would say useful, in the definition of poverty.

Comparisons of the extent of poverty between industrial countries (ICs) and developing countries (DCs) are more meaningful if they treat poverty as a continuum of deprivation, with undernutrition at the very harsh end and lack of social participation at the other, more generous, end (George and Howards 1991, chap. 1). For convenience sake, the declaration of the World Summit on Social Development in Copenhagen in 1995 signed by 117 heads of state put forward a two-level definition of poverty: an absolute and an overall definition (United Nations 1995, 57). This chapter sees poverty as multi-faceted, consisting of unacceptably low levels of nutrition, income, health and education along the lines suggested by the various reports of the United Nations Development Programme (UNDP 1997, 16–19).

Strictly speaking, it is impossible to disentangle the effects of globalization on poverty from those of demography, politics, wars or changing family patterns. All that can be done is to point out the various ways in which globalizaion has been a force in reducing or increasing the numbers of the poor in different countries. Space does not allow for the documentation of the relationships between poverty and other social problems, though this is done in some of the other chapters.

Extent of poverty

We begin the discussion with the extent of undernutrition; we then examine the magnitude of income poverty before we look at poverty in relation to both health and education. Without doubt, these forms of poverty are interrelated and affect each other in various ways.

Undernutrition

Most of the data on the global extent of undernutrition, i.e. inadequate consumption of calories for a healthy life as measured by either weight or height, come from the Food and Agriculture Organization of the United Nations and relate to DCs. A number of conclusions flow from these data.

- The proportion of the population of DCs which is undernourished declined from 35 per cent in 1969–71 to 29 per cent during 1978–81 and to 18 per cent during 1996–8 (FAO 1996, 271; FAO 2001, 62).
- The number of the undernourished declined from 917 million to 905 million and to 791.9 million during these three periods.
- The proportion of children that are undernourished has always been higher than that of the general population – 29 per cent during 1995–2000 (FAO 2001, 63).
- Similarly, the proportion of women that are undernourished is higher than that of men, both for demographic reasons and as a result of the well-known maldistribution of resources within households.

- The incidence of undernutrition varies from one region to another: in 1996–8 it ranged from 34 per cent in sub-Saharan Africa to 10 per cent in North Africa and the Middle East (ibid., 62).
- Two-thirds of the undernourished lived in Asia and the Pacific, even though the proportion of the population that was undernourished in the region was only 17 per cent in 1996–8 (ibid.).
- The sharpest decline in undernutrition was recorded in Asia – from 32 per cent in 1978–81 to 17 per cent in 1996–8. China's record has been particularly impressive and accounts for a large part of the global reduction of undernutrition. Sub-Saharan Africa has been the least successful in reducing the extent of undernitrition.
- Milder forms of undernutrition can be found in the ICs. Data from the US department of agriculture show that in the late 1990s 10.2 per cent of American households experience food insecurity, i.e. limited or uncertain access to food for varying periods of time (quoted in Buttel 2000, 16). The proportion of children under five that are malnourished (rather than undernourished) is less than 5 per cent compared to as many as 50 per cent in DCs (World Bank 2000a, 3). Objectively, IC undernutrition is milder than that experienced in DCs, even though subjectively it may be felt just as strongly by those affected by it.

The prevalence of widespread undernutrition in DCs is not the result of either overpopulation or lack of food. It is true that population growth has been high, but food productivity has been even higher as a result of intensive farming methods. Most commentators will agree with the FAO's verdict that 'hunger results not so much from insufficient food supplies, as from people's lack of access to those supplies' (FAO 2000, 308).

Income poverty

Data on income poverty in the DCs are derived primarily from the work of the World Bank, which defines as poor those whose incomes fall below $1 a day – a figure which it considers grossly inadequate for ICs. Using $1 a day as the definition of income poverty in DCs, the following conclusions emerge from the bank's most recent estimates (World Bank 2000a, 23).

- First, the number of people in DCs living in poverty rose from 1183 million in 1987 to 1198 million in 1998.
- Second, however, the proportion of the population in DCs living in poverty declined from 28.3 per cent in 1987 to 24.0 per cent in 1998. In other words, the risk of being in poverty declined slightly over the years, but because of population growth the numbers of the poor rose slightly.
- Third, since most people in the world live in Asia, it is no surprise that most of the poor also live in Asia: 75 per cent in 1987 and 66 per cent in 1998. The risk of being in poverty, however, is at its highest in sub-Saharan Africa, where 46 per cent of the population had incomes below $1 a day.
- Fourth, the risk of being in poverty declined between 1987 and 1998 in all regions with the exception of sub-Sahara, where it remained at 46 per cent, and the ex-Soviet countries of Europe and Central Asia, where it rose from 1 per cent in 1987 to 24 per cent in 1998 as a result of the neo-liberal measures applied to government policies and to the economy. The financial position of pensioners in Russia is a good indication of what happened to vulnerable groups in these societies after the liberalization of their economies and the destruction of state welfare: 'Pension arrears accumulated to an alarming degree in 1998. By the end of the year, survey evidence indicated that four-fifths of pension recipients had not received their pensions for more than 3 months' (OECD 2000, 70).
- Fifth, the extent of poverty rises very considerably if $2 per day rather than $1 a day is used as a benchmark. In China it rises from 18.5 per cent to 53.7 per cent; in India from 44.2 to 86.2; in Pakistan from 31.0 to 84.7; in Malawi from 60.2 to 88.8; in Mali from 72.8 to 90.6; and so on (World Bank 2000a, 280–2). Moreover, the poverty gap – the proportion of GDP needed to lift everyone above the poverty line – widens so much that the abolition of poverty at $2 a day is economically and politically impossible for many DCs in the immediate future.
- Sixth, if the $2 a day benchmark creates too many poor in the DCs, it results in no poverty when applied to the ICs. For this reason, two more generous income poverty lines are used by the international agencies to measure poverty in the ICs: $14.40 per day and 50 per cent of national median income. Clearly, income poverty in ICs is nowhere near as stark and visible as in the DCs. Indeed the poor of the ICs are affluent in absolute terms when compared to the poor of the DCs. Poverty, however, is

experienced as part of life in a particular society at a particular time and hence subjectively it is a relative condition.

- Seventh, during the years 1989–95, the proportion of the population in ICs with incomes below $14.40 a day ranged from a high 36.5 per cent in Ireland to a low 2.0 per cent in Italy, 14.1 per cent in the USA, 13.1 in the UK, 12.0 in France, 11.5 in Germany, 7.8 in Australia, 4.6 in Sweden, and so on (UNDP 1999, 149–51). The same benchmark resulted in very high poverty rates in most ex-Soviet countries – 50 per cent for the Russian Federation and 88 per cent in Kyrgyzstan – but low rates in some others – the Czech Republic at 1.0 per cent, Hungary at 4.0 per cent, and so on.

- Eighth, the second measure of 50 per cent of median national income leads to very similar results. The extent of poverty varies from one IC to another but it is within manageable proportions. During the same period, the highest rates were to be found among the English-speaking countries: 19.1 per cent in the USA, 13.5 in the UK, 12.9 in Australia, 11.7 in Canada, 11.1 in Ireland and 9.2 in New Zealand. Most other European ICs had poverty rates ranging from 5 to 7 per cent of their population (ibid.).

- Ninth, poverty rates in terms of 50 per cent of national median income increased in most ICs during the last two decades of the twentieth century. Summarizing the data, Makinen shows that poverty increased from the early 1980s to the mid-1990s in nine ICs and declined in five (Makinen 1999, 8). The greatest rise took place in the UK – from 6.7 to 17.3 per cent – while the sharpest decline occurred in Finland – from 6.7 to 2.4 per cent. The USA, however, had the highest rates in both the early 1980s and the mid-1990s – 15.2 and 18.6 per cent of the population. What is clear from these differential rates is that the extent of poverty in ICs is primarily the result of government policies. All these countries possess the financial means to abolish poverty, but they tolerate it because they give priority to other considerations. Poverty abolition is primarily a political issue in ICs.

- Tenth, the feminization of income poverty is universally true. Women not only form the majority of the poor because of demographic reasons but they also run a higher risk than men of being in poverty because of their inferior position in the labour market and in the social security system, as well as from the fact that they are the majority of the unpaid carers for children, the elderly and other groups. They are also more likely than men to be in poverty for longer periods and to be suffering from more severe income poverty. Their position is worse in DCs than in ICs for obvious market, legislative and cultural reasons. Over the past few decades, however, some progress has been made in improving the position of women and in narrowing the gender divide in ICs and to a lesser extent in DCs.

Health poverty

Undernutrition and income poverty lie at the heart of the woefully low health standards in DCs: 'A staggering 55 per cent of the nearly 12 million deaths each year among children under five in the developing world are associated with malnutrition' (FAO 2000, 66). This is compounded by the low expenditures on health services and by the insanitary conditions. In the 1990s, public expenditure on health in the DCs was a mere 1.9 per cent of GDP compared with 6.2 per cent in ICs (World Bank 2000a, 286–8). Bearing in mind the urban and hospital biases of government expenditures in DCs, it means that health services in the rural areas are pretty non-existent. Polluted water supplies and general insanitary conditions add to the pressures for low health standards. During the 1990s, for example, 28 per cent of the population of DCs were without access to safe water; for the forty-eight least developed countries the proportion rose to 41 per cent; and for sub-Saharan countries, it was 50 per cent (UNDP 1999, 146–9).

Despite these adverse conditions, life expectancy has improved over the years, though the gap with the ICs remains. In 1970, life expectancy at birth in DCs was fifty-three years and in the forty-eight least developed countries a mere forty-three years, compared to seventy-two in the ICs. In 1999, the corresponding numbers were sixty-three, fifty-one and seventy-eight years respectively (UNICEF 2001, 94–8). In relational terms, life expectancy in the least developed countries amounted to 60 per cent of that in the ICs in 1970; by 1999, it rose to 65 per cent – a small but hardly sufficient narrowing of the gap. There are, of course, wide variations within these group averages which show that health standards can be improved substantially in DCs if the right policies are pursued. Sri Lanka's life expectancy in 1970 was sixty-five years, but by 1999 it had reached seventy-four years, despite the low incomes per capita – a figure that was not that much lower than that of several rich countries.

The same trends apply to infant mortality rates, with an absolute improvement over the years but the gap between DCs and ICs remaining as wide as ever. In 1960, infant mortality rate per thousand live births was 173 for the least developed countries, 141 for DCs and thirty-one for ICs. In 1999, the corresponding figures were 104, sixty-three and six respectively (UNICEF 2001, 78–82). To put it differently, a baby born in 1960 ran almost six times the risk of dying in the least developed countries than in the ICs; by 1999, the risk was seventeen times higher. Again, there are wide variations in DCs, reflecting the same point as with life expectancy: income is a good proxy for health but not a perfect one. Cuba, where incomes per capita are low, saw its infant mortality rate decline from thirty-nine in 1960 to six in 1999 – a figure that was pretty similar to that of many rich countries.

The gap in health standards between DCs and ICs is most stark in the case of maternal mortality (the number of women dying every year from pregnancy-related causes per 100,000 live births), despite the improvements over the years: 'A woman in the developing world is on average 40 times more likely than a woman living in the industrialized world to die from complications of pregnancy and child-birth' (UNICEF 2001, 23). The risk is even greater in twenty-three DCs which reported maternal mortality rates that exceeded 500, including three countries where it was over 1000. Rates in ICs are below ten. The reported risk of a woman dying because of pregnancy-related causes ranges from 1100 in Mozambique and the Central African Republic to five in Sweden and Switzerland (ibid., 102–6).

Education poverty

The importance of education to the welfare of both the individual and the country has been acknowledged for some time: 'It has long been recognized that the qualities of a nation's people have an important influence on its prosperity and growth' (World Bank 1980, 37). A great deal has been achieved in raising educational standards over the years, but an equally immense task lies ahead. The proportion of the adult population in the DCs who were illiterate declined from 65 per cent in 1950, to 42 per cent in 1980, and to 36 per cent in the late 1990s.

The gender gap has also narrowed. In 1980, the adult literacy rate (the proportion of persons aged fifteen and over who can read and write) in DCs for men was 68 per cent and for women 46 per cent; by the late 1990s it had reached 81 and 66 per cent respectively. The figures were lower for the least developed countries even though the rate of progress was pretty much the same. For 1980, the figures were

47 and 24 per cent; and for the late 1990s, they were 63 and 44 per cent respectively. The problem is even more daunting for some of the least developed countries – a total of 15 per cent in the late 1990s where only one-quarter of adult women were literate (UNICEF 2001, 90–4).

Obviously school registrations have improved over the years and will continue to improve. But caution is needed in interpreting these data, for school registration is not the same as school attendance. Moreover, there is the serious problem of children not being registered at birth: 'In 33 countries of the world, more than half of the children are not even registered at birth. Even in countries with birth registration, children of ethnic minorities and children born with disabilities are often ignored' (UNICEF 2001, 59).

DCs have been spending more on education than on health over the years, though less than the expenditure of ICs. In 1997, public expenditure on education in DCs amounted to 4.1 per cent of GNP compared to 5.4 per cent spent by ICs. The corresponding figures for 1980 were 3.5 and 5.6 per cent respectively (World Bank 2000a, 284–6). As with health, however, the urban bias means that a disproportionate amount is spent in the cities and on higher education, with the result that primary education in the rural areas suffers.

Despite the substantial progress in reducing illiteracy, a great deal still remains to be done, particularly in the case of women, for 'nearly two of every three children in the developing world who do not receive a primary education (approximately 73 million of the 130 million out-of-school' are girls (UNICEF 1999, 7). At this rate, illiteracy will continue to be a major problem for many years to come. The progress made by some DCs, however, gives hope that rapid advances in this area are possible provided the right policies are pursued.

The situation is different in ICs: illiteracy has almost been wiped out and high proportions of both boys and girls move on from their secondary schools to tertiary education. There are problems of truancy, of underachievement and of wasted ability, but these can hardly rank in the same league as the education problems of DCs. It is quite legitimate to talk of inequalities in heath and education but not of poverty in these areas, as it is the case in DCs.

Globalization and poverty

Neo-liberal enthusiasts concede that globalization may well lead to more poverty in some cases, but they see this as a temporary situation which will rectify itself soon enough as the country's economy takes off on the road to industrialization. They will also remind the reader that, though poverty may well increase, 'the poor are getting less poor in relative terms globally' (Patten 2001, 2). In other words, the poor of today are more affluent than the poor of the past – an observation that is of no comfort to the poor. Marxisant writers will take a diametrically opposite view: globalization represents a race to the bottom, with wages and social benefits declining and poverty increasing as a result of the triumph of capital over labour. Moreover, the prospects for improvement are negligible so long as capitalism reigns. The evidence does not support either of these two positions. Rather it lends support to the pluralist pragmatist view that the results of globalization on living standards are diverse and varied, negative and positive; and that progress is possible, albeit at a slow and uneven pace.

There are many interrelated reasons for the ups and downs in the rates of poverty – demographic trends, family changes, growth rates and so on. Globalization is simply one of them and it is hardly possible to isolate the strength of its influence from that of the other factors, particularly in view of the fact that they are interrelated. All that can be attempted is to discuss the various ways in which globalization has contributed to the rise and fall of poverty in DCs and ICs.

1   Globalization has encouraged economic growth through the spread of technology, investment and trade. The rate of growth has been higher in the DCs than in ICs, but because of much higher population growth rates the disparities in incomes per capita remain as wide as ever. Thus in 1975 incomes per capita in real terms were $600 in DCs, $287 in the least developed countries and $12,589 in ICs; in 1997 the corresponding numbers were $1314, $260 and $27,174 (UNDP 1999, 151–5). The most shocking statistic is the decline in real incomes per capita in the least developed countries, due primarily to the fact that the annual growth of their economies was slower than the annual rise of their population. Economic growth does help to reduce poverty, but it is more effective in those countries where it is accompanied by government anti-poverty measures.

2   Globalization has contributed to the improvements in health and education standards and the reductions in the proportions of the population who are undernourished and in income poverty in other ways – through the spread of Western medicine, the encouragement of more gender-friendly ideas, and the work of

UN bodies in the areas of health, education, child welfare and so on. But, as we shall see below, some of the policies forced on governments of DCs had the opposite effect of increasing the risk of poverty.

3   The impact of globalization on the improvement of living standards has been very uneven because of the freedom that it provides to private business to invest and de-invest where it pleases. Thus improvements in living standards have been at their lowest in the least developed countries because there is less profit to be made from investing in them. Improvements have been at their highest in the ICs and the small countries of South-East Asia because investment was judged to be more profitable. The globalization of Russia illustrates the vast damage that can be heaped on society when privatization and deregulation are rushed in quickly. In the 1990s, per capita incomes declined, income poverty increased, education and health standards plummeted and crime soared: 'The story is not a good advertisement for capitalism. More precisely, it is a very bad reflection on the case for "quick bang" transition' (Marris 1999, 80–1).

4   The increased freedom offered to business by globalization has not been reciprocated by a corresponding ethical trading on behalf of business. There are numerous examples of this, such as the lack of attention to the health needs of DCs on behalf of the large pharmaceutical companies, and so on. Most of the medical research for new drugs, for obvious profit reasons, concerns the illnesses of the rich countries.

5   Globalization has increased the ability of speculative capital to move in and out of a country at will, and this has been the major cause of many a crisis in DCs, as that in Asia in 1997–9 showed. Such crises have a habit of hurting the poor and the not-so-poor rather than the rich.

6   The neo-liberal ideology underpinning globalization became the ideology of the World Bank and the IMF, with negative effects on the social services of DCs during the 1980s and early 1990s. Governments in financial difficulties and needing the support of these two institutions had to meet their conditionality criteria, which meant reductions in social expenditure and in food subsidies, deregulation of their labour markets, privatization of their public utilities and reductions in their taxation rates. It was not until the mid-1990s that the ill effects of these policies on the poor were recognized and some measures were taken to provide some protection to the poor.

7   Though globalization exerted similar pressures on ICs, they were in a better position to withstand them, with the result that welfare retrenchment has not proved as deep and painful in those countries with pro-welfare governments – evidence of the argument that nation-states make a difference in the handling of globalization pressures.

8   Irrespective of IMF and World Bank pressures for welfare restructuring, globalization has encouraged and sustained an intense spirit of competitiveness which, on one hand, helped to increase economic growth but, on the other hand, forced governments to adopt anti-welfare measures that increase poverty. The case of China is a good example of this. The political reforms of 1992 meant increased participation of China in the world economy but on terms that were competitive enough to attract foreign capital and investment. This led to changes in social security and health provisions so as to reduce social expenditure and strengthen international competitiveness. As Guan points out, however, once a regime of global competitiveness gets established, it becomes a fixture of government policy for fear that, if relaxed, it will lead to a backlash by international capital (Guan 2001, 251).

9   The neo-liberal ideology of globalization was largely responsible for the rigid policies pursued over the years in relation to the debts accumulated by governments in DCs. The result has been that many DCs have been spending more on debt repayments than on either education or health over many years now. Indeed, in 1998 fourteen countries were spending more on debt servicing than on their basic social services – education, health and personal social services (UNICEF 2001, 55). Moreover, the burden increased over the years: while the cost of debt servicing amounted to 11 per cent of the total value of exports of goods and services of DCs in 1970, it rose to 16 per cent in 1996 (ibid., 98–102).

10 Globalization has been high in the areas of finance, trade, technology and tourism but very low in relation to immigration. While Europeans flocked to the Americas, Africa and Asia when they found their living conditions insufferable, people from DCs find it extremely difficult to do the same today. In this way, poverty remains confined within national borders: 'The fact that labour, the chief resource in early stages of development, is among the least mobile (in terms of crossing borders) of all production factors means that globalization can lead to greater inequalities as well as to greater progress' (FAO 2000, 312).

11   Globalization has encouraged the growth of more gender-friendly policies through the spread of gender egalitarian values and the work of UN bodies. Thus one finds that infant mortality rates between boys and girls have become similar and that life expectancy in 1999 was greater for women than for men in all but two small DCs (UNICEF 2001, 102–6). Educational achievements between boys and girls in DCs have narrowed over the years while in ICs they are the same. Wage inequalities by gender have declined and so have poverty rates between men and women of working age. Though gender inequalities persist, they are not as wide as they used to be, and part of the merit for this must go to globalization.

12   Globalization has had the paradoxical effect of encouraging both cosmopolitanism and nationalism. Cosmopolitanism supports a world view of social issues and thus may be a force in mitigating poverty. Nationalism can have the opposite effect when it leads to civil wars and border conflicts, as it has done in many DCs. Indeed, expenditure on defence exceeds that on education or health in a large number of DCs, including many of the least developed countries: 'During a recent border war, Eritrea and Ethiopia spent hundreds of millions of dollars on weapons, while 1 million Eritreans and 8 million Ethiopians faced famine' (UNICEF 2001, 37).

13   Though the effects of globalization have varied from one part of the world to another and have, on the whole, raised living standards, they have contributed to the widening of income inequalities between the very rich and the very poor countries: 'The average income in the richest 20 countries is 37 times the average income in the poorest 20 – a gap that has doubled in the past 40 years' (World Bank 2000a, 3).

Whatever the net balance of the effects of globalization may be, the fact is that poverty in terms of undernutrition, income, health and education remains far too high in a world of plenty.

Anti-poverty policies in ICs and DCs

Four paradigms

Anti-poverty policies in DCs have been shaped largely by exogenous bodies – the World Bank, the IMF, UNICEF, the ILO and other United

Nations bodies, as well as by the major advanced industrial countries. The ideas, the political direction and the economic leverage came from outside.

Four poverty policy paradigms can be distinguished during the second half of the twentieth century: the trickle down thesis, the basic needs approach, welfare state restructuring/structural adjustment policies, and adjustment with a human face.

(a) The trickle down thesis The 'trickle down' thesis dominated poverty thinking and policy in the 1950s and 1960s. The fruits of economic growth, it was argued, are enjoyed by all, poor and non-poor. Economic growth trickles down to all sections of the community in equal terms. Hence economic growth maximization was the best way to deal with poverty.

(b) Basic needs approach By the mid-1960s, however, poverty was rediscovered in the USA and the UK, and a war on poverty was declared amid a striking political consensus (Harrington 1962; Abel-Smith and Townsend 1965). Poverty had not disappeared despite the significant rates of economic growth. By the mid-1970s, it was also evident that the same process had taken place in the DCs. Despite impressive rises in rates of economic growth, poverty reductions remained feeble and variable. UN bodies involved in poverty policies accepted that, though important, 'economic growth alone could not reduce absolute poverty at an acceptable speed' (World Bank 1980, 32). It had to be tempered and supplemented by government action designed to benefit the poor. As a result, a basic needs approach (or redistribution with growth) was seen as the road to poverty alleviation, and thus 'attention shifted to the direct provision of health, nutritional and educational services' (World Bank 1990, 2).

(c) Structural adjustment policies The basic needs approach was a short-lived policy because, by the early 1980s, the USA and the UK began to take steps to curtail the role of the state in public affairs, to reduce public expenditure, to privatize public utilities, to reduce direct taxation, to deregulate the labour market and to make the control of inflation rather than of unemployment the primary aim of economic policy. It was believed that this would raise rates of economic growth even though it would increase inequality and poverty during the initial stages. Other ICs followed, with the result that the 1980s and early 1990s were years of welfare restructuring designed both to change and to roll back the frontiers of the state.

Similar developments took place in the DCs under the structural adjustment programmes (SAPs) imposed by the IMF and the World

Bank or freely adopted by governments. The situation was more complicated in DCs because many of them became highly indebted to international bodies, governments of ICs and private institutions and thus had little choice but to adopt SAPs. Inevitably this meant reduction in public services and in food subsidies, with painful effects on many sections of the population but particularly the poor. Adjustment 'was generally tackled without regard for its distributional or poverty implications' (Cornia et al., 1987, 7).

This was a policy that had its critics from the start. UNICEF was particularly concerned because SAPs had their severest effects on children: 'The essence of UNICEF's position . . . is that policies which lead to rising malnutrition, declining health services, and falling school enrolment rates are inhuman, unnecessary, and ultimately inefficient' (UNICEF 1987, 18).

(d) Adjustment with a human face   By the mid-1990s, a new consensus of a sort emerged around the notion of adjustment with a human face. The new approach accepted that adjustment can be necessary but it should be applied in such a way that the poor are protected. It is a movement away from the early claim that the simultaneous pursuit of high rates of economic growth and the safeguard of basic social standards are incompatible. Evidence from the development histories of several countries, particularly in Asia, showed that government provision of public services could help rather than hinder economic growth. Thus the World Bank came to acknowledge that 'growth, equality, and reductions in poverty can proceed together, as they have done in much of East Asia' (World Bank 1999, 15).

The bank's latest strategy is 'for attacking poverty in three ways: promoting opportunity, facilitating empowerment and enhancing security' (World Bank 2000a, 6). Despite the high rhetoric, the details of the strategy show that it is a policy that belongs to the fourth model discussed above, which many writers on social policy have found wanting, for in essence it is nothing more but 'liberalism with safety nets' (Deacon 2000, 261).

Prospects for poverty reduction

Present policies pursued by the UN bodies stand no chance of substantially reducing poverty in DCs. There is a striking contrast between the strong language used by several international bodies to condemn the existence of poverty and the meek policies adopted for its abolition. The former director of the IMF sees poverty as 'the ultimate systemic threat' to the world community (Camdessus 2001, 36). Yet the policies of the IMF on poverty over the years nowhere live up to this expectation. What can be attempted briefly here is to sketch out the main changes that need to be adopted if poverty is to be reduced in the near future. These are divided into the economic, the social, the political and the ideological, even though they overlap.

The economic policies that are needed to reduce poverty indicate that most DCs will not be able to abolish poverty unless they receive substantially more financial and technical assistance from the ICs and the rules of world trade are made fairer to the interests of DCs.

First, the amount of aid given by ICs to DCs is woefully low. The Pearson Report of 1969 recommended that ICs should give 0.7 per cent of their gross national product in overseas aid – a recommendation accepted by the UN. In 2000, the average rate for all OECD countries was a mere 0.22 per cent. Only five countries achieved the Pearson target – Sweden, Norway, Denmark, the Netherlands and Luxembourg. Moreover, a large part of aid is given for military spending; most of aid is allocated according to political considerations; a good part of aid is 'tied' and used for the purchase of goods and services from the donor country; and only a very small part of aid goes to the poorest countries with the greatest need. Both the amount of aid and the philosophy of aid giving need to change.

Second, the amount of debt that many DCs have to service has grown so much over the years that many of them spend more on debt servicing than on health or education. This is clearly unsustainable, for it will continue to drive DCs into deeper indebtedness. Despite the many promises and targets for the reduction of debt for the poorest countries, very little has been delivered. The rhetoric far outstrips reality. The much publicized heavily indebted poor country (HIPC) initiative put forward by the IMF and the World Bank in 1996 was designed to provide special debt relief assistance to twenty of the forty-one HIPCs. Two years later, UNDP's judgement was that 'the initial promise of the HIPC initiative seems unlikely to be fulfilled. Relatively few countries will benefit in the near future' (UNDP 1998, 49). Subsequent initiatives, such as the Poverty Reduction and Growth Facility, are of the same ilk: grudging minor concessions that bring some relief to some countries but which do not go to the heart of the problem – i.e. that current debt-servicing burdens are unsustainable. The IMF and the World Bank spend as much energy acting as debt collectors as they do serving as development agencies.

Third, investment in DCs has to improve if their economies are to expand sufficiently – at least in line with their population growth rates. Investment has suffered not only because of reductions in aid and the rise in debt relief but also because very little foreign direct investment reaches the poorest of DCs. Most of it goes to the ICs and to the few large DCs where profit maximization is possible. Inevitably, investment declined in many parts of the developing world: 'Between 1980 and 1996, in the developing world with the exception of Asia, the ratio of gross domestic investment to GDP dropped significantly' (UNDP 1998, 17).

Fourth, the demands made by multinational companies on DCs in terms of taxes, wages and labour standards are excessive. How to attract foreign direct investment without conceding these excessive demands remains an unresolved problem for DCs. As Townsend points out, 'the challenge is to find some means of arbitrating between transnational corporations and nation states' (Townsend 2000, 225).

Fifth, the rules of world trade need to take more into account the needs of the DCs. The aim of the World Trade Organization (WTO) of facilitating free trade, by reducing import duties and barriers, remains unfulfilled, particularly in agricultural products and textiles that are the major products of DCs. The heavy subsidy paid by ICs to their farmers not only makes it difficult for DCs to compete but it also undermines their agriculture. In addition, the price of primary commodities that are the main exports of DCs has fallen in relation to that of manufactures which are the main exports of ICs. Attempts by DCs to rectify some of these disadvantages at recent meetings of the WTO met with little success, despite the fact that 'the developing countries appeared readier . . . to negotiate and strike deals than either the Americans or the Europeans' (Bayne 2000, 145). It is not unexpected that WTO conferences are marked by popular protests and that many activists consider the WTO as a total failure for the poor – it has failed 'the most conservative of tests: to do no further damage' (Wallach and Sforza 1999, 63).

The monetary losses to DCs from these economic disadvantages are substantial: 'The loss to developing countries from unequal access to trade, labor and finance was estimated by the Human Development Report 1992 at $500 billion a year, 10 times what they received in foreign assistance' (UNDP 1997, 87). At the social policy level, the most important reform needed to abolish poverty in DCs is the gradual introduction of some form of basic income combining wages and benefits. Improving employment opportunities through economic expansion is the first line of attack against poverty, but economic growth by itself is not sufficient. It has to be supplemented by state income policies. Such a basic income will have to be funded to a large extent by taxes laid on the sales of multinational and other corporations.

The second important area of social policy that needs to be addressed is population control. Though population growth is declining in many DCs, it is still too high bearing in mind the fact that immigration to ICs will continue to be severely controlled. High population growth may not be the root cause of poverty but it exacerbates it and makes attempts to deal with it more difficult. Linked to population growth is the issue of migration. The current policy of ICs of erecting 'Berlin walls' to keep immigrants out is 'just as loathsome' as the old and needs to be replaced by a more generous and co-operative policy approach (Gorringe 1999, 76).

The third area relates to education and health. Though great progress has been made over the years in improving basic standards in both areas, there is the urgent need to develop policies that target women, ethnic groups, specific countries and diseases. Women in DCs still lag behind men in health and education standards; ethnic groups usually are worse off than the general population; many of the least developed countries should be enabled to catch up with the rest of DCs; and the eradication of illnesses such as malaria need the special attention of the international medical community.

On the political front, it is first important to develop further the power and the reach of the UN and similar bodies, backed up more strongly by the international community. The technological changes of the last quarter of the twentieth century enabled the globalization of economic, social and cultural life to an extent that it outpaced the development of global governance. This needs to be rectified: 'Reinventing global governance is not an option – it is an imperative for the 21st century' (UNDP 1999, 97).

Second, and related to the first, the belief that governments cannot control the operations of private entrepreneurs, be they in the field of business or crime, needs to be exposed for what it is – ideology rather than reality. Acting together governments can do a great deal. Politics still matters even though nation-states may not be as sovereign as they were in the past.

Third, governments of DCs need to improve their administrative and efficiency record. Corruption and maladministration have for years marred the political landscape of many DCs. Though poverty seems to be a fertile ground for this, there are many examples of governments in many DCs that managed to rise above it. It is after all the legal responsibility of national governments in DCs to abolish poverty in their borders, though the international community has at least a moral responsibility to bear some of the cost.

Fourth, the national resources devoted to poverty alleviation could be greatly enhanced if military expenditure could be reduced. It is not very helpful for military expenditure in DCs to be similar to that of ICs as a proportion of their national wealth – 2.9 per cent of their GNP as against 2.4 per cent in 1997 (World Bank 2000a, 306–8). Reductions in debt repayment and in military expenditure would release substantial sums that could be used to reduce poverty.

The reduction of poverty in ICs is primarily an ideological and political issue, for these countries possess the financial resources to reduce if not to abolish poverty. A glance at poverty rates in different ICs confirms this. In the mid-1990s, the USA and the UK had the highest rates of poverty among DCs while the Scandinavian countries had the lowest rates (Makinen 1999, 8), despite the fact that all these countries have similar incomes per capita. Similarly, the rate of poverty for particular groups depends on the kind of income maintenance provision that different countries make. In 1996, while 33 per cent of lone parent families were in poverty in the UK, the corresponding proportion in Denmark was a mere 3 per cent (Chambaz 2001).

It is not possible to generalize about the prospects of poverty reduction in ICs because each country has its own agenda. It is true that the European Commission speaks eloquently about the need to reduce poverty, but its anti-poverty programme does not amount to much. The USA seems set to continue to rely on the market for its anti-poverty programme – a policy that failed in the past and will do so in the future.

On the ideological front, mankind will benefit hugely from the rejection of the extreme forms of neo-liberalism that accompany the current process of globalization. The belief that gross inequalities are necessary for economic growth still dominates the work of many national and international bodies despite the ample evidence that this is not the case. Gross inequalities are not inevitable, and 'we do have *some* choice' (Atkinson 2002, 25). Similarly, the ideology that liberalization of government and other services is beneficial to all is not only untrue; it is not practised even by those who preach it. While DCs are pressurized to privatize and liberalize their trade and services, most ICs spend huge sums of money subsidizing their farmers. It is a policy of 'you liberalise, we subsidise' (Elliott 2002, 4).

Conclusion

Globalization is one of many factors that can affect the nature of human welfare in a country. It has contributed to the general rise in living standards in the world, even though in a very unequal way. The least developed countries benefited less than the richest countries, with the result that the income gap between them has widened over the years. At the same time, however, globalization has helped to raise living standards substantially in some parts of the developing world, particularly East Asia.

The effects of globalization on poverty reduction have been mixed. Education and health standards have risen substantially but the extent of undernutrition and of basic income poverty has not declined that much. There is, however, a greater awareness of poverty and a stronger stated desire to reduce it, even though the actual policies pursued do not live up to the rhetoric. ICs have to accept that poverty reduction in DCs is in their own interest. In an increasingly globalized world, self-interest and mutual interest walk hand in hand more than ever before.

Globalization is here to stay, but it needs to be regulated and to be guided by a more pro-welfare ethos if it is to serve the public interest on a global scale. Present practices mean that poverty will continue to blight the lives of millions for many years (Townsend and Gordon 2002a, 413). Poverty in DCs is of such severe nature that it is universally condemned. Its reduction is not only morally correct but it also makes economic sense to all countries, including the ICs. As always, the reduction of poverty is a gradual and erratic process – a daunting but not an impossible task.

Further reading

Marris, R. (1999). *Ending Poverty*. London: Thames & Hudson.

Randel, J., German, T., and Ewing, D. (eds) (2000). *The Reality of Aid, 2000*. London: Earthscan.

Townsend, P., and Gordon, D. (eds) (2002). *World Poverty: New Policies to Defeat an Old Enemy*. Bristol: Policy Press.

World Bank (2000). *World Development Report: Attacking Poverty*. New York: Oxford University Press.

5

Globalization of Crime: Terror in a Contracting Globe

Mark Findlay

Overview

This chapter speculates on the place of crime within global themes of change, in particular recent interpretations of international terror. The duality and paradox of globalization in its present phase is examined as a backdrop for international terror and the current global 'war' response. The cultural bias of globalization is discussed, along with cultural stereotyping, which specifically features in the US monopolization of anti-terrorism.*

The place of crime and control as features of globalization is specified through the comparative analysis of changing cultures. The split presently revealed in globalization, between American imperialism in crime control and the internationalization of criminal justice, has particular resonance in the context of international terror.

More generally, within contemporary international political priorities and dualist socio-economic development, crime as a feature of globalization appears crucial to the process of social differentiation and the control agendas by which differences in world cultures are reinforced. Crime is a characteristic of globalization and criminalization has become a force for global change.

It is argued that terror crimes, now represented as a paramount global social problem, reflect and reproduce similar material and

---

* While this chapter looks at the relationship between crime and globalization, its focus on terrorism not only adds currency to its arguments, but what is said about the crime control responses to terrorism has relevance for globalized crime at large.

institutional interests such as those at the heart of globalization (in the form of Western modernization). It is not so much that globalization causes crime but rather that both globalization and crime share common imperatives which merit comparative analysis. Particularly in the context of transitional cultures essentially responding to global political and developmental agendas, this synergy holds significance for the shape of societies into the new century and their terrains of conflict.

Crime and globalization

In examining the relationships between globalization, crime and cultural change, the uneven nature of globalization is revealed, particularly as a motivation for selective socio-economic development and the control over cultural integrity it provides. This then is exposed as a natural, if all too often ignored, environment for world crime such as terrorism, where democracy and civilization are broadcast by the dominant cultures in globalization as the victims. In turn, the determination of what is most serious about world crime is now more dependent on global political priorities and alliances than culturally reliant concepts of harm to mankind and international social justice.

Essential for modernization promoted by strong to weak nation-states, the consumerist ethic of globalization generates new contexts for crime. Modernization is crucial as a sub-text for the current phase of globalization. As international strategies of socio-economic development betray, modernization is central to economic reordering and criminal diversification in transitional cultures (See Findlay 1999, chap. 2).

However, in the case of terrorism as the archetypal contemporary global crime, this chapter speculates that the cultural imbalances produced through modernization are largely shielded against any responsibility for the context in which global terror is generated. More immutable and no less problematic cultural differentiators such as religious fundamentalism are disproportionately identified as the motivation behind anti-Western/Israeli terrorism. With a Western culture-centre, therefore, the contemporary form of globalization is not given sufficient significance in the analysis of control responses which global terror has generated.

The secularism of globalization and its attendant distortions of democratic political ideology have led to a world where terrorism is the great threat, and world war is now a legitimate method of crime control. The West has broadened its interpretation of terrorism as being anything which attacks its culture and makes it afraid and the terrorist is demonized in the language of evil. Democracy is protected and advanced through the violent overthrow of authorities and cultures which are said to harbour such evil.

International agencies and regional bodies are bypassed in the military resolution of terrorist crime as a global social problem. However, the sectarian approach to crime control by military intervention is undermining any global pretence at cultural harmony, so important for the commercial imperatives behind globalization. This highlights the paradox of cultural integrity under challenge from globalization and, at the same time, resilient against globalization, crime and control.

Globalization or a divided world?

As with many emergent and contested themes in the analysis of crime and culture, globalization is both simple and complex. Put simply in its contemporary manifestation, globalization is the collapsing of time and space, the process whereby, through mass communication, multinational commerce, internationalized politics and transnational regulation, we seem to be moving inexorably towards a single culture. Regarding its relationship with crime in particular, the more complex interpretation of globalization is as paradox – wherein there are as many pressures driving us in the direction of the common culture as those keeping us apart (Findlay 1999; epilogue).

In its current phase, globalization is largely an economic paradigm, meaning modernization and the marketing of predominant consumerist values. These values and their benefits exacerbate the division in the world between rich and poor. Western economic and military dominion in its recent political incarnation as the 'global alliance against terrorism' is implicating states in more than these mutual interests in modernization. The American-sponsored war on terror is committed to (and reliant on) the sectarian advancement of a common paradigm of 'justice' against a demonized cultural fundamentalism. In reality these demonized cultures are anything but homogeneous in fundamentalist interpretations of religion, politics or social harmony. They seem more unified in their opposition to Western materialist values and cultural and political domination.

While selectively identified, terrorism is now *the* crime against democracy, and its control is advanced in global war terms and not (as in the past with, say, Northern Ireland) reliant on criminal justice discourse and control resolutions alone. However, the theme of bringing the criminals to justice is resplendent throughout the discourse and symbolism of political responses to terrorism, and criminal sanctions sit alongside the 'dead-or-alive' preferred outcomes.

The force of modernization is marked in transitional cultures. So, too, crime as a consequence of modernization in transitional cultures is evident, troubling and little recognized. New crimes in old cultures arise as a consequence of the imposition of cash economies and the flourishing of an under-resourced public sector ripe for corruption (Findlay 1999: chaps 2, 4). In weak or non-neo-liberal state structures (such as those organized around fundamentalist religious/political ideology), resistance through crimes of terror is criminalized by the 'global alliance'. Using criminality as a discriminator, and its superior military power as the crime-control strategy, this alliance defines and polices global terrorism on the one hand, while on the other its members can be criticized for selectively endorsing state terrorism as a legitimate control response in a climate of global war. In this sense global crime-control agendas divide the world down lines which are not dissimilar to that which marks out modernization. An interesting aspect of this in the contemporary context of terrorism is the manner in which the American-led alliance has discarded some of the fundamental safeguards inherent in regional and international criminal justice institutions and procedures in preference for the military police/tribunal/prison model.

The war on terrorism is a conflict between modernized and transitional cultures; transitional in the sense of political destabilization, economic underdevelopment and conflict between religious institutionalism. Modernized cultures have contributed to the transitional state of these cultures beyond the *terror as response paradigm*. Examples are the significance of regional trade access, and the control of energy sources in the case of the Soviet and the US interests in Afghanistan.

The influence of modernization over developing cultures in transition can be initially destabilizing of custom and tradition. Crimes such as corruption and fraud, domestic violence and drug abuse (characteristic of modernized societies) now attach to and arise out of this process of destabilization, and crime control is expected to restore order. Fundamentalist or anarchistic resistance to consumerist and sectarian globalization (such as the recent riots against globalization at meetings of world trade and economic interests) may galvanize endangered cultures (Ignatieff 2001). The colonial and orientalist institutions and processes of criminal sanction and penalty marketed as part of the criminal justice infrastructure for modernization tend to undermine custom, along with producing new forms of crime. Transitional cultures governed by weak states are particularly susceptible to the modernization–crime–cultural strain equation (Dauvergne 1998).

The more complex interpretation of any relationship between globalization, crime and cultural change recognizes the paradoxical manner in which the essence of these cultures transforms crime and control, or is strengthened and endorsed through reaction to their influence (Findlay 1997). Common themes of religious integrity and economic oppression may foster allegiances among cultures traditionally excluded from, or exploited through, modernization. On the other side of the global–cultural divide, globalization, modernization, development, crime and its control are now interrelated in such a predictable and consistent fashion that they significantly influence global culture and responses to crime. At present if there is a claim to a global culture, no matter how tenuous, in the current phase of globalization, it incorporates those societies which endorse neo-liberal, consumerist values.

In its harmonious state, globalization tends to universalize crime problems and generalize control responses. For instance, the US-led war on terrorism is selective but at the same time universalized as an inevitable, unavoidable and unquestionable response to a challenge to 'civilization' and 'democracy'. Like the war on terror and its global alliance, the harmony of globalization is as yet more convincing at a symbolic level. Crime represents unequivocal symbols around which global ethics are confirmed through control strategies – global answers to world social problems, as it were. Crime control claims an irrefutable mandate for global order and a symbolic terrain across which order rules.

Once this crime–control equation was the domain of nation-states. With agendas such as the war on drugs it became the responsibility of regional and international agencies (for example, Interpol, Eurojust and the UN Office for Drug Control and Crime Prevention). Now the war on terror has seen the USA and its allies claim responsibility for global crime control out of the hands of nation-states and the international community. Along with this there is a new control agenda set to ignore aspirations such as the International Criminal Court (ICC). This is well evidenced by the intention of the USA not to put prisoners captured during the Afghanistan conflict before an international tribunal, in favour of US military tribunal adjudication.

The injection of a military solution to the problem of terrorism confirms that an appreciation of crime within globalization is only partial unless control is considered. In its early phases international crime control was limited to police co-operation around nominated global crime problems. The territoriality of policing worldwide made it almost impossible to forge an institution for global policing. Some say this is also due to the fact that much of international 'peace keeping', whether sponsored by the UN or carried out by superpower alliances, is more about policing than world peace. Another reason is found in the ambiguity of global crime and the implication of many states (and their justice agents) in its profit dimensions.

With the emergence of international institutions such as the Commonwealth Secretariat and the OECD as promoters of economic crime control, the mechanism of model legislation became significant. In respect of money laundering in particular these agencies have been successful on a regional level in developing and marketing common legislative instruments which they have then used at jurisdictional and international levels.

Regional bureaucracies such as the European Union have identified priority crime-control concerns. The trafficking in women and children, for instance, has generated a range of regional co-operative endeavours involving member crime-control agencies. At the international level the UN has employed crime-prevention conferences and resultant international declarations to identify broad control strategies in areas such as organized crime.

United Nations crime agencies have also employed research networks and capacity building to advance a more uniform 'language' of global crime and control. The international victims of crime surveys in particular have endeavoured to identify crime as a world issue, from which strategic campaigns can be mounted for control, drug law enforcement providing a prioritized focus.

NGOs such as Transparency International have endeavoured to capture from reluctant (and often implicated) state and regional bodies the running on particular global crime issues. In the case of Transparency International, corruption is reported on and exposed, and crime-control agencies are challenged to regulate where in the past they have been happy to ignore the problem. Amnesty International adopts similar campaign and direct action strategies against torture and state crimes. Greenpeace is one of many global environmental NGOs which target competing commercial and state interests which it determines as crimes against the global environment. In these circumstances issues of victims' rights move well beyond the individual and harm is seen as more universalized.

Control is more than a response to crime. It is in many situations the political and economic prize. Reflect on the intense political lobbying which preceded the settling of the Rome Statute enabling the International Criminal Court (Schabas 2001). Crime and its control, as global political concerns, are now essential features of the predominant global culture.

The significance of crime and control in challenging (or perhaps confirming) any commonality of culture, central to globalization as a market endeavour, is best tested where the host culture is resilient but, through globalization, pressured to transform. What follows is a brief insight into the connections between crime and globalization within transitional cultures. This requires an appreciation of the way in which crime promotes globalization as a market process. Crime is more than merely a characteristic of globalization in that both globalization and crime may work towards common market outcomes. In such settings globalization has tended to influence crime and control, and their inclusive/exclusive agendas, by promoting the maintenance of a common market model. In order to contextualize this within transitional cultures it is necessary to test some unifying and grounded themes arising from the crime–globalization interaction.

The crime–globalization nexus

Globalization creates new and favourable contexts for crime. In particular, this is the consequence of what Harvey refers to as the 'compression of time and the annihilation of space' (1989, 293–5). Commercial crime relationships, for instance, are set free to benefit from opportunities not dissimilar to those enjoyed by multinational enterprise beyond the jurisdiction of the individual state and the limitations of single markets.

The process of time–space compression which is globalization has now enhanced material crime relationships to an extent where they require analysis in a fashion similar to that of any other crucial market force. The claim of globalization is that 'spatial barriers have collapsed so that the world is now a single field within which capitalism can operate, and capital flows become more and more sensitive to the relative advantages of particular spatial locations' (Waters 1995, 57–8). The context of crime is such a location.

The globalization of capital, from actual money to the electronic transfer of credit, and of transactions of wealth, from the exchange of property to info-technology as well as the seemingly limitless expanse of immediate and instantaneous global markets, has enabled the transformation of crime beyond people, places, and even identifiable victims. Crime now is as much a feature of the emergent globalized culture as is every other aspect of its consumerism.

Common themes for crime and globalization are commodification and profit. The market place is an essential context for modernization and the version of culture it promotes. Crime's place within the market appears to be crucial for an understanding of the nexus between crime and globalization. Even where crime relationships are those of power and domination, the materialist consequences of crime are rarely denied. These consequences sit well with the motivations behind modern materialist cultures, and with cultural resistance to them.

The collapsing of time and space, while at the same time profound cultural difference is celebrated through such global realities as world debt, forces hard up against each other the intolerant and the implacable features of world cultures. World political and economic domination through modernization has tended to reignite the most ancient of antipathies.

Conventional resolutions of global conflict, such as wars of state against state, have been replaced in this phase of globalization by crime as warfare and warfare as crime control. American-directed international policy, and its influence over international agencies, has driven a selective war response to terrorism, while at the same time concealing the criminogenic consequences of Western-centred modernization. The effort of international agencies to generate a monocultural global community with liberal, democratic sectarian values at its heart has largely ignored crime as resistance which has confronted this trend.

Crime and the global culture

Crime is not an indicator of culture or of its stage of advancement. It is often wrongly assumed that global crime is more likely to feature in advanced societies, or at least be exploited by industrialized against developing cultures. If global crime is equated with economic exploitation, then poverty and socio-economic disadvantage are its indicators and the developing world regions are the home for most crime victims. But such a definition of global crime, while telling, is too simplistic.

Advanced industrialized societies have in recent generations witnessed an increase in violent crimes against the person, property crimes of all types, and crimes against communities. Writers on urbanization identify the fear of crime as an important collective consciousness in modern cities. Those theories of crime which see one of its principal social generators as the intersection between wealth and poverty argue that the social inequities of modernism will mean more crime as a society develops. The question is whether it is the process of modernization or the achievement of certain levels of material advantage that determines the nature and extent of crime in advanced industrial societies.

Globalization is changing our understanding of culture and its significance as a context within which crime is constructed and played out. Until recently, and in recognition of the diversity of world cultures, it was safe to say that crime is culturally specific, and to confine contextual analysis thereby. Now, the distinction between criminalization and resultant punishment as differentiating the individual, whereas global crime and control agendas rely on more generalized cultural distinction, invites an appreciation of the role of crime which is culturally specific as well as more universal. Different but parallel levels of analysis allow for these apparent competing visions. Contextual grounding within the process of globalization as a force for change in culture enables the reconciliation of crime as a feature of the universal and the particular culture, an influential feature of both and each.

An example of this is the contemporary treatment of terrorism as a global concern of crime and control. Confined within cultures and jurisdictions (even in regional backwaters), terrorism might be addressed in jurisdictional terms as a feature of culture or cultural conflict. In this sense the terror of Northern Ireland was deemed by the occupying culture as an irrational consequence of religious difference. The response of the international community was to leave it to the British to regulate, along with the occasional mediation from the Irish Catholic lobby in the USA. No such non-interventionist approach would satisfy the call for a response to the September 11 attacks on the World Trade Center. Here democracy and Western culture were under attack from fanatical opponent cultures of evil. The response was argued not simply as just but as one on which free cultures depended. The USA, the champion of the free, identified itself beyond being a victim of terror. The global alliance against terror, constructed by the USA and its close cultural allies, confirmed for America the position of champion. International agencies were sidelined while states were called to show solidarity with the US response and therefore be counted as 'for' or 'against' terror. The principal cultures of the world were required to line up with the USA or with terror. Terrorism as the global crime and war as the global response had become the most telling global cultural discriminators. Cultures were bifurcated across a terror–war line drawn hard by the dominant culture. Yet the dilemma here is that criminalization is about discrimination and globalization is said to work towards global harmony.

In the likelihood that 'in a globalised world there will be a single society and culture occupying the planet' (Waters 1995, 3), a more integrative and dynamic contextual analysis for crime, particularly as it sits within any universal culture, is required. The place of crime within globalization will no doubt also suggest the need for a more partisan analysis of the impact of globalization on culture.

This is all the more immediate in the transitional phase of globalization which defies cultural integration. Our world is still far from the universalized culture in all quarters. Globalization is a transitional state. It is illusory and potentially distracting at this stage of the globalization process to concentrate only on 'the collapsing' of time and space without recognizing the diversity of human consciousness which remains (see Giddens 1996/1997).

> Globalisation as a concept refers both to the compression and the intensification of consciousness of the world as a whole ... both concrete global interdependence and consciousness of the global whole in the twentieth century. (Robertson 1992, 8)

The intensification of consciousness may also apply to nationalism and state/cultural revival. This may work against the unification of culture through global consciousness at the same time as it is being broadly claimed (by global political, economic and regulatory organizations and 'communities'). The crime and control consequences of this tension are apparent through the formulation and confrontation of international terror.

Globalization is paradoxical in the way it unifies and delineates, internationalizes and localizes. A criticism of the contemporary application of terms such as globalization to studies of crime and culture is the tendency for it to be envisaged as a simple paradox between the local and the global. While presenting a useful analytical tool, such a dichotomy is further away from today's world than considerations of the transnational, regional and cosmopolitan. Crime demonstrates a similar duality. While crime on the streets might be viewed as a local issue and crime in the multinational boardroom more as global, there remain important contextual themes common to both, inextricably essential to an understanding of either. This is where an interactive appreciation of crime in context is important to an understanding and analysis of crime as a force for globalization and vice versa, rather than being restricted to representations of crime as criminals, offences or victims – aliens in the 'global village'.

Elaborating on the paradox and harmony themes of globalization, international terror has been described as a response to globalization and the political domination and sectarianism which has fuelled the process of modernization ever since the mercantile phase of globalization during the middle of the nineteenth century. However, while terrorism may be an extreme (and extremist) response to globalization, so globalization is a response to internationalized terror. War is no longer between state and state, nor is crime control between state and individual. Extraordinary political and economic alliances are forged for legitimacy in a climate where world superpowers avoid international institutions in order to reconstruct and manipulate world order for clear national interests.

While international organizations may retain the focus of world governance during this phase of globalization, cultural dominance through economic and military alliances flexes the international muscle. The state is, and is no longer, the core context of government within global politics. Multilateral state alliances are forged to combat individuals and collectives representative of transitional cultures and dominated world views.

The state as the definer of crime and the monopolist of punishment gives way to global declarations of collective (cultural) deviance, represented, for example, in the current debate about what terrorism is. The ruling state seems central to these definitions, where resistance to any state and in any form is terror. Such definitions commend the international state and its action as beyond terrorism, provided it is not deemed 'rogue' and beyond global ideologies of democracy. Those who are outside this imagery are also excluded from the reordering of world security, and are seen in terms of terror or their support for it (Milne 2001).

The emphasis in globalization literature on the role of the bureaucratized state tends to disguise the importance of corporations and multinational markets as an equally significant force in the transition of cultures. The global agenda for modernization and market economies complements the aspirations of corporate as much as state-centred politics. This is a powerful recognition when addressing the relationship between development and crime in transitional cultures. Where development means commodification and modernization it will be selective, dependent and discriminatory. It will produce in transitional cultures, either resisting or on their way to modernization, apparent inequities which may in turn generate crime and require control if development is to proceed and claim legitimacy.

Terrorist cultures are not coincidently cultures of the Third World and of underdevelopment. It can be said that the terrorist is fighting for autonomy, political identity and self-determination and in retaliation against alien interests, socio-economic exploitation and repression. In turn the terrorist can be represented as attacking democracy, free enterprise, political integrity and modern civilized values.

Globalization, development and crime as social problems

One significant cultural theme in globalization is development. An essential but often overlooked by-product of globalized development is crime. In this connection both crime and development can be seen as social problems resulting from globalization (Findlay 1999).

More than modernization, development is a paradigm affecting all world cultures and an international financial dogma intruding on all societies in transition. Equally relevant to globalization and crime, however, are the selective and discriminatory nature and outcomes of development. These may be criminogenic and productive of new and globalized control agendas consistent with the promotion of modernization.

Along with development, free-market economics and the reconstruction of centralized economies motivate change, particularly in Eastern Europe. The discourse generated around these themes of change reflects a tendency to marginalize crime as a 'foreign import' or a 'black market aberration'. This, in turn, diminishes the significance of a crime market within these emergent economies, and ignores the opportunity of using crime as a critical measure of free-market economics to achieve reconstruction.

Global priorities such as economic reconstruction largely define the direction of modernization within contemporary cultural and social development in whatever paradigm. So too are they integral to current representations of crime and crime control, particularly when crime is targeted as a challenge to the realization of such priorities or, as with the search for motives behind the recent extremities of global terror, is seen as an attack on the icons of modernization. However, the place of crime within themes of change is never so straightforward.

Crime is not an irrational response to the universal benefits of modernization. Nor is it an immoral challenge to the 'democratic' hegemony of Western political and cultural supremacy. Control responses on the other hand may arise out of and reassert that hegemony. This is the key to understanding the reinterpretive influence of crime and control in globalization. Control is the essential mechanism in representations of global crime and the reordering of international criminal justice. Beyond this, however, there is a lot more at stake in terms of cultural development than is evidenced through the international crime and control agenda.

As Giddens suggests (1996/1997), whereas globalization was initially the province of Westernized cultures, it is now outside and beyond the exclusive control of any particular cultural influence, certainly in terms of globalization as action and reaction. It is the international influence of consumerist and sectarian market economics, rather than the particular impact of culture, which presently fuels globalization (in a somewhat similar fashion to the way in which it shapes transnational criminal enterprise).

For instance, corruption, if it is essential to the maintenance of a local black market, will exist as the giving and receiving of material advantage. Where corruption is a feature of government, it transforms beyond local exchanges of advantage into processes of influence which become political networks. For corruption to replace the work ethic of the community and the sense of duty of the public official, it challenges the themes of rights and responsibilities which are identified characteristics of model democratic, globalized culture. On the other hand, it may be entirely compatible with the enterprise/ profit priority of modernization and corporate culture.

Cultures in transition, particularly those assailed by pressures to modernize, are living with a transformation of crime and control so often impossible to disentangle from world economic and political priorities. How this transformation simultaneously works towards the paradox of universal culture and resilient individual cultural difference is worthy of comparative analysis. Unfortunately, as the interpretation of international terrorism demonstrates, such comparison can only effectively progress from a detailed understanding of the transitional cultures influenced by globalization and presenting a focus for its resistance to the globalization of culture through common control agendas.

Relationships of crime

Relationships that are criminal essentially depend on choice and the manner in which this is constrained. Arising from considerations of crime as choice is the need to reveal the stages through which crime relationships are moulded, opportunities are responded to, and consequent choices are transacted. In the same way that choice is essential to crime relationships, it is crucial for considerations of control. Strategies for crime control, local and global, and the institutions created to support these, reveal the way in which choices about crime and choices about control are interdependent. Attached to this is the discriminatory representation of what forms of common action and behaviour will be designated deviant or legitimate, and the international political context for this.

Crime is interactive and as such depends on personal relationships and institutional reactions. Unless crime is discussed in terms of interaction, its dynamic influence within global social change may be overlooked. In both local and global language crime and criminality are talked about as if one party to a relationship, or one institution in an administrative process, is responsible or responsive. As a result perpetrators are stereotyped, victims are marginalized, control agencies are distorted, and justice policy is misdirected. This is a reason for the attraction of crime and control discourse for global politics.

For contexts wherein laws regulate behaviour, crime is a trigger for the inception of control relationships. Sometimes the reverse is also true. Usually crime is characterized as a breach of legal prohibitions which are graduated in terms of their seriousness or the severity of the harm resulting from their violation. While the measure of crime seriousness is a culturally relative exercise (and remains so for global crime-control agendas), violence against individuals is more often than not an aggravating feature of crime in most community settings. Put in the context of violence against the state and global state ideologies, violence against the person moves from an intimate perpetrator–victim relationship into a culture against culture connection.

The significance of regulation and control (through criminalization) represents a utility for globalization. Crime control in the context of globalization is about reshaping opportunities and consequent choices. Both the motivation for and the consequences of such choices are the endorsement of globalized political authorities and economic interests, which promote modernized cultural priorities globally. In this respect the regulation of crime reveals crucial connections between global politics, criminalization and wider aspirations for control, through which crime and cultures may be restructured in terms of the predominant view of world order.

Therefore, the social positioning of crime is not simply a matter of determining the seriousness of crime or its consequences in a particular cultural setting. The status of the offender or the victim, the

priorities of criminal justice agencies, and the perceptions of governments and communities influence the representation of crime and the
reactions to it. For example, in both developed and developing
societies significant investments of control resources are directed
against minor property crimes and public order offences, as well as
certain crimes of serious violence, individual against individual. At
the same time, theft by corporations, environmental destruction, or
violence by state agencies against individuals may not receive a
similar intensity of control effort or state response. The harm caused,
the seriousness of the behaviour, or the extent of victimization does
not explain such differential treatment. Nor will the laws against
criminal activity necessarily clarify the position. It is the social
context of crime which holds the key to its significance, local or
global.

Globalized situations of crime

The unification of global culture is politically motivated through
Westernized priorities. One such is the eradication of recreational
drug abuse. Whether in a medical or social order context, a uniform
view against certain proscribed drugs is enforced even in cultures
where traditions of drug production and consumption differ from
those in the modernized West. In addition, the commercial realities
which influence developing agrarian economies may generate an
alternative commercial expedient in drug production and export. In
these settings international crime-control priorities may not make
good economic sense.

Drug crime operates in a highly selective and discretionary political and social context. This context is essential to the perpetuation
of drug economies, as it is to the maintenance of international political priorities. Without criminalization the profit motive behind drug
trafficking would not be ensured and the creation of international
law-enforcement policies under the authority of uniform legal prohibitions would not be possible. Governments would therefore have to
expose their drug control politics to a more sensitive form of analysis, not diverted or distracted by neutral and universal concepts of
crime and punishment.

Criminalization is an essential element within discretionary and
selective drug control. Without it, the meaning of the supply and
demand stages of drug economies would be ambiguous. In fact, the
whole monopolistic structure of drug markets, and the distortions of

price and purity of supply which arise as a result of market regulation, would not be prevalent without the globalized and selective criminalization of drug sale and use patterns.

This has led to an internationalized trade (supply and demand) structure, where global prohibitions create global market conditions to exploit regional supply and national demand through transnational enterprise.

The criminalization of drugs and the drug trade on an international level provides an example of the clearest indication of crime's importance for global politics. For instance, the recent history of the criminalization of opiate abuse and trade (see Ward and Dobinson 1988) is all about international influence (political and medical). Even today the agenda for the 'war on drugs' is as colonial and imperialist as any contemporary military excursion. The recent employment by the US government of the Central Intelligence Agency, along with military aircraft and personnel, to collaborate with Colombian authorities in raids against the cocaine cartels is an example of the politicization and militarization of drug law enforcement.

The hypocrisy of the global drugs-as-crime problem does not stop at the slippage between medical mission and political intervention. Global economic priorities almost force-feed agrarian-based developing economies to cash crop. The markets for legitimate cash cropping (such as coffee, sugar and cotton) are reliant on the fickle tastes of the developed world. One such market which is uniquely stable and growing is the drugs market. The principal producers of the fashionable drugs of choice are in the developing world, and the vast market for these lucrative cash crops is in the developed world. Yet, where in other economic situations such supply and demand relationships would be fuelled by legitimate (rather than illegitimate) capital, and barriers to free trade would be attacked, with criminalized drugs the opposite is the case. Global development and economic theory is ignored, or reversed, for the sake of political and health-control agendas.

In the context of both local and globalized crime control, consistency is sacrificed. Multinational economic priorities determine that alcohol and tobacco are legitimate while cannabis and opiates are not. Interestingly, it is in the developing world, where the crime and health consequences of tobacco and alcohol are most acutely felt, that the argument behind their aggressive marketing rests in unbridled free-marketeering. The same approach and motivation is criminalized when dealing in proscribed drugs.

Further, the recognition of market structures as the context for controlling the drug trade requires a recognition of the impetus for the trade and its control in a globalized context. The outcomes are for oligopoly markets, multinational trading, relationships of commercial interest, and the weakness of state regulation.

Local or global crime – connecting crime and changing cultures

When crime is analysed within a global context, the world seems to become more harmonious and at the same time more diverse. When globalization and its impact on crime are contrasted with localized frames of reference, this enables consideration of transitional and contesting images and representations of crime, such as homicide and genocide, individual and organized crime, and corruption of officials or governments.

Cultures too, and their transition, are influenced by global representation. One of the most obvious features of social development through modernization has been the establishment and growth of the city, replacing rural existence. The city is the environment of the modern and as such the preferred domain for global life. At the same time urban environments provide one of the clearest contexts within which the connections between crime and youth, crime and gender, and crime and economic disparity might be explored. The city is the image and the context of the modern within which crime is a feature and an impetus for urban change.

As both crime and urbanization are dynamic social phenomena, their relationship has been widely discussed in terms of 'drift' (Matza 1964). Fluid commitments to crime are often demonstrated in similar ways, as are the choices made by young unemployed males to move to the city. The fear of crime, now one essence of modern city life, is an important stimulus for the exodus. Further, the exodus alters the image of the city in terms of crime danger and vulnerability.

Urbanization trends in developing countries tend to reflect the popular perceptions of the relatively limited developmental opportunities in rural areas. City populations explode as a result, and the limited services within these centres in turn rapidly negate those opportunities which may have once existed. In addition, the newly arrived resident is disconnected from familiar rural life supports and is unfamiliar with the formal, institutional welfare alternatives which the city affords, limited as these might be.

To the difficult socio-cultural adaptations required of young rural migrants is added the economic reality of restricted employment opportunities, shortages of accommodation and the relatively high cost of urban living. Further, the immigrant worker often does not bring with him those skills and training essential for wage labour in an emerging city. Is it surprising in such a context that crime becomes 'work'?

Urban drift might best be seen in certain developing contexts as a progress of frustration and eventual violent dislocation, from one context of blocked opportunity to another of diminished or distorted opportunity. The tendency for cultural unification and the implication of common values essential to globalization stands challenged by the marginalization and cultural vilification as a byproduct of modern economic development, and the protection of supportive climates of world order. How are we then to understand globalization as paradox and the role of crime within it?

Globalization is paradox

Within this atmosphere of paradox we are presently witnessing a recasting of globalization away from international organizations and bureaucracies and into political and economic alliances at war, with threats to safety and security, be these from the drug trade, terrorism, corruption or urban decay. War is waged against these threats to global order, and the civilian cultures that remain are reconstructed in image and value structures compatible with modernization. At the same time there is a consequent trend away from the individuality (and rights and freedoms) of modernization and a retreat into territorial safety, with a focus on world order, spatial control and cultural regularization.

Paradox is an important device in the reconciliation of the intangibles that are globalization and crime. This is especially apparent when relating crime to cultural marginalization and resistance. Social and economic development promotes certain interests and marginalizes others. If the analysis of globalization and culture recognizes the functional potential of crime as a response to marginalization and control as a reassertion of cultural dominance, then it becomes more than an exploration of strain, opportunity and conflict, much more than identifying and solving global social problems.

Paradox is also contextual when it comes to the current phase of globalization. Terrorism is represented as the crime against the global community. And yet if we search further for the true nature of global terrorism, as with the global community against which it is directed, there is a big leap from common symbolism to the diversity of the actual. This gulf between the reality and the rhetoric of global terrorism makes control initiatives detached and problematic. Global terrorist networks are interpreted as franchises of a singular fundamentalist brotherhood. The answer to this should be the capture and castigation of celebrity ringleaders. This will bring down the organization and defeat the threat. Only then will the global community reside in peace.

The paradoxical reality is a generation, not a fanatical franchise, turned to terror. The modernized world, for decades the promoter of crime through insensitive development strategies in the southern or Third World, is now the target, the victim. The challenge is not to award individual liability but to be creative enough to confront the social problems which precede terrorist outrages or which stand as their justification. The developed Western world, the target of terror, may only protect itself from globalized crime when the marginalization produced through modernization is recognized. The other world, the home of global terror, envisages this emergence of globalized crime as a rational response to the state terror of the West. A prosecution and punishment paradigm confronting this divide seems doomed to failure through fuelling what it sets out to control. Restorative justice may be the successful alternative, yet only after the 'global community' is seen for what it truly is – a brand name for the victors in the Security Council. It is not an inclusive world fellowship which recognizes diversity and tolerates difference while working out from the dominant languages, cultures, religions and populations, rather than profits and military predominance of globalization in its current phase.

Future trends

There is something not quite convincing about speculation on future trends in the incidence and resolution of global crime problems. This is specifically so at such a transitional stage of globalization, and when notions such as the 'international community' are being fundamentally redefined along quite sectarian lines.

The safest approach to any such speculation is around the identification of features of globalization having irrefutable connections with the major social explanations of crime:

Crime and opportunity – It was suggested earlier in this chapter that a unique feature of this phase of globalization is the collapsing of time and space. Information technology, and the worldwide web, facilitate this. All crime that is possible and more attractive through instantaneous communication methodologies will grow as does our reliance on these technologies. The reality of electronic funds transfer replacing paper money for all sorts of commerce has opened up vast possibilities for theft and fraud. Conventional, jurisdictionally based crime-control institutions and agencies are lagging behind the developments in crime and information technology. New agencies are being created and stimulated by multinational commercial and financial interests which have so much to lose as victims of this crime wave. If the integrity of information technology for legitimate commerce is challenged by crime then the fundamental profit motive for modernization is under challenge.

Crime and socio-economic disadvantage – Modernization is driving the worlds of the North and the South further and further apart. The inequities of world debt regimes are making it more impossible for the poorer nations and regions to extricate themselves from cycles of disadvantage and exploitation. To that extent the nature of victimization as a result of many fundamental global crime problems (particularly for women and children) will be directed from rich to poor. In addition, it is likely that the level and extent of this victimization will go largely unnoticed because initially it does not possess a profit dimension.

Crime and social marginalization – Advanced industrial societies are witnessing a rejection by the young of conventional politics, and more generally of foundation social institutions. Marginalization and alienation are dividing modern societies by race, religion, age, drugs of choice, sexuality, etc. Crime as a feature of social marginalization and as its by-product will grow within advanced industrial societies. Conventional, state-centred crime control is failing this challenge, and the need to move away from popular punitive law-and-order strategies towards those which are restorative and inclusive will become inevitable if these societies are to survive.

Crimes of the powerful – The recognition that with the abuse of power comes crime is at the heart of many of the more prominent recent crime-control initiatives such as the International Criminal Court. However, behind this recognition is concealed a real debate about what the crimes of the powerful are and who should be punished for them. The more that criminalizing the abuse of power rests with Western political interests, the more common will be the rejection of formal international criminal justice agencies for the resolution of crime problems. Justice will continue to be sought by those who feel aggrieved and disenfranchised in the form of direct action. Terrorism will grow as the alternative justice resolution process at a global level.

Further reading

Bauman, Z. (1998). *Globalization: The Human Consequences*. Cambridge: Polity.

Findlay, M. (1999). *The Globalisation of Crime: Understanding Transitional Relationships in Context*. Cambridge: Cambridge University Press.

Held, D., McGrew, A., Goldblatt, D., and Perraton, J. (1999). *Global Transformations: Politics, Economics and Culture*. Cambridge: Polity.

Pierson, P. (1994). 'The new politics of the welfare state'. *World Politics*, 48, 143–79.

6

Globalization and Drugs

Larry Harrison

Introduction

Among the first of the health and social problems to be associated with cross-frontier trade, and to be the focus of transnational policies, were those associated with the use of psychoactive substances such as opium and its derivatives. This chapter outlines the scale of illicit drug use worldwide, before reviewing the historical and socio-cultural literature on the impact of globalization on patterns of drug use. It proposes that there was a direct relationship between the development of world markets and the trade in addictive substances, and that there is a relationship between globalization and both the demand side and the supply side of the drug market. The chapter then details the way in which transnational policies were developed to counter these problems. The effectiveness of the current international drug-control policy is examined, and the possibility of future developments explored.

The extent of drug-related problems

In the second half of the twentieth century, the growth in the numbers of people experiencing problems in relation to psychoactive substance use was exponential. When the British government first became concerned about illicit drug use in 1958, for example, cannabis smoking was seen largely in a few ports where there was a regular supply;

there was no organized, nationwide distribution network for cannabis or any other illicit drug; and injecting drug use was extremely rare. Just under 350 people were known to the British Home Office in 1958 as being dependent on opiates and/or cocaine throughout the United Kingdom (Interdepartmental Committee on Drug Addiction 1961). Just over forty years later, the number of people who had problems with injecting drug use had increased to over 43,000 (Corkery 1997). Surveys indicated that one in three UK adults of working age had used an illicit drug at some time in their lives, and there was evidence that drug use had become normative among young people in England (Ramsay and Spiller 1997; Parker et al. 1995). In a forty-year span, cannabis smoking and the use of opiates such as heroin, stimulants such as cocaine, hallucinogens such as LSD, volatile inhalants such as butane gas and sedatives such as barbiturates had been added to the traditional drugs used in the British Isles – alcohol and tobacco – to produce an extended menu of psychoactive substances which were available in the illicit and licit markets. As Kam and Harrison (2001) noted, a change in the use of intoxicants on this scale is a cultural shift of seismic proportions.

There were similar trends in other countries. Approximately 4.3 per cent of the world's population were believed to use illicit drugs by the beginning of the twenty-first century (United Nations Office for Drug Control and Crime Prevention 2000). There was a world trend towards rising levels of substance use, an increase in the number of female substance users, a falling age of initiation into substance use, and a growth in cannabis and in multiple drug use (World Health Organization 1996). As the United Nations Office for Drug Control and Crime Prevention (2000, 55) commented, 'drug abuse' is now a 'global phenomenon' which affects almost every country, although its extent and characteristics differ from region to region.

Drug dependence is a complex bio-psycho-social phenomenon, but rapid change in the pattern of drug use, of the kind seen in the UK over the last forty years, is usually due to a change in the cultural norms governing intoxication. In traditional society, the intake of drugs such as alcohol or coca is circumscribed by ritual and ceremonial, and problem use rarely assumes epidemic proportions. In late modernity, however, consumption becomes a matter for personal choice, and the assessment of the risks associated with intoxication becomes a task for the individual. It is possible, therefore, that the process of globalization, as a cultural as well as an economic phenomenon, is related to the changes in recreational drug use that have been observed across the world, as people in many different societies increasingly take the risk of experimenting with non-indigenous psychoactive substances (World Health Organization 1996). The social dislocation associated with globalization and modernization could create the conditions which foster problematic substance use (Alexander 2000).

Globalization and the demand-side of the drugs market

Writing in 1848, Marx and Engels observed that the creation of a world market was changing the nature of production and consumption:

> The bourgeoisie has through its exploitation of the world market given a cosmopolitan character to production and consumption in every country . . . All old-established national industries have been destroyed or are daily being destroyed. They are dislodged by new industries . . . that no longer work up indigenous raw material, but raw material drawn from the remotest zones; industries whose products are consumed, not only at home, but in every quarter of the globe. In place of the old wants, satisfied by the productions of the country, we find new wants, requiring for their satisfaction the products of distant lands and climes. In place of the old local and national seclusion and self sufficiency, we have intercourse in every direction, universal interdependence of nations. (Marx and Engels 1934, 12)

The decline of self-sufficiency, which was already becoming apparent in the mid-nineteenth century, gathered pace at the close of the twentieth. The globalization of world markets, which was such a marked feature of the 1990s, intensified the interdependence first noted by Marx and Engels. Industrialized countries depend on the industrial raw materials, manufactured products and labour, as well as the markets, of the developing world to sustain their standard of living, while the economies of developing countries depend on trading networks that bind them to the industrialized countries (Giddens 1993). This has resulted in 'the rapidly developing and ever-densening network of interconnections and interdependencies that characterise modern social life' (Tomlinson 1999, 2).

Such technical and economic developments have a cultural impact. From a socio-cultural perspective, globalization is a process in which 'the constraints of geography on social and cultural arrangements recede and in which people become increasingly aware that they are receding' (Waters 1995, 3). Globalization involves the phenomenon of disembedding, which is read as the main dynamic of modernity by Giddens (1990, 1991). Giddens (1990, 21) defines disembedding as the 'lifting out of social relations from local contexts of interaction and their restructuring across indefinite time and space'. Since advanced technologies and communication networks relay information rapidly to different corners of the world, individuals can communicate with people whom they would never otherwise know, in different cultural contexts and different time zones. Thus individuals are no longer tied in the same way to the norms and values of local communities.

Interaction with global communities fosters scepticism towards tradition as well as the absorption of different cultural practices. As a result it facilitates the breakdown of traditional social bonds, which used to be tied to a specific space and time: 'as our experience of space and time is being dramatically reconstituted . . . our embodied experience of space and time is fundamentally restructured' (Burkitt 1990, 129). Discontinuities with traditional life are further accelerated by rapid social change, the global scale of the transformation, and the uniqueness of modern institutions (Giddens 1990).

According to Featherstone (1991), in a consumer culture the individual's consumption behaviour is symbolic. The benefit-oriented nature of the capitalist system transforms people into consumers by altering their self-images and encouraging consumption in the directions of wants rather than needs: 'under a consumer culture, consumption becomes the main form of self-expression and the chief source of identity' (Waters 1995, 140). Thus, by weakening traditional society through the phenomenon of disembedding, globalization creates both a crisis of identity and a means by which this may be resolved, through the self-conscious formulation of a lifestyle based on a pattern of consumption.

In traditional society, the use of psychoactive substances is usually stable, hedged around with norms, rituals or prohibitions that govern intoxicated behaviour, that regulate who may become intoxicated, on which substances, and in which circumstances. Thus, coca use among peasant communities in the Andes is not attended with the kind of problems associated with cocaine use in the late modern capitalist state (Negrete 1983). When rapid social change disrupts traditional practices, or when these are dismantled from without, by invasion or colonization, there is often a collective loss of control over substance usage. The same thing happens when technology creates previously unknown substances or routes of administration: new risks are produced.

This is not to argue that traditional societies are a kind of lost Eden, in which substance-related harm is unknown, nor to suggest that modernization is the sole cause of alcohol and drug problems. There are examples of traditional communities which have competitive drinking practices, for example, which can foster high levels of alcohol consumption or destructive drinking patterns (Douglas 1987b; McAndrew and Edgerton 1969). But, on the whole, socially prescribed drunkenness or drug use is not associated with a high prevalence of social and psychological problems, even if it does have negative health consequences. Drug 'epidemics', when the prevalence of drug use seems to increase exponentially, are associated with high levels of problems, and are often a feature of societies undergoing a process of transformation.

It seems that when drinking or drug taking loses its ritual and traditional boundaries, and the onus for managing risk shifts to individuals, there is a lessening of community controls over substance use. As mass communications transform the networks of people with whom we interact, traditional society is weakened and individuals are no longer bound in quite the same way to local communities, values and norms. Rapid innovation and cultural diffusion can take place, and, as Marx (1972) observed in the nineteenth century, out of these global interactions new, internationalized cultural forms emerge.

This hypothesis is difficult to test. Culture is one of the most important influences on substance use, but many of the anthropological research techniques needed to investigate the cultural transmission of the norms and values relating to substance use are still being developed, and there is currently a lack of basic data, even in relation to the relatively accessible cultural practices surrounding drinking (Douglas 1987a). Nevertheless, the phenomenon of individuals being increasingly prepared to take the risk of experimenting with newly available, non-indigenous intoxicants seems to be in harmony with underlying social trends.

In the next section, we examine supply-side changes to the market for addictive substances. First, we consider how the trade in addictive substances helped to create a world market. We then show how the historical drive to create a market for Western goods in South-East Asia, and thus to incorporate Asia into a global system of trade, led to the production and marketing of opium on an organized commercial basis and created the financial and transport infrastructure to support large-scale opium trading.

Globalization and supply-side factors

The initial drive for the globalization of trade and for the construction of consumerism, both of which were necessary for capitalism to
flourish, was made possible by the discovery of addictive substances
such as tobacco and opium, together with what Mintz (1985) calls
the 'drug foods' – that is, coffee, tea, cocoa and sugar. The marketing of addictive substances facilitated the process of manufacturing
what Marx and Engels (1972) called 'new wants', and thus provided
a motive for traditional societies to abandon subsistence agriculture
and create surpluses that could be traded. Addiction was the cutting
edge of consumerism and, therefore, a driving force for modernization. It is not an exaggeration to say that colonialization, in particular, depended on the promotion of dependence-producing substances,
because, apart from precious metals, this was the only trade that generated the profits which could underpin colonial market expansion.

This can be seen clearly in relation to tobacco. Every English
colony in America and the Caribbean was founded upon tobacco.
Apart from gold and silver, it was the only commodity produced in
America in the early seventeenth century which was profitable
enough to justify the transatlantic crossing, as contemporary English
commentators realized (Harcourt 1613, 105).

The health consequences of smoking were known in England by
1601, when anatomies performed on Londoners who had died pre-
maturely revealed pathological changes to the lungs (Harrison 1986).
Nevertheless, the crown's policy of discouraging tobacco consumption on the grounds that 'it hindereth all the Kingdom in Health' was
reversed by parliament during the English civil war, when it was
realized that the tobacco trade was central to England's future as a
colonial power (ibid.). Within a few years, tobacco had become
indispensable to the English economy: 'were the planting or traffic of
tobacco now hindered, millions of the Nation, in all probability, must
perish for want of food, their whole livelihood almost dependent on
it' (Miller 1659, i).

The tobacco trade was the mainstay of British shipping in the
struggle against the Dutch to control transatlantic trade, and it made
slavery both necessary, because tobacco was a labour-intensive crop,
and lucrative, because the three-way trade between Africa, the
Americas and Europe meant that English ships never travelled
without a profitable cargo: manufactured goods from England to the
west coast of Africa; slaves from Africa to America; and tobacco on
the return leg to England. The tobacco interests were a major force

in English politics from the 1620s, when they defeated attempts to prohibit tobacco imports on health grounds (Harrison 1986). The principal tobacco merchants were the principal slave traders – men such as Micajah Perry, lord mayor of London and member of parliament, who campaigned in favour of the slave trade and lobbied successfully against tobacco taxes (Donnan 1932).

It was the phenomenal growth of the tobacco trade in the seventeenth and early eighteenth centuries, closely followed by the trade in sugar, which together with tobacco accounted for about seven-eighths of colonial trade (Beer 1958), that made possible the rise of the British Empire. Similarly, the opium trade enabled the British to achieve their pre-eminent position in the late eighteenth and early nineteenth centuries. Just as tobacco supported the first English colonies in the New World, and laid the foundations of the slave trade, the profits from which kick-started the Industrial Revolution, the opium trade permitted the expansion of the British Empire in Asia.

In expanding trade with Asia, the West had faced a number of problems. First, there was a trade deficit with China, because Western nations imported Chinese goods but were unable to offer much that the Chinese wanted in return, apart from silver. Second, there were substantial territories in South-East Asia where the cash economy hardly existed, where subsistence agriculture obtained, and where exchanges were governed by ritual (Trocki 1999). As Trocki (1999, 61) notes, 'capitalism cannot develop as long as peasants simply squat on land, growing enough food to feed themselves.' It was necessary to 'prime the pump . . . to initiate the cycles of production, consumption and accumulation that we identify with capitalism' (ibid., 172). This was achieved through the transformation of opium into a mass-produced commodity in British India, manufactured under an East India Company (later British government) monopoly. Such was its success in opening China to Western trade that within a fifty-year period British opium had become China's most costly import and the political economy of South-East Asia had been transformed.

The scale of the nineteenth century opium trade is often overlooked. In 1836, for example, China imported opium valued at £4 million in contemporary prices, which made it the world's most valuable single commodity trade in the mid-nineteenth century (Wakeman 1978). For much of the nineteenth century opium was the most valuable export of British India, representing about 14 per cent of all revenue and subsidizing the administration (Owen 1934). The government monopoly's profit on a chest of opium, which in the 1850s cost about 250 rupees to produce and sold at auction for around 1600 rupees (Marx 1972, 220), was over 500 per cent.

During the last fifty years of the nineteenth century, the net revenue to the government of India never fell below £1.7 million sterling, or approximately £112.8 million at 1998 prices, and was as high as £7.3 million in 1871, or £464.8 million at 1998 prices (Rowntree 1905; conversion formula from Twigger 1999). Indeed this may have been an underestimate, since Marx (1972, 219) calculated the opium revenues to be worth $25 million to the British Indian government in 1856, although the basis for his estimate is unclear. More importantly, opium reversed the balance of trade with China, creating a substantial deficit in trade with the West. It forced open the door to trade, and, when the Chinese attempted to enforce their prohibition on opium, the British fought the Opium Wars of 1839–42 and 1858–9 to defend British interests.

The total quantities of opium exported to China increased rapidly in the nineteenth century, from a little under 10,000 chests in 1829 to over 100,000 chests at its peak in 1879, before Chinese domestic production began to replace the imported product. Effectively, the Chinese were unable to restrict opium imports after the Treaty of Nanking, and after the Second Opium War of 1858–9 they were obliged to legalize opium.

Part of the reason for this explosion in opium use was the supply-side changes introduced by the East India Company, which placed the production of opium on a quasi-industrial footing. In many parts of India, opium had been transformed from the product of a cottage industry into a mass commodity. The cultivation of opium poppies was organized systematically, on a large scale, on low-grade agricultural land, utilizing a plentiful and inexpensive indentured labour force (Trocki 1999). The collection of raw opium and its subsequent processing, packaging and pricing were standardized and centrally controlled, and there was more or less secure access to a mass market in China after 1842, using the fastest and most sophisticated sailing ships available.

The real achievement of the opium traders, however, was to create political and economic structures 'which were inimical to the traditional "gift economy" of Southeast Asia and the agrarian economy of China' (Trocki 1999, 53). In opium they had a product for which there was high demand, and which created or accentuated the need for trade in communities that had previously regarded themselves as self-sufficient. Opium became an exchange medium and a form of money, as well as a consumer commodity, and in some regions labourers were partly paid in opium, which was a further incentive for them to abandon subsistence farming in favour of wage labour. The opium trade thereby contributed to the creation of a wage economy among rural populations at the same time as it produced massive accumulations of capital (ibid., 167).

There was a direct relationship, historically, between the drive to bring Asia into the world trade system, the introduction of the capitalist economic system and the commodification of opium (Trocki 1999). The social production of wealth was accompanied by the social production of risks, as Beck (1992) notes, but in the initial phase of capitalist development the risks associated with opium consumption fell disproportionately on China and the poorer nations of South-East Asia. Indeed it is arguable that it was this which made the continuation of the opium trade acceptable to the British in the late nineteenth century, when there was increasing awareness of the health risks of opium smoking and moves to restrict domestic consumption (Berridge 1999). The fact that most of the risks of opium consumption were external to the United Kingdom was certainly an important consideration for Warren Hastings in the eighteenth century, when he expressed the view that opium should only be permitted for foreign commerce and its domestic use restricted (Rowntree 1905, 17). In the same vein, a British House of Commons Select Committee noted in 1832 that 'it does not seem advisable to abandon so important a source of revenue, a duty upon opium being one that falls principally upon the foreign consumer' (House of Commons Select Committee on the Affairs of the East India Company 1970, 70).

Although it remained controversial, successive British governments protected the opium trade, arguing that Great Britain was not called upon to be a self-appointed custodian of Chinese morals (Rowntree 1905, 264). Should Her Majesty's government cease to trade in opium, it was argued, the market would simply be supplied by Persian and other foreign competitors. If the Chinese must be poisoned, observed one British member of parliament, then it was better that they were poisoned for the benefit of British subjects, rather than those of any other power (Owen 1934, 301).

Evidence has been presented in support of the proposition that the drive to establish world markets involved the commodification of dependence-producing substances and the commercial promotion of substance use. However, those who doubt the importance of supply-side factors may see these commercial activities as simply a response to the high level of demand for addictive substances. Essentially, this was the seventeenth-century English government's rationale for tolerating tobacco cultivation in its colonies: a large number of people spent their money on tobacco, 'not caring at what price they buy that drug' (James I, 1604). The crown decided to permit tobacco growing temporarily, until the colonists could diversify into other commodities. Yet within sixty years, the English government actively promoted tobacco use around the world, using diplomatic pressure to persuade other European nations to repeal anti-tobacco legislation and open their markets to colonial tobacco (Harrison 1986). Similarly, the nineteenth-century British government defended its involvement in the opium trade in parliamentary debates by representing the opium monopoly as a reluctant vendor, which did the minimum to keep pace with Chinese demand. Blame was deflected to the imperial Chinese government, for maintaining a policy of ineffective prohibition rather than opting for regulation through taxation. In reality, the drug was actively marketed by the British, even though it was illegal in China, and considerable effort went into market research to determine which kinds of packaging were most popular with Chinese consumers (Owen 1934).

From the seventeenth century onwards, the objective of British policy was always to maximize revenue. When punitive tobacco taxation, introduced in 1604 with the supposed aim of limiting tobacco consumption, started to reduce taxation revenues in 1608, the duties were reduced substantially (Dietz 1964). Similarly, when the opium monopoly was threatened by the increase in Chinese poppy cultivation in the 1870s, immediate steps were taken to increase production in Bengal, in order to maintain market share through lower prices. Far from being a passive participant in the opium trade, the British Indian monopoly sought to stimulate demand and maximize profits. Supply-side factors such as mass production and energetic marketing did much to promote opium use in China.

The policy response

In the early years of the twentieth century, United States commentators argued that the global nature of the opium trade meant that it was unmanageable without international regulation. Although the British and Chinese governments reached a bilateral agreement to limit the opium trade in 1907, US President Theodore Roosevelt called for an international commission on opium to be convened in Shanghai in 1909, at which a course of action could be agreed collectively.

At the Shanghai Opium Commission, the British resisted American attempts to debate the question of the Anglo-Chinese bilateral treaty and the timetable for phasing out British exports of opium to

China. As McAllister (2000) shows, Shanghai and the subsequent international conferences provided the occasion for some adroit political manoeuvring, in which the USA pushed for prohibition while others defended their interests in the opium trade or acted to deflect attention from themselves. The 1912 Hague Convention for the Suppression of Opium and Other Drugs succeeded in restricting the production and distribution of raw opium, and the manufacture, sale and use of medicinal opium, morphine, heroin and cocaine, but consensus was achieved only by avoiding a precise definition of 'legitimate use' and agreeing that the convention would not come into force until it was ratified by all parties (McAllister 2000).

Ratification proved to be a slow process due to the onset of the Great War, and eventually the victorious nations made use of the Versailles peace treaty to compel Germany and Turkey to accept the measures which they had resisted (McAllister 2000). Under the terms of the Versailles treaty, the opium question was placed under the jurisdiction of the League of Nations. The USA, which had refused to participate in the League of Nations, was therefore potentially excluded from the debate, but the league allowed the Americans to send delegates to its Advisory Committee on the Traffic in Opium and Other Dangerous Drugs in a 'consultative capacity', and the USA was invited to most international conferences on narcotics convened by the league (Anon. 1923). Thus began a charade which lasted for the next twenty years, in which the USA participated in negotiations over narcotics control within the committee structure of the League of Nations, while neither accepting the authority of the League, nor dealing with it directly.

The 1925 Geneva Convention on Opium and Other Drugs extended the scope of drug control further, by proscribing cannabis. This was a result of lobbying by Egypt and Turkey, encouraged and supported by the USA (Kendall 2003). While the announcement of this accord was hailed as a victory in America, it was followed by the disappointing news that European powers had refused to set any definite time limit for the suppression of opium smoking in their Far Eastern colonies, a move which led to the American delegation walking out of the conference in protest and the USA refusing to ratify the convention (Anon. 1926a). The 1925 convention was notable, however, for establishing a way to implement the earlier agreements through a system of regulation. It created the framework of an international drug control and reporting system, under the auspices of the League of Nations, which compiled annual statistics on the production of drugs and monitored compliance with treaty obligations. This institutional framework was the forerunner of the current international control system inherited by the United Nations when it was established in 1945. The UN Single Convention on Narcotic Drugs of 1961 then consolidated two League of Nations bodies, the Permanent Central Opium Board and the Drug Supervisory Body, into the International Narcotics Control Board (INCB), which administers the UN's present drug-control system.

The final component of the international system of control was achieved in 1931, when agreement was reached over regulating the manufacture of opiates and cocaine. The 1931 Limitation of the Manufacture of Narcotic Drugs Convention sought to permit a degree of competition while maintaining prices and limiting production, so that no 'excess' was available to be diverted into illicit markets (McAllister 2000). The principle of restricting the use of a selection of psychoactive drugs to medical and scientific purposes, through internationally agreed supply-side controls, has remained at the core of the international drugs policy ever since, even though the control system has been refined and reinforced by a succession of international treaties over the last seventy years and the list of proscribed drugs has grown ever longer.

Within the UN, the development of policy proposals designed to strengthen international drug control is currently the responsibility of the Commission on Narcotic Drugs. The UN Drug Control Programme attempts to strengthen international action through crop monitoring, alternative development projects, anti-money-laundering operations and educational activities. Both agencies form part of the UN Office for Drugs and Crime, established in 1997 as the Office for Drug Control and Crime Prevention (ODCCP 2002). This structure brings together two of the UN's central functions, and locates drugs policy firmly within the realm of law enforcement rather than health.

The policy process for international drug control

The policy process has been a political one of bargaining, coercion, negotiation and compromise, rather than a rational approach in which scientific evidence informed policy choice. Indeed, although there were frequent references to medical science in the speeches of conference delegates, early twentieth-century policy on drug use was determined by ideology rather than science. In support of their 1926 call for a ban on the manufacture of heroin, for example, the American delegation argued that half of all urban violence in the United States was caused by illicit heroin use, and was attributable to heroin's pharmacological action on the brain (Anon. 1926a). This claim had no basis in empirical research.

Similar unfounded claims were made in the debate on cannabis in 1924, when the assembled nations took a major decision on the future of cannabis without any scrutiny of the scientific evidence (Kendall 2003). Nor was there any discussion of the nature of drug dependence at the early League of Nations conferences. Nations manoeuvred to protect their own interests, but the parameters of the debate in which they engaged were determined largely by the US temperance lobby. The demand for drugs was seen as a function of supply, and it was assumed that drug use would cease once effective prohibition was in force.

This was always a simplistic view, which located the problem in the nature of the psychoactive substance, ignoring the psycho-social and environmental determinants of drug dependence, and failing to consider fundamental economic laws about the behaviour of markets (Frey 1997). It was held with such conviction, however, that debates over the nature of drug dependence, or the effectiveness of prohibition, were actively discouraged within the international forum (McAllister 2000).

In Britain, those most active in the campaign against opium, such as Joseph Rowntree (1905), were also leading figures in the temperance movement. In the USA, the anti-opium campaign was a branch of the temperance movement, and activists such as Bishop Charles Brent, head of the US delegation to The Hague, believed America had a moral mission to rid the world of recreational opium use. The USA would, through the exercise of moral leadership, guide the world towards the prohibition of drug use (Anon. 1909; Anon. 1926a).

Although part of the explanation for the rise of anti-opium sentiment in Britain and the USA lies in the successful campaigning of such moral entrepreneurs as Bishop Brent, their activities are not a sufficient explanation for the direction taken by US, and later British, foreign policy. Other psychoactive substances believed to cause death and disability were traded internationally at this time but were not the focus of state opprobrium. While there were lobbies against tobacco smoking in the USA, for example, as in most other industrialized nations at the beginning of the twentieth century, they did not receive the government support offered to the crusade against opium (McAllister 2000).

Unlike Britain, the USA had no interest in the production of opium, but where tobacco was concerned it was one of the world's major producer nations. Restricting tobacco smoking was not seen as being in America's economic interest in the early twentieth century, whereas eliminating the opium trade was. American traders could see that the domination of China's overseas trade by opium absorbed the wealth needed for the importation of US goods. Not only was the USA unable to share in the opium trade to any great extent, but US goods were also being effectively excluded from the Chinese market (McAllister 2000). The anti-opium crusade was supported, therefore, because its objectives coincided with the goals adopted in other areas of public policy, such as economic policy.

There were also convergent goals in US foreign policy. The US opposition to European imperialism meant that America was not inclined to look favourably on the opium trade, and did not trust the European powers to regulate themselves. Thus, in 1927 an American woman active in the World Anti-Narcotic Union accused the League of Nations of not making progress against the illicit drug trade because 'every member surrounding the table of the Narcotics Committee, with the exception of the Italian delegate, represents interests vested in the opium traffic' (Anon. 1928, 1).

By supporting China against the imperialist powers, the USA hoped to gain a diplomatic advantage which would open the Chinese market to US goods. Hopes were raised when the president of the Chinese National Opium Prohibition Commission went to Britain in 1913 to lobby for the abrogation of the 1907 bilateral treaty governing imports of Indian opium and expressed feelings of gratitude towards America. 'Now that the Chinese people have realized the evil that opium is doing to the country', he was quoted as saying, 'they find it hard to forgive England for insisting on its importation . . . From many points of view British influence in China is decreasing, solely on account of the resentment against the opium traffic . . . Can you wonder that America gains in our developing markets what Great Britain loses?' (Anon. 1913, 3).

For their part, the British foreign and colonial policy makers fought a long rear-guard action in defence of the Indian opium trade, believing that its critics did not understand the complexities of the opium market, and that the problems associated with opium use were being grossly exaggerated. In the end, however, the British reversed their policy and accepted curbs on opium exports, even though many in the colonial civil service remained sceptical (Anon. 1926b). The policy reversal was not just because of the growing influence of the anti-opium movement in Britain, significant though this was in the run-up to the Liberal Party's electoral victory in 1906, but because of strategic considerations. The collapse of central government in China, to which the opium trade was contributing, was judged to be a threat to British interests in the Far East. The British joined the

Americans in wanting to secure China's territorial integrity, even if the price of this was the sacrifice of Indian export revenues (McAllister 2000).

Policy effectiveness

> Globalisation offers the human race unprecedented opportunities. Unfortunately, it also enables many anti-social activities to become 'problems without passports'. Among these are drug abuse, which brings misery to millions of families around the world every year, and drug trafficking, which cynically promotes and exploits that misery for commercial gain. If the international community is to deserve its name, it must respond to this challenge. Happily, it is beginning to do so. (Annan 2000)

At the beginning of the twenty-first century, the international drug-control policy remains anchored in the supply-side paradigm. Efforts have been made in recent years to include elements of demand-side management, such as public education, but law enforcement consumes by far the largest proportion of the drug budget in most countries. The USA, for example, spends over 70 per cent of its combined federal and state drug budget on law enforcement, and the situation is similar in most Western nations (Murphy 2001). This is despite mounting criticism of supply-side initiatives, which have failed to prevent the prevalence of illicit drug use increasing to unprecedented levels worldwide. In the USA, expenditure on enforcement continues to increase, and the numbers imprisoned for drug offences have quintupled in recent years, while illicit drug prices have fallen by half since 1980 (Reuter 2001). This suggests that the policy is failing to reduce the availability of illicit drugs, and a recent report by the US National Academy of Sciences concluded that there was an urgent need to collect data on the effectiveness of US drug enforcement so that drug-control policies could begin to be evaluated (Manski et al. 2001).

Criticisms of the effectiveness of drug control policies are not accepted by the UN or by the International Narcotics Control Board (INCB 1997), which stresses the important contribution that the criminal justice system can make in preventing the supply and consumption of illicit drugs. In its annual reports, the UN Office for Drugs and Crime remains optimistic about the progress being made, arguing that 'we must end the psychology of despair that has gripped the minds of a generation and would have us believe that nothing can be done to roll back, let alone stop, the consumption of drugs' (United Nations Office for Drug Control and Crime Prevention 2000,

1). In relation to its crop substitution and socio-economic development programmes, the UN reports major successes in a number of nations, including Pakistan – 'virtually poppy-free in the year 2000' – and claims that, 'although the media sometimes like to focus on disappointments in drug control, the fact is that most alternative development projects have been successful' (ibid., 1, 152).

The reality of the UN's crop-substitution and development programmes is rather different. Farrell's (1998) analysis suggests that, globally, the annual risk of crop eradication is consistently below 10 per cent. Reviewing over two decades of United Nations development programmes in eleven countries, Farrell concluded that, using any measure of performance, they have had little impact, and are unlikely to be much more successful in the near future.

The one area in which the UN has had undoubted success, however, is in securing adherence to the international drug-control treaties. Virtually every country in the world has adopted the prohibition model and criminalizes the recreational use of cannabis, cocaine and opiates. By 1 November 2001, 175 states had signed up to the 1961 Single Convention, and only sixteen states had not (INCB 2002). Six of the latter were signatories to the 1988 convention, but had yet to sign earlier ones, leaving only ten states which had yet to commit themselves to signing any of the drug-control treaties, and most of these already had drug policies that were in line with treaty requirements (ibid.). To introduce an unpopular and costly policy against determined opposition, gain the support of almost every nation, and maintain the policy in the absence of any evidence of effectiveness is a diplomatic success almost without parallel (Reinarman and Levine 1997).

There are a number of reasons why a policy which appears to be failing to achieve its aims might succeed both in resisting systematic evaluation and in attracting international support. The introduction of drug prohibition and the strengthening of treaty provisions over a seventy-year period has been largely due to support for these policies in the USA; but even at the height of the Cold War, when US power was most contested, there was little challenge to the policy. This is possibly because maintaining consensus over the need for collaboration on crime prevention and drug control has always been important to the survival of transnational organizations. When the League of Nations was established, Article 23 (c) of its covenant explicitly mentioned the control of 'dangerous drugs' as a major concern, and, although the USA remained outside the league, the latter's secretariat attempted to sell drug control to the Americans as one of the benefits of joining (McAllister 2000). Similarly, international drug control was intended to be a major function of the United Nations when it was founded in 1945. The newly established UN appointed a commission to investigate illicit drugs, which in the first three years of the UN's existence undertook an exhaustive investigation of the social, economic and political aspects of international drug control. From the very beginning, the UN was committed to the prohibition strategy, which required a global agency such as itself to regulate the world drug trade.

At an early stage, the moral entrepreneurs who had promoted prohibition were replaced in the policy networks by a 'gentleman's club' of administrators, law-enforcement officials and diplomats (Bruun et al. 1975). The domination of the policy discourse by an administrative clique with a direct interest in the continuation of the status quo has been a negative development. The UN and ICNB bureaucracies pursue their own interests, and promote policies which are largely in harmony with the interests of the USA, the chief sponsor of international drug control. For this reason, the ICNB has opposed a number of harm-minimization initiatives which have emerged in Europe and which are less acceptable to the USA for cultural reasons. These include the provision of injecting rooms, where addicts are provided with sterile injecting facilities in city centres, with skilled first aid and medical assistance on site; needle exchange, one of the most important ways of countering the risk of HIV transmission through shared injecting equipment; the downgrading of cannabis offences; and experiments in the maintenance prescribing of diamorphine, or pharmaceutical heroin, to heroin addicts.

Rather than leave research evaluation to the academic process of peer review, the INCB has attempted to pressure governments to halt such projects. Thus, in relation to the provision of injecting rooms in Frankfurt and some other European cities, the ICNB has reminded governments of their obligation to combat drug trafficking under the 1988 UN convention:

> By permitting injection rooms, a Government could be considered to be in contravention of the international drug control conventions by facilitating in, aiding and/or abetting the commission of possession and use crimes, as well as other criminal offences including drug trafficking. In this regard, it should be recalled that many decades ago, the drug control conventions were established, inter alia, precisely to eliminate places such as opium dens, where drugs could be abused with impunity. (INCB 2000, 26)

Given the potential contribution of properly administered injection rooms to a harm-minimization programme, this is hardly a balanced response.

Similarly, the INCB called for an independent assessment by the World Health Organization (WHO) of the Swiss government's trial of heroin maintenance prescribing. It then issued a press statement to publicize the WHO's view that the trial had failed to adopt a sufficiently rigorous methodology, arguing that, while the INCB always supported scientific research that could contribute to policy formulation, trials of this type were unlikely to do so (United Nations Information Service 1999). So that there was no danger of this being misconstrued as an argument in favour of conducting further trials with better methodology, the INCB went on to remind governments of a UN Commission on Narcotic Drugs resolution that the use of heroin on human beings should be prohibited. There is growing research evidence, however, that the prescription of heroin can be beneficial for selected groups of addicts, and a dearth of evidence to support a policy of prohibiting the medical use of heroin (Haemmig 1995; McCusker and Davies 1996; Metrebian et al. 1998; Perneger et al. 1998). Again, the UN and the INCB are promoting policies that are not informed by the available scientific evidence, but have long been an objective of US foreign policy.

The international drug policy that evolved in the twentieth century as a product of high-level diplomatic negotiations embodies a political rather than an instrumental rationality. The costs of the 'war on drugs' probably exceed the benefits, and more efficient solutions are possible, but a change in policy is not politically feasible. The world is locked into the present system, which focuses on use reduction rather than harm reduction, through a series of international treaties which would need extensive renegotiation. This would be opposed by the USA, France and other Western nations which favour more punitive policies towards drug users, and by an international policy network centred on the UN Office for Drugs and Crime and the INCB.

At the beginning of the twenty-first century, the US-led consensus appears to be faltering, as the Netherlands, Germany, Switzerland and the UK move in the direction of harm reduction. There has yet to be any sign of a European nation abandoning the prohibition model, however, or even calling for a review of international policy. Given the complexity of international drug policy, with interlinked economic, political and cultural determinants, the future is hard to predict. It is likely that the policy of prohibition will not survive in its present form, however, as the world decline in the Protestant religion leads to changes in the ideological landscape, large-scale intervention in the drug market becomes more of an anomaly within the global economy, and newer methods of managing the risks associated with the use of intoxicants come to the fore.

Conclusion

Globalization generated a unique set of risks, historically, when the drive to expand world trade and introduce a cash economy led directly to the commodification of drugs such as opium. The systematic organization of the cultivation, processing, marketing and transport of opium in British India contributed to the first of the modern drug 'epidemics', the addiction to opium smoking, which overwhelmed China at the end of the nineteenth century.

The 'Opium Evil' was seen as a direct consequence of the unregulated cross-frontier trade in drugs, and transnational agencies were established to deal with the threat. The policy instrument was a collective agreement to intervene in the market for opiates, cocaine and cannabis, in order to prohibit recreational drug use. The drive to establish control of the drug market was led by the USA, which had an ideological investment in prohibition, even though this ran counter to the free-trade market solutions favoured in other areas of the US economy. The reasons why some psychoactive drugs such as cannabis were proscribed, while other drugs such as tobacco (and after 1933 alcohol) were promoted, owed much to the economic interests of such powerful nations as the USA.

Globalization, which gave rise to high levels of drug consumption, also generated a transnational response: the twentieth-century international treaties on drug control. These treaties, and the agencies established to police them, operated in the interests of richer, non-agrarian nations, and many of the current problems associated with illicit drug use, such as the transmission of blood-borne diseases through needle sharing, may be the unintended consequences of law enforcement. Yet the development of harm-minimization policies aimed at targeting such negative consequences have been discouraged by such transnational agencies as the INCB. The history of drug control shows that it is quite possible to reach international agreement over global social policies, but one of the negative aspects is that such agreements may act as a brake on policy innovation and perpetuate outdated and ideological policy formulations.

Further reading

Douglas, M. (1987). *Constructive Drinking: Perspectives on Drink from Anthropology.* Cambridge: Cambridge University Press.

McAllister, W. B. (2000). *Drug Diplomacy in the Twentieth Century.* London: Routledge.

McAndrew, C., and Edgerton, R. (1969). *Drunken Comportment: A Social Explanation.* Chicago: Aldine.

Trocki, C. A. (1999). *Opium, Empire and the Global Political Economy: A Study of the Asian Opium Trade, 1750–1950.* London: Routledge.

7

Globalization and AIDS

Kathy Attawell

The HIV/AIDS epidemic has been described as a global emergency. After twenty years, there are no signs that the spread of HIV is slowing down. In the worst affected countries, HIV prevalence rates continue to rise and AIDS is having a devastating impact on every aspect of life. In countries that until recently had seen little HIV, assumptions that the epidemic would not have a major impact or would remain confined to marginalized groups, such as drug users, are being challenged as infection rates increase rapidly.

This chapter provides an overview of the epidemic in different regions of the world. It then discusses some of the global factors that have contributed both to the spread of HIV/AIDS and to efforts to tackle the epidemic. It concludes by highlighting issues that require concerted international action to ensure an effective response to the HIV/AIDS epidemic.

The extent of the HIV/AIDS epidemic

At the end of 2001, an estimated 40 million people worldwide were living with HIV/AIDS, 95 per cent of them in developing countries (see table 7.1). The epidemic continues to spread and, in 2001, 5 million people were newly infected with HIV. It is also increasingly affecting women, young people and children. Women represent 43 per cent of those living with HIV. Almost half of new infections are in young people aged fifteen to twenty-four years, and one in ten in

Table 7.1   Global HIV/AIDS estimates, December 2001

Region	Number of people living with HIV/AIDS
Sub-Saharan Africa	28,500,000
South and South-East Asia	5,600,000
Latin America	1,500,000
Eastern Europe and Central Asia	1,000,000
East Asia and Pacific	1,000,000
North America	950,000
Western Europe	550,000
North Africa and Middle East	500,000
Caribbean	420,000
Australia and New Zealand	15,000
Total	40,035,000

Source: UNAIDS 2002

children aged less than fifteen years. By the end of 2001, 14 million children had lost one or both parents to AIDS (UNAIDS 2002).

HIV/AIDS affects every region of the world but, as table 7.1 shows, sub-Saharan Africa is hardest hit. Twenty-four of the twenty-five countries in the world with the most severe epidemics are in sub-Saharan Africa. HIV/AIDS has claimed almost 15 million lives and is the leading cause of death in sub-Saharan Africa. In 2001, 3.5 million people in the region were newly infected with HIV.

The impact is most severe in Southern and Eastern Africa. In Botswana, Lesotho, Namibia, South Africa, Swaziland, Zambia and Zimbabwe, more than one in five of the adult population is infected with HIV. In West and Central Africa, where prevalence rates have been lower, there is evidence of its recent and rapid spread. In Cameroon, infection rates in pregnant women had reached 11 per cent in 2002. Nigeria, the most populous country in sub-Saharan Africa, already has an estimated 3 million people living with HIV (UNAIDS 2002).

Almost 7 million people in Asia and the Pacific are infected with HIV. Unlike in sub-Saharan Africa, where transmission is largely through heterosexual intercourse, Asian countries are experiencing severe epidemics in vulnerable populations such as sex workers, injecting drug users (IDU) and men who have sex with men. More than 20 per cent of sex workers in Ho Chi Minh City, Vietnam, and more than 50 per cent of IDU in Myanmar, Nepal and Thailand are infected with HIV (UNAIDS 2002).

The implications of the epidemic, in terms of numbers affected, are particularly significant in the world's most populous nations,

India and China. In India, the National AIDS Control Organization estimated HIV prevalence to be 2.46 per cent in 1999 (NACO 2000). While this is relatively low, India's large population means that more than 3 million people may be infected. In China, 850,000 people are infected with HIV, although this may be an underestimate. As a result of widespread sharing of needles and syringes, there are serious localized epidemics in IDU in several provinces, and prevalence rates of over 70 per cent have been reported. There is also a serious HIV epidemic in Henan Province, where thousands of rural villagers have been infected through selling their blood to collecting centres that did not follow basic donation safety procedures (UNAIDS 2002).

In Latin America and the Caribbean, the epidemic is well established. In several Caribbean countries, including Haiti and the Bahamas, adult HIV prevalence rates are second only to those in sub-Saharan Africa. In Latin America, where the epidemic had until recently mostly affected IDU and men who have sex with men, heterosexual transmission is increasing.

Eastern Europe and Central Asia is experiencing the fastest-growing epidemic in the world. In 2001, there were an estimated 250,000 new HIV infections in the region, most of them in the Russian Federation. Countries experiencing a recent rapid rise in infection rates include Latvia, Estonia, Kazakhstan, Azerbaijan, Tajikistan and Uzbekistan. Ukraine, where 250,000 people out of a population of 50 million are infected, is the worst affected country in Europe. Most infections in the region are related to unsafe injecting drug use, but sexual transmission is on the increase (UNAIDS 2002).

In the Middle East and North Africa, prevalence remains low, although infection rates are increasing in some vulnerable groups. While transmission is mainly sexual, transmission through injecting drug use has been reported by all countries except Yemen and Sudan. In 2001, ten prisons in Iran reported HIV infection in IDU, with prevalence as high as 63 per cent in one (UNAIDS 2002).

In high-income countries, rates of infection are low relative to those in most of the developing world, and the epidemic is increasingly concentrated in poor and deprived communities. In Spain, Portugal and Italy, injecting drug use is a significant factor in HIV spread. The UK is seeing a rise in HIV cases resulting from heterosexual transmission, in part because of infections acquired in regions such as sub-Saharan Africa and in part because of reduced attention to preventive campaigns. In the USA, African Americans make up 13 per cent of the population but accounted for 54 per cent of new infections in 2001. In 2000, young disadvantaged African American and Hispanic women accounted for 82 per cent of new infections in women (UNAIDS 2002).

The impact of HIV/AIDS

HIV/AIDS is reversing development gains and threatening the capacity of poor countries both to benefit from and to withstand the negative effects of globalization.

In sub-Saharan Africa, the epidemic is having a severe impact on economic growth. World Bank studies estimate that national income may fall by a third in countries with an adult HIV prevalence rate of 10 per cent (World Bank 2000b). The World Health Organization Commission on Macroeconomics and Health noted that, without HIV/AIDS, Africa's income per capita would have grown at 1.1 per cent per year, nearly three times the growth rate of 0.4 per cent per year achieved in 1990–7 (World Health Organization 2001).

Business is experiencing labour shortages and a reduction in productivity as workers become sick or die. Profitability declines as companies spend more on sick leave, insurance, health care, recruitment and training of replacement workers. Uncertainty about the impact of HIV means that foreign investors are increasingly wary of investing in enterprises in the worst affected countries, and this is likely to be particularly significant in competitive international markets.

HIV/AIDS also affects household income, creating or exacerbating poverty, as families increase expenditure on medical care and funeral costs, and adults become too sick to work. In Zambia, two-thirds of urban households that have lost their main breadwinner to AIDS have seen their income fall by up to 80 per cent. In Rwanda, households where there is a family member with HIV/AIDS spend twenty times more on health care annually than those without an AIDS patient (UNAIDS 2002).

The epidemic is dramatically reducing life expectancy. Were it not for HIV/AIDS, average life expectancy in sub-Saharan Africa would be sixty-two years. Instead it is about forty-seven years. The epidemic is also radically altering population growth and structures, and by 2003 Botswana, Zimbabwe and South Africa were experiencing negative population growth. In the hardest-hit countries, more than a third of young adults will die as a result of the epidemic.

HIV/AIDS is also reversing gains in health and education. AIDS is responsible for 64 per cent of deaths in children under five in

Botswana and 70 per cent in Zimbabwe. Based on current trends, the United Nations Children's Fund anticipates that infant mortality will increase by 75 per cent and under-five mortality by over 100 per cent in the worst affected countries by the year 2010. Orphans and children from families affected by HIV/AIDS are more likely to be malnourished and less likely to go to school or to receive health care. Without education and family support, these children are condemned to a lifetime of poverty and are themselves at greater risk of HIV infection. The epidemic is creating teacher shortages and in some countries has reduced primary school enrolment by 20 to 40 per cent. An estimated four to five teachers die of AIDS each day in Zambia, and 30 per cent of teachers in Malawi are infected with HIV. In Swaziland, AIDS has reduced school enrolment by more than a third, mostly affecting girls.

The impact on the health sector is particularly severe, increasing demand for health care as the number of people with HIV-related illnesses rises. In some sub-Saharan African countries, HIV/AIDS patients occupy up to 50 per cent of hospital beds. Health-care costs for people with HIV/AIDS are consuming a growing proportion of health budgets. In the mid-1990s, it was estimated that treatment for people with HIV consumed two-thirds of public health spending in Rwanda and over a quarter of health expenditures in Zimbabwe. In 1997, spending on HIV/AIDS alone exceeded 2 per cent of GDP in seven of sixteen African countries where total health expenditure from public and private sources on all diseases accounts for 3 to 5 per cent of GDP. In most countries this means fewer resources for other health needs. Health services also face the costs of absenteeism and training replacement doctors and nurses as staff become sick or die from HIV/AIDS. The World Bank has estimated that replacing skilled health personnel will increase health care costs by 0.5 to 1 per cent (World Bank 1997).

Recent thinking on global sustainable development and poverty reduction underlines the importance of building human capital through improved health and education. HIV/AIDS is undermining human capital for generations to come, through the combined effects of loss of skilled and educated people and loss of educational opportunities for children affected by the epidemic.

The epidemic also has serious implications for food security, as people with HIV reduce agricultural activities and families of those who are sick and dying are forced to sell land and livestock to pay for medical and funeral costs. Subsistence farming is highly labour intensive and particularly vulnerable to the effects of HIV/AIDS. In some countries, the epidemic has reduced agricultural production by as much as 60 per cent and is responsible for the loss of up to 50 per cent of agricultural extension staff. In Namibia, the rise in sickness and death due to HIV/AIDS has resulted in widespread sale of animals to support those who are ill and to provide food for funerals, jeopardizing the livestock industry and longer-term food and economic security. In West Africa, in Côte d'Ivoire, there have been reports of lower production of cash crops, such as cotton, coffee and cocoa, while in Burkina Faso some 20 per cent of rural families are estimated to have reduced their agricultural work or abandoned their farms because of AIDS.

HIV/AIDS contributes to instability, by increasing poverty, social disruption and marginalization. Some predict uncertain futures for societies with a burgeoning number of orphans without skills or education. In Botswana, the epidemic has depleted the number of judges able to hear cases, and trials are being deferred or abandoned. Social instability threatens the rule of law and contributes to conditions for conflict. The United Nations Security Council has recognized HIV as a threat, particularly in conflict and peacekeeping settings, debating the issue in January 2000 and subsequently adopting Resolution 1308, which states that 'The HIV pandemic is exacerbated by conditions of violence and instability, which increase the risk of exposure to the disease through large movements of people, widespread uncertainty over conditions, and reduced access to medical care . . . If unchecked, the HIV pandemic may pose a risk to stability and security' (United Nations Security Council 2000).

The influence of global factors on the spread of HIV/AIDS

The HIV/AIDS epidemic is driven by a range of complex and inter-related factors. Some of these factors – poverty and social exclusion, labour migration and population mobility, conflict and complex emergencies – discussed below, are associated with the effects of globalization.

Poverty and social exclusion

The HIV/AIDS epidemic has developed during a period of rapid globalization and growing polarization between rich and poor. New forms of social exclusion associated with these global changes have reinforced pre-existing social inequalities. Poverty and social exclusion increase vulnerability to HIV/AIDS in a number of ways.

The poor and marginalized are the most likely to be affected by HIV/AIDS and the least likely to have access to education, health services, information and the means to protect themselves from HIV. Poor health and nutritional status weakens the immune system, increasing susceptibility both to HIV infection and to HIV-related illnesses once infected. Other sexually transmitted infections (STIs) increase the risk of infection with HIV; the poorest are particularly vulnerable to STIs and in some contexts may be unable to afford to pay for treatment. In many countries, poverty forces women and girls who lack education and employment opportunities to sell sex in order to survive. Many poor countries lack the infrastructure and the resources to address the causes of HIV spread and the impact of AIDS.

HIV/AIDS is a growing problem in societies experiencing economic and social disruption. In the countries of the former Soviet Union, mass unemployment and economic insecurity, social and political change, and deterioration of public health and other services have created the conditions for rapid spread of HIV. The opening of borders has also drawn these countries into global drug-trafficking networks, contributing to an increase in injecting drug use.

Labour migration and population mobility

The rapid spread of HIV is linked to increased labour migration and population mobility, which are a consequence both of poverty and of the development of the global economy and growth in international trade and travel.

Globally, the United Nations Joint Programme on HIV/AIDS (UNAIDS) estimates that there are 150 million economic migrants working outside their own countries. The majority of these migrants are from poor countries where employment and economic prospects are limited. Eight per cent of the population of the Philippines is working overseas, most of them women. Large numbers of men from South Asia work in the Gulf States. Malaysia has over 2 million migrant workers, mainly from Bangladesh, Indonesia and the Philippines.

Even higher numbers of people move within national borders, and rural to urban migration is a growing phenomenon. China is experiencing massive population mobility, with as many as 100 million people temporarily or permanently away from home (UNAIDS 2002).

The risk of individuals engaging in risky sexual behaviour with multiple partners is enhanced in settings where men work away from home for lengthy periods of time, and migrant workers are particularly vulnerable to HIV. An estimated 28 per cent of Filipinos and 41 per cent of Bangladeshis with HIV have been migrant workers (UNAIDS 2002). The beginning of the HIV epidemic in rural Mexico can be traced to the return of agricultural labourers from the USA. Southern Africa, where the epidemic is particularly severe, is characterized by male migration from neighbouring countries to work on the mines in South Africa. A thriving sex industry has developed around these mining communities, where thousands of men live in single-sex hostels. Sexual exploitation of female migrants, both in transit and at their destination, makes them highly vulnerable to HIV. Migrant workers are also at higher risk of HIV because of lack of access to information and services. In Brunei, where overseas labour accounts for around 25 per cent of the population, migrants were found to have low awareness of HIV risk in encounters with sex workers and of the need to use condoms (ibid.).

Forced movement of people is also a factor. An estimated 1 to 2 million people are trafficked for prostitution or forced labour each year. Trafficking of women and girls from Nepal to work in the sex industry in Indian cities such as Mumbai has contributed to HIV spread in rural Nepal. In one study, 30 per cent of Nepali women who had worked in the sex industry in India had been coerced, and those who had been coerced were three times as likely to be HIV positive than other women who had worked as sex workers (UNAIDS 2002).

The development of more efficient and affordable transport may inadvertently increase the spread of HIV, and the worst affected countries in sub-Saharan Africa are also those with the best infrastructure. In Malawi, road construction has been linked to the spread of HIV. Mobile workers are particularly vulnerable; truck drivers in South Africa and India have been found to be at higher risk of HIV than other population groups. Rates of HIV infection are also higher in areas of significant population movement, such as border crossings and seaports. Population mobility is a key factor in the spread of the epidemic in Central America, an important transit zone between the rest of Latin America and North America. High rates of infection have been reported in port towns in Papua New Guinea, port cities connecting Indonesia and the Philippines, and trucking centres bordering India and Nepal (UNAIDS 2001).

Conflict and complex emergencies

Complex emergency situations, whether caused by natural disasters or conflict, exacerbate factors that increase vulnerability to HIV, such as poverty, population movement, social instability and powerlessness. Ethiopia, affected by drought and famine as well as war, has more than 1 million AIDS orphans and a rapidly growing HIV epidemic. Conflict plays a particularly significant role because of military and civilian population movements, family displacement and social disruption. HIV infection rates are often two to three times higher in combatants than in the civilian population, due to higher rates of risky sexual behaviour. Women and girls are at increased risk of rape, sexual exploitation and forced prostitution in conflict situations, or may be forced to sell sex to survive when they have been displaced from their homes.

Many of the countries most affected by HIV have experienced war in the recent past or are currently involved in conflict. More than twenty countries in sub-Saharan Africa are at war or have personnel involved in war. Sudan has a widespread epidemic, driven in part by conflict and resulting large-scale population movements. UNAIDS has recently reported high rates of HIV infection in Angola and anticipates similarly high rates in Rwanda, Burundi, the Democratic Republic of Congo and other countries emerging from conflict. In the Balkans, the psychological and socio-economic impact of conflict has increased vulnerability to HIV, especially among young people. Recent assessments by UNICEF and WHO found high rates of injecting drug use and sharing of injecting equipment (UNAIDS 2002).

Global and regional responses

Globalization and global and regional links have also played a positive role in responding to HIV/AIDS. Growing recognition of the significance of the epidemic and its impact has catalysed a range of actions by intergovernmental and government bodies, civil society organizations and the private sector.

International institutions

Existing global institutions, such as UN agencies, have taken action to respond to HIV/AIDS according to their specific mandates.

UNICEF, for example, focuses on women and children, drawing attention to the needs of AIDS orphans and supporting programmes to prevent mother-to-child transmission of HIV. The International Labour Organization (ILO) focuses on promoting codes of conduct to protect the rights of workers with HIV and on working with business and trade unions to support HIV/AIDS workplace initiatives.

New international bodies and mechanisms have also been created to assist the international community and nation-states to address the epidemic and to promote a co-ordinated response. UNAIDS, the Joint United Nations Programme on HIV/AIDS, was launched in January 1996 to advocate for global action and to lead an expanded response to the epidemic. UNAIDS is co-sponsored by eight organizations – the ILO, United Nations International Drug Control Programme (UNDCP), United Nations Development Programme (UNDP), United Nations Educational, Scientific and Cultural Organization (UNESCO), United Nations Population Fund (UNFPA), UNICEF, WHO and World Bank – and works at international level to track the epidemic, facilitate joint action and disseminate best practice.

UNAIDS works closely with other international organizations, regional bodies, bilateral donor agencies, national governments, non-governmental organizations, the private sector and people living with HIV/AIDS. This reflects an increasing trend towards global and regional partnerships, based on recognition that an effective response to the HIV/AIDS epidemic requires action at all levels and by all sectors.

Regional bodies and South–South collaboration

Regional bodies have also provided a useful forum for joint action to address common issues, mobilize resources, and share expertise and experience. The Association of South-East Asian Nations (ASEAN) has developed a regional plan to tackle HIV in mobile populations, focusing on seafarers and truck drivers. The Pan-Caribbean Partnership Against HIV/AIDS, launched in early 2001 and co-ordinated by the Caribbean Community Secretariat (CARICOM), is linking the resources of the international community, governments and civil society to boost regional and national responses. In 1997, the Southern African Development Community (SADC) Council of Ministers adopted a joint Code on HIV/AIDS and Employment to establish common standards in the workplace and provide the basis for national legislation on employment rights of people living with HIV/AIDS.

There has been an increase in other forms of South–South collaboration. In 2001, India and South Africa signed a declaration of intention to co-operate in technology transfer and import of inexpensive HIV drugs and an Indian manufacturer of generics has agreed to provide antiretroviral drugs to the Nigerian government at low cost. In Latin America and the Caribbean, national AIDS programmes have established a mechanism to share technical assistance, and Argentina is collaborating with Chile, Paraguay and Uruguay to set up harm-reduction programmes for injecting drug users.

Non-governmental organizations and networks

International non-governmental organizations (NGOs) and global networks that bring together national and regional NGOs have played a significant role in generating a response to the HIV/AIDS epidemic from UN and donor agencies and governments in the industrialized and developing world.

A wide range of organizations, among them international NGOs such as Oxfam, have lobbied for reduced drug prices. Global NGO networks, such as the International Council of AIDS Service Organizations (ICASO), and international networks of organizations of people living with HIV/AIDS (PHA), such as the Global Network of People Living with HIV/AIDS (GNP+) and the International Conference of Women Living with HIV/AIDS (ICW), have played a key role in advocating for human rights and access to treatment for PHA. Persistent lobbying by ICASO, GNP+ and ICW has ensured that PHA have a voice at international meetings and are represented on international bodies, such as the UNAIDS board, and funding mechanisms, such as the recently established Global Fund to Fight AIDS, Tuberculosis and Malaria (GFATM).

On a smaller scale, regional NGO networks are working to address specific issues. Examples include the Global Alliance against Traffic in Women, a regional network of organizations in South and South-East Asia working to highlight the issue of trafficking, and Co-ordination of Action Research on AIDS and Mobility (CARAM), a network of NGOs in Asian countries that provides support to migrant workers. Other regional and international linkages are providing opportunities to work jointly to tackle HIV/AIDS. In sub-

Saharan Africa, the African Forum of Religious Health Organizations Working in Reproductive Health was launched in September 1999 at the eleventh International Conference on AIDS and STD (ICASA) in Lusaka, Zambia. The forum, which also works with international faith-based development agencies such as Christian Aid and CAFOD in the UK and multilateral organizations such as the World Council of Churches, is encouraging religious leaders and organizations to play a role in HIV prevention and to promote compassion and support for people living with HIV/AIDS through their congregations and links with communities.

The private sector

The private sector has also recognized the need for co-ordinated global action.

The Global Business Coalition on HIV/AIDS, established in 2001, which brings together seventy-five international companies and works in partnership with UN agencies, donor organizations and NGOs, aims to improve the effectiveness of the business response to HIV/AIDS.

Some global companies with interests in countries affected by the epidemic have already taken action. In Brazil, Volkswagen instituted an AIDS care programme in 1996, including free antiretroviral therapy, and as a result hospitalizations fell by 90 per cent and the cost of treatment and care fell by 40 per cent. Body Shop International has provided assistance to one of its suppliers in India to develop a workplace policy, which involves non-discrimination, employment of people with HIV/AIDS and provision of free medical care, life insurance and pensions. The Lesedi project in South Africa began as a partnership between a US NGO, Family Health International, and the Harmony Gold Mining Company in Virginia. Now other mining companies, the National Union of Mineworkers and provincial and national health departments have adopted a similar approach to reducing HIV risk among mineworkers and surrounding communities.

Trade unions are also working at global level. For example, the International Transport Workers Federation is negotiating with governments and transport companies to protect workers' rights, and the Commonwealth Trade Union Council is promoting co-ordinated action by its members.

Impact of global and regional responses

These global and regional responses have resulted in some progress, and some key examples – generating greater political commitment, increasing allocation of financial resources for HIV/AIDS, and improving the affordability of antiretroviral drugs – are highlighted below.

The global information revolution has made an important contribution, enabling activists and NGOs to mobilize and co-ordinate international advocacy and lobbying, as well as facilitating networking and exchange of information. International and regional meetings and conferences have also played a part in getting issues on to the agenda. Successive international AIDS conferences have, for example, drawn attention to global inequities in access to antiretroviral drugs and put pressure on pharmaceutical companies, UN agencies and national governments to negotiate lower drug prices.

Growing political commitment

Growing recognition that tackling the HIV/AIDS epidemic is essential for global development and increasing political engagement reflect many years of global activism by international and national NGOs and networks and community and PHA organizations, as well as the efforts of multilateral and bilateral agencies.

AIDS is now on the agenda of international gatherings such as the G8 and G77 and Commonwealth heads of government meetings, and of regional bodies such as the Organization for African Unity, ASEAN and CARICOM. The UN Millennium Summit identified the epidemic as a critical issue, and the UN General Assembly held a Special Session on HIV/AIDS (UNGASS) in June 2001, which resulted in the Declaration of Commitment on HIV/AIDS. The Declaration of Commitment reaffirmed the pledge made by world leaders in the Millennium Declaration to halt and begin to reverse the spread of HIV by 2015.

In the New Partnership for Africa's Development (NEPAD), launched in October 2001, African leaders pledged to eradicate poverty and to place their countries on the path to sustainable growth and development. Tackling HIV/AIDS is high on their agenda, and NEPAD builds on the International Partnership on AIDS in Africa (IPAA), an initiative involving African governments, UN and bilateral donor agencies, the private sector and civil society, to slow the spread of HIV/AIDS, promote care and mobilize society at country level. Another recent initiative that reflects the commitment of African leaders to tackling HIV/AIDS was the Organization of African Unity Summit on HIV/AIDS, TB and Other Related Infectious Diseases in Abuja, Nigeria, in April 2001, where a commitment was made to increase health expenditure to 15 per cent of national budgets.

The UNGASS declaration and other commitments provide a common mandate and an important benchmark for political accountability. For example, following UNGASS, Caribbean heads of government issued the Nassau declaration and are focusing on ways jointly to negotiate affordable prices for antiretroviral drugs, international NGO networks such as ICASO are monitoring implementation of the declaration, and NGOs in Latin America are using it as a tool to support lobbying for access to HIV treatment. International agencies, NGOs and activist organizations have also successfully used other international commitments, for example, international human rights frameworks, to advocate for changes in national laws and discriminatory policies.

Increased funding

Substantial efforts have focused on increasing financing for developing country efforts to tackle HIV/AIDS. The Global Fund to Fight AIDS, Tuberculosis and Malaria (GFATM), established in January 2002 with the intention of generating additional resources, is the outcome of commitment generated at the Genoa and Okinawa G8 meetings and by the UNGASS declaration. As of April 2002, the fund had received pledges of almost US$2 billion, including 53 per cent from industrialized countries, 27 per cent from UN organizations and 7 per cent from private foundations. So far, the fund has committed $616 million over two years. Sixty per cent of the $238 million allocated in the first year is for HIV/AIDS.

Another initiative is the World Bank Multisectoral AIDS Program (MAP) for Africa, which came into effect in 2001. MAP made available $500 million in no-interest IDA loans to thirteen sub-Saharan African countries for expanding prevention, treatment and care. A further $500 million was allocated in 2002, as well as support for regional and cross-border initiatives, and $155 million was also made available in the Caribbean under a similar initiative.

Among other mechanisms being employed to increase resources available for HIV/AIDS are the Highly Indebted Poor Country (HIPC) Initiative and Poverty Reduction Strategies. Data from ten low-income African countries suggest that these countries were budgeting about $32 million or 5 per cent of HIPC savings for AIDS activities in 2001. Donor agencies are encouraging national governments to mainstream HIV/AIDS into Poverty Reduction Strategies, which are now required for debt relief and loans from the major financial institutions.

Access to drugs and vaccines

Improving access to antiretroviral drugs has become a global priority. Countries such as Brazil have challenged the World Trade Organization (WTO), asserting their right to invoke compulsory or voluntary licensing arrangements on patented drugs and medicines under the terms of the Trade-Related Aspects of Intellectual Property Rights (TRIPS) Agreement. As a result, in November 2001, all 142 WTO member states endorsed the Doha Declaration on the TRIPS Agreement and Public Health, which stresses that TRIPS can and should be interpreted and implemented in a manner supportive of WTO members' right to protect public health and to promote access to medicines for all, and states explicitly that 'public health crises, including those related to HIV/AIDS . . . can represent a national emergency' for which governments can issue a compulsory licence authorizing, including under certain conditions, the use of patented products.

The principle of preferential pricing for low-income countries has now been largely accepted by the pharmaceutical industry as a result of concerted lobbying by NGOs and activists, pressure from international agencies such as UNAIDS, competition from generic manufacturers, and court action by AIDS treatment campaigners in South Africa and elsewhere. The Accelerating Access Initiative, a partnership between UN agencies and pharmaceutical companies, is negotiating to increase affordability and to support procurement agreements between countries or groups of countries and drug manufacturers. UNAIDS is promoting multiple approaches, which involve tiered pricing, regional procurement to secure price reductions through large-volume purchases, and licensing agreements between patent-holding companies and manufacturers in low- and middle-income countries.

In response to the impact of HIV/AIDS on productivity and profitability, as well as to lobbying for access to treatment, large companies are increasingly offering antiretroviral treatment to their workers. In July 2002, the mining companies De Beers and Anglo American announced plans to fund comprehensive health programmes, including antiretroviral treatment, for their workers in South Africa and, in September 2002, the Coca-Cola Africa Foundation and Coca-Cola's forty bottling companies in Africa announced a similar programme.

Global action has also helped to focus attention on vaccines. The International AIDS Vaccine Initiative (IAVI) aims to mobilize funding and industry participation to accelerate the development and distribution of preventive vaccines. Since 1996, IAVI has invested $20 million in a series of vaccine development partnerships between researchers in industrialized and developing countries and has negotiated intellectual property agreements to ensure products will be available in developing countries.

Future challenges

Much has been achieved and some countries have demonstrated that effective action can make a difference. In Uganda, for example, HIV prevalence in pregnant women in Kampala fell from 29.5 per cent in 1992 to 11.25 per cent in 2000 (UNAIDS 2002). Uganda has implemented a comprehensive national effort backed with high-level political commitment, including the personal involvement of President Museveni, which has engaged all sectors of society from the outset. Uganda has given particular emphasis to promoting access to condoms and voluntary counselling and testing services, to improving treatment of sexually transmitted infections (STIs), and to providing HIV/AIDS life skills education to school children. Success in reducing the spread of HIV is attributed to behavioural changes, notably a decrease in individuals' sexual partners, increased condom use, and the postponement of sexual debut among young people.

Key elements of the effectiveness of the response in Uganda and other countries such as Senegal and Thailand are political commitment and leadership, partnerships between government and the private sector, NGOs, civil society and donor agencies, integration of HIV/AIDS issues into national budgets and sector strategies, building the capacity of health systems, ensuring reliable supplies of drugs and commodities such as condoms, and mobilizing community involvement.

However, despite these success stories, the HIV/AIDS epidemic continues to spread, and there is scope for far greater global commitment and action. Significant challenges, in particular increasing resources and improving access to drugs and basic commodities such as condoms, must be overcome if the UN Millennium Summit target is to be achieved. These are not new issues, but the HIV/AIDS epidemic makes them more urgent.

Increased resources

The WHO Commission on Macroeconomics and Health identified a range of priority prevention and treatment interventions that could achieve maximum impact on the HIV epidemic. Scaling up preventive interventions to cover 70 per cent of vulnerable populations could halt or reverse the epidemic in most countries. Prevalence in most African countries would remain nearer to 5 per cent rather than rising to 10 per cent, avoiding 12 million new infections by 2015. In countries with more severe epidemics, reduction to levels achieved in Uganda, where the prevalence rate fell from 31 per cent in 1990 to 5 per cent at the end of 2001, is feasible. Effective treatment could reduce HIV-related illness and increase the length and quality of life for people with HIV, as well as decreasing related economic and social costs.

However, resources currently available are inadequate to achieve this level of coverage. In sub-Saharan Africa, annual expenditure on HIV prevention programmes from all sources is $500 million. The World Bank and UNAIDS estimate that comprehensive coverage with basic components of HIV prevention and care would require $1.5 to 2.3 billion per year. Providing antiretroviral therapy would require an additional $1.5 to 2.4 billion, depending on drug prices.

Developing countries will be unable to increase expenditure on HIV/AIDS without global action to address economic constraints and a substantial increase in development aid. Unfortunately the prospects are not promising. According to UNDP estimates, Official Development Assistance to the twenty-eight countries most seriously affected by AIDS fell by a third between 1992 and 2000. Current aid levels are far below estimated needs in the health sector, especially given the growing demands placed on health services by the HIV/AIDS epidemic and the impact of HIV/AIDS on health system capacity. Not all countries with significant HIV/AIDS epidemics are eligible for debt relief under the HIPC Initiative, notably several sub-Saharan African countries where HIV prevalence is above 20 per cent. Contributions to the GFATM have so far fallen short of the original goal of increasing spending on HIV/AIDS in low- and middle-income countries to $7 to 10 billion a year (ICASO 2002).

Progress in honouring donor and government commitments to tackle HIV/AIDS must be carefully monitored to ensure that rhetoric is matched by resources. International responses and the range of different global and regional initiatives must also be well co-ordinated, so that additional resources are used as effectively as possible.

Access to drugs and commodities

Despite efforts to improve access to treatment, fewer than 30,000 people in Africa, 30,000 in Asia and the Pacific, and 1000 in Eastern Europe and Central Asia are benefiting from antiretrovirals. In comparison, 500,000 people in high-income countries and 170,000 in Latin American and the Caribbean, more than 105,000 in Brazil alone, are receiving antiretroviral treatment. The Brazilian policy of providing antiretroviral drugs through the public health system has dramatically reduced AIDS deaths, improved the quality of life for people with HIV, and avoided an estimated 234,000 hospitalizations in 1996–2000. In 2001, the Brazilian Ministry of Health estimated that savings on treatment for opportunistic infections and hospital treatment were $50 million more than the cost of purchasing anti-retrovirals (UNAIDS 2002).

However, affordability is a critical issue in low-income countries where many people are infected with HIV. In 2003 even at reduced prices, the cost of antiretroviral treatment was around $350 a year for each HIV/AIDS patient, far in excess of the per capita health expenditure of most poor countries. For example, annual public and private health spending in the poorest African countries is less than $10 per capita (World Health Organization, 2000). Some countries are providing antiretroviral drugs, but expanding coverage is a major challenge. In Nigeria, the government is subsidizing the cost of drugs for treating 10,000 adults and 5000 children by $250 per patient per year, but it is estimated that there are 3 million people infected with HIV in the country.

Affordable drugs alone are not enough. Consideration also needs to be given to the costs related to treatment, including counselling, testing and monitoring the drug regimen. At present the cost of managing antiretroviral therapy is estimated to be double the cost of the drugs themselves. Effective delivery of antiretroviral drugs also requires well-functioning health systems, but the health infrastructure in many poor countries is weak as a result of years of inadequate investment and, in some cases, of conflict.

In addition there is a critical need to improve access to other essential drugs to treat HIV-related infections such as tuberculosis. WHO estimates that one-third of the world's population still lacks access to essential drugs and other health commodities. In the poorest parts of Africa, over 50 per cent of the population does not have reliable access to basic drugs.

As with antiretroviral drugs, key issues to be addressed include financing for health, prices and health systems. Prices are a significant factor and, in developing countries, the final cost to the consumer of a drug or commodity may be two to five times the producer or importer price, reflecting the effects of taxes, import duties, distribution costs, and dispensing charges. Increasing the affordability of key pharmaceuticals will require strategies such as reduced taxes and tariffs, tiered pricing and bulk purchasing, and global organizations can play an important role in brokering these strategies. Increasing investment in research and development to develop the new drugs and vaccines needed in developing countries also requires an enabling global context and international collaboration to build on promising approaches.

There is a need to improve access to commodities such as condoms. Although between 6 and 9 billion condoms are distributed annually, up to 24 billion condoms are needed for all populations to be able to protect themselves from HIV and other STIs. In sub-Saharan Africa alone, the condom gap has been estimated at 2 billion a year (UNAIDS 2002).

Conclusion

Despite the benefits of globalization for some, more than 1.2 billion of the world's people live on less than a dollar a day, and the HIV/AIDS epidemic is spreading most rapidly and having the most severe impact in the countries and population groups least able to withstand the negative effects of globalization. Stagnating economic growth, high debt service burdens, high levels of aid dependency, inadequate investment in the social sectors, poor infrastructure and increasing poverty limit the capacity of the poorest countries, especially those in sub-Saharan Africa, to prevent the further spread of HIV and mitigate the worst effects of the epidemic.

While existing global institutions and new international mechanisms have facilitated co-ordinated action to respond to the epidemic, generating greater political commitment, increased funding for HIV/AIDS and more affordable treatment, the response has not matched the scale of the problem. Reducing HIV vulnerability and mitigating the impact of the epidemic will require greater efforts by the international community as well as by national governments to increase resource allocation, improve access to drugs and basic commodities for the poor, and address the wider issues that drive the epidemic. Tackling the epidemic will also require greater efforts to improve access to basic services, such as education and health care, to prevent conflict, to ensure good governance and a voice for the poor in decisions that affect their lives, to support human rights and to enable marginalized groups to organize themselves collectively to challenge stigma, prejudice and discriminatory policies and practices. Most importantly, since HIV/AIDS is inextricably linked with poverty, it will require effective action to reduce global poverty. However, as discussed in chapter 3, this will only be achieved if poor countries have increased access to high-income country markets, direct financial investment, debt relief and development aid and if governments take steps to reduce inequalities, enhance access to productive resources, boost employment opportunities and strengthen social systems and infrastructures.

Further reading

Barnett, T., and Whiteside, A. (2002). *AIDS in the Twenty-first Century: Disease and Globalization*. Basingstoke: Palgrave.

Lee, K., Buse, K., and Fustukian, S. (2002). *Health Policy in a Globalising World*. Cambridge: Cambridge University Press.

Loewenson, R., and Whiteside, A. (2001). *HIV/AIDS Implications for Poverty Reduction*. New York: UNDP.

8

Globalization and Family Violence

Jan Pahl, Claudia Hasanbegovic and Mei-Kuei Yu

Family violence occurs in every part of the globe, but it is only recently that it has ceased to be seen as a private trouble and has become a public issue. More recently still, it has become something which could be described as a global social problem. There are still countries and cultures which deny its existence or minimize its extent and impact. However, over the last quarter of the twentieth century, in one country after another, this type of violence was 'discovered', and it has come to be regarded as a social problem and as appropriately tackled by social policies.

Violence within the family can take many forms, including child abuse and elder abuse, but in this chapter we shall be concerned with its most common form, which is violence by a man against his wife, his ex-wife, or the woman with whom he lives. Many different words have been employed to describe this sort of violence. Terms such as 'family violence' and 'domestic violence' are widely used, but have been criticized on the grounds that they are gender neutral and do not convey the fact that men are the main perpetrators and women the main victims. More recently there has been concern that terms such as 'abused women' imply passive victims, and this has led to the use of phrases such as 'women survivors of male violence in the home'.

At international levels the term most commonly used is 'gender-based violence' or 'violence against women'. This was defined by the United Nations Declaration on the Elimination of Violence against Women as:

Any act of gender violence that results in, or is likely to result in, physical, sexual or psychological harm or suffering to women, including threats of such acts, coercion or arbitrary deprivation of liberty, whether occurring in public or in private life. (United Nations 1993, 2)

Violence against women within the family can take many different forms, among them physical assault, rape and sexual violence, psychological or emotional violence, torture, financial abuse, including dowry-related violence, and control of movement and of social contacts.

However, in a book on social problems we must also consider how the name given to a problem affects the way in which it is perceived. The words 'domestic violence' or 'wife abuse' shift attention from the people who cause the problem to the place where it takes place or the people who are its victims. Writing about 'battered women' is like calling mugging the problem of 'people who walk about carrying money' or car theft the 'problem of people who leave cars unattended'. This point is relevant when we think about appropriate action. Short-term social policy may focus on the women and the children, because they need help most immediately. But in the long term we should remember that the problem might be more accurately defined as the problem of 'men who are violent to the women with whom they live'. This perspective on the issue has led to the development of initiatives focused on the men and on modifying their violent behaviour (Dobash et al. 2000).

In this chapter we shall mainly use the terms 'domestic violence', 'violence against women' and 'abused women', but we do so in the context of the points made above. We recognize that women can be, and are, violent against men and that the men involved usually find this very distressing. However, when a woman does use violence against a man this is often in the context of self-defence or as a desperate attempt to protect children. A World Health Organization report concluded that 'the overwhelming burden of partner violence is borne by women at the hands of men' (World Health Organization 2002a, 15).

How did violence against women come to be defined as a social problem? There are many possible answers to this question, but the following have certainly been important in the UK. First, feminist activists of the 1970s identified this as an issue which would give practical expression to their more general concern about the position of women: many of the early refuges began life as 'women's centres' but were used to provide a haven for women and children escaping from violence (Hanmer and Sutton 1984; Pahl 1978, 1985). Second, the opening of refuges made visible what had previously been hidden; this was particularly so in the case of the refuge opened by Erin Pizzey in Chiswick, which received widespread publicity on television (Pizzey 1974). Third, the growth of Women's Aid, as a co-ordinating body for the expanding number of refuges, brought the activists together to share ideas and experience and to work for increased political visibility for their analysis of the issue (Women's Aid 2002a, 2002b). Fourth, feminist scholars and activists were energetic in researching the issue and in pressing for more effective and appropriate action by all the different agencies which have responsibility for women and family life.

Globalization and domestic violence

Globalization is relevant to debates on domestic violence in three different ways. First, the identification of the issue in some countries has stimulated awareness in others. In the next section of this chapter we shall examine the extent and distribution of this form of violence and consider its impact on the health of women and children. We shall show how the research which has been done in individual countries, when brought together by international organizations, has had a powerful effect in underlining the global nature of this problem.

Second, debates about the causes of domestic violence have taken place at many different levels, but the growth of a global debate has been significant. Later in the chapter we shall discuss the explanations which have been put forward. We shall show that the development of a global debate has had a profound impact on ideas about causation by revealing the similarities between male violence across countries which otherwise are very different from each other.

Third, policy responses have varied enormously between countries, as we shall see, but global and regional organizations have been important in shaping debates within member countries. We shall trace the growth of the global movement against violence against women, consider some of the policy responses which have been proposed and try to evaluate the impact of directives produced by international organizations. We shall illustrate this section with original case studies from England, Taiwan and Cuba.

Finally we shall consider future trends. Is there any evidence that violence against women is decreasing in its extent or its intensity? Is globalization likely to influence future trends in domestic violence?

What has been the impact of social policies enacted at global and regional levels?

The extent and distribution of domestic violence

Studies of the extent of violence against women have now been conducted in many different countries, with results which are surprisingly similar. Table 8.1 shows the results of several such studies; it is drawn from a number of sources, but especially from the *Violence against Women Information Pack* produced by the World Health Organization (2002b).

It is likely that the figures given in table 8.1 underestimate the problem, for many reasons. Some women may believe that they deserve the beatings, or accept them as a 'normal' part of marriage. Other women are ashamed of their situation or refrain from speaking about the abuse because they fear that their partner will further harm them in reprisal for revealing 'family secrets'. In many countries there are no legal or social sanctions against violence by an intimate partner and so revealing the abuse serves no purpose. Considering these factors, estimates of the prevalence of physical abuse by a partner are probably conservative.

It is also important to remember that most of the studies listed in table 8.1 were focused on physical abuse. Yet many women have reported that the physical assaults were less distressing than the other forms of abuse which they experienced, such as threats of harm to themselves or their children, acts designed to humiliate and degrade them, rape and sexual abuse, being denied money for children's food, being prevented from seeing family or friends, or being continuously shouted at and kept awake.

It is estimated that globally around one in four women is likely to experience violence at the hands of her partner (World Health Organization 2002a).

The effects of domestic violence

Violence within the family can have significant effects on the health of women and children. At its most extreme it is a cause of death, especially for women. In the UK about half of all homicides of women are killings by a partner or ex-partner; one in five of all murder

Table 8.1 Violence against women

Canada	25 per cent of ever-married/common-law partnered women reported being physically assaulted by a male partner (Johnson 1996).
Chile	26 per cent of women reported at least one episode of violence by a partner (Larrain 1993).
Colombia	19 per cent of women had been physically assaulted by their partner in their lifetime (DHS III, 1995).
Egypt	35 per cent of married women reported being beaten by their husbands in their marriage (El-Zanaty et al. 1995).
India	18 to 45 per cent of married men admitted physically abusing their wives (Narayana 1996).
Israel	32 per cent of married Arab women reported at least one episode of physical abuse in the last year (Haj-Yahia 1996).
Kenya	42 per cent of women reported having being beaten at some time by a partner (Raikes 1990).
Korea	38 per cent of wives reported being physically abused by their spouse in the last year (Kim and Cho 1992).
Mexico	30 per cent of women reported at least one episode of physical violence by a partner (Rodriguez and Becerra 1997).
Nicaragua	52 per cent of ever-married women reported being physically abused by a partner (Ellsberg et al. 1996).
Switzerland	20 per cent of women in a relationship reported being physically assaulted (Gillioz et al. 1997).
Thailand	20 per cent of husbands admitted to abusing their wives at least once in their marriage (Hoffman et al. 1994).
Uganda	41 per cent of women reported being beaten or physically harmed; 41 per cent of men reported beating their partners (Blanc et al. 1997).
United Kingdom	30 per cent of women had at some time had acts perpetrated against them which came into the category of domestic violence (Mooney 2000).
United States	28 per cent of women reported at least one episode of physical violence from their partner (Straus and Gelles 1986).
Zimbabwe	32 per cent of women reported physical abuse by a family or household member (Watts et al. 1996).

Source: World Health Organization 2002b

victims (male and female) is a woman killed by a partner or ex-partner (Victim Support 1992).

Domestic violence also causes much morbidity, both physical and mental. Physical injuries can range from minor cuts and bruises to severe injuries requiring hospitalization. One list of the effects on women's physical health included wounds and fractures, unwanted pregnancy, gynaecological problems, miscarriage, chronic pelvic pain, permanent disability, asthma, and sexually transmitted diseases, including HIV/AIDS. Among the effects on women's mental health were depression, anxiety, low self-esteem, sexual dysfunction, eating disorders, post-traumatic stress disorder and drug and alcohol abuse (International Planned Parenthood Federation 2002). Compared with women who are not living with violent men, women who have been abused by their partners are five times more likely to commit suicide (World Health Organization 2002b; see also Stark and Flitcraft 1996).

Health can also suffer if children witness or are aware of domestic violence between their parents. The Women's Aid Federation, which co-ordinates refuges in England, has been concerned for some time about the effects of domestic violence on children. Among children staying with their mothers in refuges, 70 per cent had themselves been abused by their father; even those who do not suffer abuse are likely to be aware of what is taking place (Women's Aid 2002a). Such children are likely to suffer from confused and torn loyalties; they may feel ashamed, guilty, isolated and alone; they may respond by trying to protect their mothers, by phoning the police or, most dangerously, by trying to restrain their fathers (Hague and Malos 1998).

Among common health problems of children who witness domestic violence are increased levels of anxiety, headaches, abdominal pains, asthma, peptic ulcers, stuttering, enuresis, withdrawal, fear and sadness. Behavioural problems can include boys becoming more disobedient and destructive, girls becoming more nervous, anxious and withdrawn, and both sexes becoming more inclined to run away from home (Jaffe et al. 1990; Mullender and Morley 1994).

Most of the research about the nature and distribution of domestic violence and about its impact on women and children has been undertaken in individual countries. However, a global perspective creates a powerful impression. In country after country we can see how similar are the prevalence rates, suggesting that on average around one-quarter of women worldwide experience domestic violence at some time in their lives. And though researchers may be working in different countries, they find very similar patterns in terms of the impact on the health of women and children. The World Health Organization concluded that the costs to society of violence against women are tremendous, in terms of medical care and treatment, police and court processes, social services costs, including child protection, and the loss of productivity when women have to take time off work (World Health Organization 2002b).

The causes of violence against women

Much has been written about the causes of violence against women, but there is space here only to outline the main points. We shall go on to assess the impact of the global movement against violence against women and consider whether the development of a global debate has changed ideas about causes.

A useful summary of the arguments for and against different explanations is provided by Hague and Malos (1998). They begin by summarizing traditional attitudes to marriage, in which the husband was seen as the breadwinner and as head of the household, with the right to control 'his' wife. This was the perspective which lay behind the evidence put forward in 1974 by the police in England to the Select Committee on Violence in Marriage. The Association of Chief Police Officers suggested that 'We are, after all, dealing with persons "bound in marriage", and it is important for a host of reasons, to maintain the unity of the spouses' (Select Committee Report 1975, 366). However, a detailed historical survey prompted two of the leading researchers in this field to conclude that traditional attitudes led to a situation in which the wife became the 'appropriate victim', while the man's violence could safely be explained away as justified, excusable or unimportant (Dobash and Dobash 1980). Traditional attitudes such as these can still be found in every part of the world, but they are more common in some parts than others.

One argument is that violence is caused by *individual pathologies*, which lead to deviance from a non-violent norm (Hague and Malos 1998, 51). The individual in question may be the man, who may be suffering from psychiatric illness or may simply have learned as a child to see violence as normal behaviour. Alternatively it has been argued that individual women may provoke or collude with the man's violence, or may accept the violence because of having grown up in a violent family. There is some evidence that violence can be learned in this way, or transmitted from one generation to another (Straus et al. 1980; Shen 1997). However, most of those who grow up in violent homes do not go on to abuse their partners, while a violent man is twice as likely to have had a non-violent than a violent childhood home (Stark and Flitcraft 1996). The fact that such a high proportion of men are violent against their partners must undermine the idea that their behaviour is a product of psychiatric illness.

A second approach focuses on *social structural explanations*, and suggests that violence against women is the product of such factors as poor education, low income, unemployment, bad housing and so on. Straus et al. (1980) developed a profile of the violent family in order to predict families in which violence would be more likely. The factors which predicted violence included unemployment, low income, being a manual worker, being worried about economic security, having two or more children, being under thirty, coming from a non-white racial group, and a number of others. This approach has been criticized for failing to recognize that violence takes place in middle-class families but is more likely to be concealed or to be resolved without recourse to any outside agencies. In support of this position a study in London showed that there was no difference between professional, lower middle-class and working-class men in terms of their self-reported use of domestic violence (Mooney 2000, 185).

A third set of explanations has been described as *moralist*, that is, as related to the breakdown of the family (Hague and Malos 1998, 56). This draws on the work of New Right commentators and sees domestic violence as part of a decline in family values, and as the result of a more general collapse in the moral order of society (Abbott and Wallace 1992). However, historical evidence suggests that violence against wives was, if anything, more common and more severe in the past than it is now. Certainly in nineteenth-century England violence was widely accepted, and the right of men to beat their wives was not legally rescinded until 1892 (Dobash and Dobash 1980).

Fourthly, *feminist explanations* of domestic violence see the traditional family, built on male dominance and female subordination, as a fertile breeding ground for violence. There are many different strands within the feminist debate. Some stress the historical position of women within marriage, while others point to the continuing responsibility of women for child care, which places them in a weaker economic position. Some argue that the roots of violence against women lie in patriarchy and in a pattern of gender relations characterized by male power and abuse of power, and female dependence, both financial and psychological. Others would stress the role of cultural factors such as *machismo* and the normative approval given to male violence (Hague and Malos 1998, 58).

Debates about the causes of domestic violence continue, but it is clear that at international level feminist explanations have become the most influential. The United Nations Declaration on the Elimination of Violence against Women set the analysis out clearly:

> Violence against women is a manifestation of historically unequal power relations between men and women, which have led to domination over and discrimination against women by men, and to the

prevention of the full advancement of women. . . . violence against women is one of the crucial social mechanisms by which women are forced into a subordinate position compared with men. (United Nations 1993, 1)

How and why did the feminist analysis of domestic violence become the dominant explanation at international level? There must be many answers to this question. However, experience at international meetings suggests that most countries sent delegates who were already specialists in domestic violence and who saw the feminist explanation as fundamental to an understanding of the issue in their own country. Bringing them together from around the globe underlined the fact that domestic violence takes strikingly similar forms in different countries. Despite different family patterns, different cultures and traditions, and different social and economic structures, delegates to international meetings described very similar patterns of male violence in the home.

The Declaration on the Elimination of Violence against Women set the problem firmly in the context of women's human rights. It went on to argue the need for 'a clear statement of the rights to be applied to ensure the elimination of violence against women in all its forms, a commitment by States in respect of their responsibilities, and a commitment by the international community at large to the elimination of violence against women' (United Nations 1993, 2). In the following section we examine some of the ways in which global and regional bodies have tried to deal with the issue.

International initiatives to deal with violence against women

International concern about this issue can be traced back to 1979 and the Convention on the Elimination of Discrimination against Women (CEDAW), often described as a bill of rights for women. This paved the way for the World Conference of the United Nations Decade for Women, held at Copenhagen in 1980, which stated that domestic violence constituted an intolerable offence to the dignity of human beings. Accordingly the programme of action for the second half of the United Nations Decade for Women, adopted at the Copenhagen conference, advocated research into the extent and causes of domestic violence, with a view to its elimination, and the provision of effective help for women (United Nations 1980).

Subsequently the issue was discussed at a number of international meetings, and progress was reviewed at the Nairobi Conference to Review and Appraise the Achievements of the United Nations Decade for Women (United Nations 1985). The result was a resolution to the United Nations General Assembly which advocated concerted and multidisciplinary action within and outside the United Nations system to combat the problem and urged the introduction of specific criminological measures to achieve the fair and humane response of justice systems to the victimization of women within the family (Resolution 40/36, adopted on 29 November 1985).

The issue was carried forward in a number of different international contexts. In 1985 the Women and Development Programme of the Commonwealth Secretariat convened an Expert Group Meeting on Violence against Women, held in London (Commonwealth Secretariat 1992). In 1986 the UN Centre for Social Development and Humanitarian Affairs organized an Expert Group Meeting on Violence in the Family, with Special Emphasis on its effects of Women. The meeting was held in Vienna and its report aimed to 'provide an overall picture of violence against women in the family as a world issue rather than as an issue that is confined to one country or one cultural system' (United Nations 1989, 1).

More recent international actions have focused on violence against women as an infringement of human rights or as a threat to health. CEDAW underlined the importance of the issue in 1992, when it set out a resolution dealing with domestic violence and its elimination. A landmark was the adoption in 1993 by the United Nations of the Declaration on the Elimination of Violence against Women. This was the first human rights instrument to deal exclusively with violence against women. It affirmed that violence impairs or nullifies the enjoyment by women of their fundamental human rights (United Nations 1993). Also in 1993 the World Conference on Human Rights stated that gender-based violence is incompatible with the dignity and worth of human persons. It called for legal measures, national action and international co-operation in such fields as economic and social development, education, health care and social support.

In 1994 the UN Commission on Human Rights appointed a Special Rapporteur on violence against women. The Special Rapporteur can receive and request information from governments, organizations and individuals and can initiate relevant investigations (United Nations 1997). In the same year the Inter American Convention on the Prevention, Elimination and Punishment of Violence against Women was passed. This was the first international instrument specifically designed to eradicate domestic violence, and it presented states with a detailed list of their duties with respect to this issue.

In 1995 the Fourth World Conference on Women, held in Beijing, devoted an entire section to violence against women. It described violence against women as an obstacle to the achievement of equality, peace and development and set out a number of measures which governments should take to prevent and eliminate violence (United Nations 1995, 1). In 1996 the World Health Assembly made violence against women and children a public health priority (World Health Organization 2002b), while in 1997 domestic violence was condemned as an infringement of women's human rights. In 1999 the Optional Protocol to the Convention on the Elimination of all Forms of Discrimination against Women made it possible for individuals who have exhausted national remedies to petition the committee directly about alleged violations of the convention by their governments. In 2000 the European Commission launched a four-year programme to combat violence against women and children, which has provided funding of 4 million Euros for NGOs working in the field (European Commission 2000). Evidence to support this initiative came from the *World Report on Violence and Health* (World Health Organization 2002a).

Box 8.1   The main international actions on violence against women

1979   Convention on the Elimination of all Forms of Discrimination against Women
1985   UN General Assembly resolution on violence against women
1986   UN Expert Group Meeting on Violence against Women in the Family
1993   UN Declaration on the Elimination of Violence against Women
1994   Special Rapporteur on violence against women appointed
1994   Inter American Convention on the Prevention, Elimination and Punishment of Violence against Women
1995   Fourth World Conference on Women at Beijing
1996   World Health Assembly made violence a public health issue
1996   Commission on Human Rights condemned violence against women
1999   Optional Protocol to the Convention on the Elimination of all Forms of Discrimination against Women
2002   World Health Organization *Report on Violence and Health*

However, other, and more powerful, international forces have also been important over these years, many of them linked to the processes of globalization explored in other chapters of this book. Among these other forces we would cite the movement of capital and labour around the world, the globalization of culture, and the structural adjustment policies imposed by the International Monetary Fund and the World Bank. In the case studies which follow we will attempt to assess the relative importance of these different forces on the problem of violence against women.

Case studies in England, Taiwan and Cuba

Our case studies are all are based on original empirical research, undertaken in three very different countries in the years from 1999 to 2001. The studies are reported at greater length elsewhere (Hasanbegovic 2002a; Yu 2002). The research set out to explore women's experience of violence in the home and their views on the services which might have been expected to help them. The research methods included around twenty interviews in each of the three countries, the collection of life histories, and the analysis of laws and documents. Across the three countries the interviews were strikingly similar when the women described the violence they had endured, but strikingly different when they talked about the responses which they encountered when they had sought help and an end to violence.

England could be said to be the country which 'rediscovered' violence against women. The catalyst was the setting up of the first women's refuge in the world and the development of the Women's Aid movement from 1974. Women's Aid is a non-governmental organization (NGO) which provides a helpline for women experiencing violence, supports the work of local refuges, and campaigns for change in policy and practice with regard to domestic violence. In 2001 there were over 400 refuges in England, used by 54,000 women and children in that year (Women's Aid 2002b). By contrast with other countries, the refuge movement has always been relatively important in England, being seen as having greater expertise and experience than any other agency, and as offering abused women a more comprehensive service. The development of the refuges was supported by the state system of income maintenance, which enabled women who left home to claim enough money to feed themselves and their children and pay for their accommodation.

Partly because of the strength of Women's Aid, and partly because it was not clear which government department should take prime responsibility, other agencies were relatively slow to develop effective policies to deal with domestic violence. However, pressure by Women's Aid, and by feminist activists, journalists and researchers, led to a series of changes in legislation and professional practice. Key steps included the 1985 Housing Act, the 1990 Home Office circular to police forces, and the 1996 Family Law Act. Domestic violence came to be defined primarily as a crime, and thus the government department which takes prime responsibility is the Home Office. The Department of Health, which is responsible for social services as well as health care, was relatively late in developing policies and guidelines for dealing with the issue (Department of Health 2000; Pahl 1995).

In Taiwan, by way of contrast to the UK, domestic violence has been seen primarily as a social problem requiring state intervention. Identification of the issue did not really begin until the late 1980s. At this time academic research, action by NGOs, and international debates began to draw attention to the issue, and local government became involved in funding groups which were setting up shelters. Increasing public concern led to the passing in 1998 of the Family Violence Prevention Act (FVPA). The Act stipulated that every local government authority must set up a Family Violence Prevention Centre (FVPC). The function of these centres was to prevent family violence, to promote the protection and safety of all victims of family violence and to play a role in advocating policy in this field. Responsibility for the FVPCs was given to social services departments, so social workers became the lead professionals in the field of domestic violence. However, progress in setting up shelters/refuges was slow, so that by 1999 there were only twenty-eight in the whole country, used by 545 women during the preceding year.

Cuba experienced radical changes in all aspects of life after the revolution of 1959. The equality of women was a core principle of the revolution, and policies to achieve this goal have eroded, although not eliminated, patriarchy (Basail Rodríguez 1999). Women have been fully incorporated into the labour market, have become largely economically independent, and have achieved equality in education and in social and political participation (Alvarez Suarez 1998; Caño Secade 1997; Larguía and Dumoulin 1986). A wide range of legal reforms accompanied these changes. The clearest attempt to challenge patriarchy in intimate relations was the Family Code of 1975, which insisted on men's equal participation with women in housework, child-rearing and support of the family.

The revolution also set up the goal of achieving a society free of crime. This included better co-ordination of neighbourhood-based organizations and state institutions to prevent crime. The Cuban Penal Code Book identifies discrimination against women as a crime, and the revolutionary political commitment to this principle was extended in 1966 to setting up public trials to judge a man on the grounds of a woman's maltreatment (Van der Plas 1987). Although no specific domestic violence law exists in Cuba, the implementation of the Penal Code in family violence covers a wide range of family abuses, including marital rape and economic domestic violence. The effect is that domestic violence has been tackled as anti-social behaviour and as a crime (Oliva et al. 1994; Aguilera Ribeaux 2001).

In Cuba the response to domestic violence has been characterized by a community-based approach, which brings together neighbours, neighbourhood organizations, family doctors, the police, the Federation of Cuban Women and the Council of Social Prevention. This response is accompanied by policies to protect women and to support them in finding remunerated jobs. In effect the Cuban revolution changed the boundaries between private and public. The goal of intervention is to challenge and halt male violence. This results in empowerment for battered women, who find it possible to manoeuvre strategically in, and/or leave, abusive relationships. There are no refuges or shelters, since it is considered that women should be able to stay in their own homes and be protected there. In general, the women interviewed for the Cuban research felt protected by the community and the law, and saw the police and the courts as essential to controlling and preventing further violence (Hasanbegovic 2001, 2002a).

There were three significant differences between the countries in their approach to domestic violence. First, social workers were more involved in Taiwan than elsewhere, and were seen as case managers, with the responsibility to link together all the resources needed to help a particular woman. Other agencies, such as the police and the health services, were expected to refer women to the social services, and it was only through a social worker that women could get access to a FVPC. By contrast, in England social services were just one of a number of agencies to whom a woman might turn for help. Dealing with violence in the family was often seen in terms of child protection rather than in terms of empowering women: in the interviews many women expressed the fear that contacting social services might lead to their children being removed from them.

Second, the role of the police was rather different in each of the three countries. The FVPA made it mandatory for the police in

Taiwan to record cases of domestic violence and to make a report to the FVPC. In addition the police were likely to refer the woman to a hospital, since medical evidence would be important in applying for a civil protection order and returning the woman to her own home; the refuge was seen as very much a last resort. In England domestic violence tended to be seen predominantly as a crime, and as such the police were likely to be the lead agency; police practice has improved over the past few years, and the legislation has become more effective. However, the interviews showed that refuges still play a central part and the police were more likely to refer the woman on to a refuge than to any other agency.

In Cuba, enabling women to live safely in their homes was seen as a priority, and the police, the court, and the neighbours were expected to provide protection. The research in Cuba showed that professionals and the Federation of Cuban Women were shocked by the idea that women and children should have to leave home while their abusers remained (Hasanbegovic 2002b).

Third, there were differences in term of health care. In Taiwan health professionals were crucial, not just in treating women, but also in giving them the evidence that they would need to support their case. Women would be referred to hospital social workers, reflecting the fact that domestic violence was seen as a social problem. By contrast, in England the definition of domestic violence as a crime has led to a situation in which it is only recently that the health services have taken domestic violence seriously (Pahl 1995). In Cuba family doctors live in the neighbourhoods they serve, and pay periodical visits to their patients in their own homes in order to give advice about health care and family problems, including domestic violence (Hasanbegovic 2002a).

It is difficult to assess the impact which international measures to deal with violence against women have had in the three countries. The UK government signed both the 1979 Convention on the Elimination of all Forms of Discrimination against Women and the Declaration on the Elimination of Violence against Women, but was overdue in reporting on the action which it had taken to implement the convention. It is possible that the 1990 Home Office circular resulted partly from the need to be seen to take action, and certainly the 1990s saw a plethora of policy and practice guidelines, seminars and training sessions, and multi-agency initiatives (Hague 1999). At the time of writing the UK had not signed the Optional Protocol to the Convention on the Elimination of all Forms of Discrimination against Women.

Taiwan did not have the opportunity to sign the various UN documents, but has shown determination in getting effective legislation into force, again perhaps in order to be seen to be taking action in this field.

Cuba signed the Convention on the Elimination of all Forms of Discrimination against Women in 1980 and the Optional Protocol to the Convention in 2000, and has reported periodically to the Commission on the Elimination of Discrimination against Women. However, when the UN Special Rapporteur on violence against women visited Cuba in 1999, she did not support the Cuban perspective on refuges. In her recommendations to the Cuban government, she asked for the establishment of refuges for abused women all across the island (United Nations 2000b). This recommendation was unwelcome to the government, which argued for the right of Cubans to decide on the best ways of protecting and empowering women (United Nations 2000c).

Conclusion

How realistic is it to see violence against women as a global social problem and how effective have global social policies been in creating solutions? In answering these questions we return to the criteria set out in chapter 1 by the editors of this book. The editors saw global social problems as distinguished by four criteria.

First, the causes of the problem are found in global social processes. This is true of domestic violence, in the sense that the roots of the problem lie in male dominance and in discrimination against women, in a pattern which is found in every part of the globe, though to a varying degree depending on the local culture. International declarations have presented convincing arguments to support this explanation, which is likely to have influenced ideas at national levels. At present there is no hard evidence about whether the problem is increasing or decreasing, though it seems to be the case that women are more willing to report violence now than at any time in the past.

However, globalization may be playing a part in increasing the risks to women. Research has identified a relation between domestic violence and the implementation of structural adjustment policies in developing countries (Beneria 1991; Kuenyehia 1994). Women's unequal access to economic power has been identified as one predictor of domestic violence (Levinson 1989), and the feminization of poverty has been acknowledged as a burden for women's equality (United Nations 1995). Therefore, it is possible that in some circumstances globalization may increase women's vulnerability to male violence. This certainly seems to be the case in Cuba. In 1989, with the collapse of the Soviet Union and the Eastern European bloc, Cuba underwent one of its most difficult times since the revolution in 1959. Strategies for economic survival were named the 'Special Period in Times of Peace', and involved opening the economy to a globalized capitalist world. Many women dropped their paid jobs and went back into their homes to cope with the increasingly difficult social reproduction of the family. A shadow economy, in which American dollars became the currency, emerged alongside the official economy, in which wages were paid in pesos. While women mostly remained in the latter, since at least one member of the household had to have employment in the official economy, many men ventured into the better-paid dollar economy. This created an imbalance of economic power within the couple, which made women more vulnerable to domestic violence (Pearson 1997; Navarrete Calderon 1999; Hasanbegovic 2002a).

Second, a global social problem spreads across national boundaries despite efforts by the nation-state to the contrary. In the case of violence against women it was not the problem which spread but rather recognition of the problem. Many countries which initially denied the existence of domestic violence within their boundaries have been forced to recognize its reality; the few countries which persist in denying that domestic violence takes place are probably those in which such violence is both taken for granted and also very shameful and hidden.

Third, global social problems are said to be those which are difficult to solve at national level. This does not exactly apply to violence against women. What has become clear is that, while women's experiences of violence are remarkably similar from one country to another, effective policy responses vary greatly. As we saw in the case studies, policy responses reflect long-standing legal, political, economic and cultural differences between countries. Nevertheless, countries have learned much from each other about possible solutions to the problem of violence against women, though policy solutions which reflect a North American and European perspective may not easily influence countries with very different cultural traditions.

Finally, global social problems are said to be those where supranational bodies have made efforts to assist member states to deal with them. This is certainly so, in that many international agencies have been active in identifying the problem and making recommendations for solutions. How effective these recommendations have been is still unsure.

It has been suggested that the most useful approach might be to regard such international agreements as 'soft law'. This means that, while they do not have the binding power of treaties, they do 'provide the parties to international agreements with the power to justify and persuade' (Hillgenberg 1999). This would mean that much of the force of international declarations and conventions lies in the use which is made of them at national levels. Certainly, the changes from 1980 to 2000 are striking in terms of the extent to which international bodies have recognized the seriousness of the problem, have committed themselves to taking action, and have begun to work towards finding solutions to violence against women. At national levels our case studies showed significant developments in policy and practice, modified in the case of Cuba by the impact of economic globalization. However, much of this activity is relatively recent: future readers of this chapter will have a longer perspective over which to judge whether there has been any reduction in violence against women.

Further reading

Dobash, R. E., Dobash, R. P., Cavanagh, K., and Lewis, R. (2000). *Changing Violent Men*. London: Sage.

Hague, G., and Malos, E. (1998). *Domestic Violence: Action for Change*. Cheltenham: New Clarion Press.

Mooney, J. (2000). *Gender, Violence and the Social Order*. Basingstoke: Macmillan.

United Nations (2003). *A Call to End Violence against Women*. New York: United Nations; available at <www.unifem.org/campaigns/november25/>.

World Health Organization (2004). *Gender-Based Violence*. Geneva: WHO; available at <www.who.int/gender/violence/en/>.

9

Globalization and Racism

Norman Ginsburg

From one perspective globalization and racism seem entirely anti-thetical. Globalization in a broad sense carries with it, perhaps, notions of an essential universalism of human values and attributes, which break down barriers of nationalism, and ethnic intolerance and absolutism. Hence globalization holds out the promise of a world of individuals, households and communities bound together by mutual respect, universal human rights and increasingly global governance. Globalization in this sense is linked with the Enlightenment values of Western political liberalism, the fundamental belief in the equal worth of all persons. Racism, by contrast, carries with it notions of particularisms and differences in human values and attributes, chal-lenging implicitly or explicitly the equal worth of all persons. Racism has often been translated into ethnically discriminatory and exclu-sionary practices both by states and in civil society. The twentieth century witnessed brutally racist regimes, movements and behaviour across the globe. Arguably, however, in recent decades anti-racism has gained in strength and has become something of a global move-ment itself, suggesting that globalization and racism may indeed be antagonistic processes.

From a contrasting perspective, historical and contemporary evi-dence seems to suggest that globalization and racism not only co-exist quite readily, but also actually seem to bolster each other. Hence European colonialism, an example of globalization if ever there was one, was associated with and inspired by notions of racial superior-ity, translated into the brutality of slavery, expropriation of native peoples and forced migration. The economic globalization of the contemporary period seems to have been accompanied by an upsurge in racism across the globe, and it is more than plausible to suggest linkages between these two processes. First, the rise of so-called Islamic fundamentalism as a global form of cultural and political resistance to Westernized globalization has been accompanied by the growth of anti-Muslimism and revitalization of white supremacist discourse. Second, anti-capitalist globalization movements have linked economic globalization to the increasing economic inequalities and injustices within and between nations, which are very often racialized. Increasing migration of people fleeing oppression and/or seeking economic betterment is a third aspect of globalization, which is linked to increasing xenophobia, and racialized exclusionary immigration and asylum policies in the West. There are obvious links between the pressures encouraging migration and the growth of global inequality and ethnic absolutism. Migrants are usually either fleeing authoritarian or ethnic absolutist regimes, or trying to leap the widening gulf between rich and poor nations, or both. Migration is dealt with in chapter 10; here we will look at other aspects of globalization and racism beyond the vitally significant issues associated directly with migration.

So, from one perspective globalization and racism are opposing forces, and from another they are symbiotically intertwined. In my view neither perspective is fully adequate; both have much to offer in understanding the complexities before us. Here we will review some of the evidence on racism as a global phenomenon, consider the possible links to globalization, and then discuss some of the contemporary global and regional responses to racism.

Concepts

Before proceeding further, it is advisable to clarify a little how the two key concepts of globalization and racism are being used here. 'Globalization' will be used in a broad, neutral sense to denote the phenomenon of increasingly swift and global flows of goods, information, people, services, cultures/sub-cultures, etc., and the accompanying deterritorialization, i.e. the emergence of 'supranational social spaces' (Scholte 2000, 3). This is broadly the line adopted in chapter 1. By contrast the term 'economic globalization' will be used to denote the recent economic and cultural advances of Western transnational corporations across the globe, particularly in the last three decades. This is widely associated with the rise to pre-eminence of neo-liberal economic thinking, the liberalization of capital move-ment and free trade, and phenomena such as 'McDonaldization' and growing income inequalities within and between nations.

Racism denotes beliefs and practices based on notions that partic-ular racialized or ethnic groups are biologically and/or culturally inferior or superior. The designation of racialized groups is specific to particular social and historical contexts, and in that sense there are many forms of racism, which evolve, ebb and flow continually. Racism operates at different levels in society, and it is useful to dis-tinguish some of these – direct or individual discrimination; institu-tional racism in organizations, including state racism, i.e. racism institutionalized in government policies; and structural racism sus-tained by economic processes or 'structures' such as corporate capi-talism or colonialism. The emphasis here will be on governmental and structural racism, which may not be explicitly racist, but never-theless results in unjust treatment and unequal outcomes on a racial-ized basis. This is not meant to ignore or set aside direct racism in the form of individual prejudice and discrimination. A major opinion survey across the European Union in 1997 revealed that almost 33 per cent of respondents described themselves as 'quite racist' or 'very racist' (European Commission, 1997); 18 per cent of respondents agreed that 'legally established immigrants from outside the EU should all be sent back to their country of origin', a proportion which increased to 20 per cent when the survey was repeated in 2000. However, the proportion of respondents who agreed that 'immigrants enrich the cultural life of the country' increased from 33 per cent in 1997 to 48 per cent in 2000 (EUMC 2001, table 19). There are obvious methodological problems with such opinion survey data, not least the reference in the questionnaire to 'immigrants' rather than ethnic minorities. Nevertheless it is reasonable to suggest that insti-tutional, state and structural racism are all sustained by the opinions and prejudices of individual people as confirmed in such surveys. There is a dialectic between institutional and structural processes on the one hand, and individual consciousness and attitudes on the other. Equally important, these surveys suggest a growing consciousness of the positive aspects of the developing multiculturalism and multi-ethnic societies in Europe.

The extent and distribution of racism globally

What is usefully referred to as structural racism manifests itself most obviously and starkly in the socio-economic differences between rich and poor countries. The World Bank in its World Development Indicators distinguishes 'high-income' states from 'middle-income' and 'low-income' states. High-income states had a Gross National Product per head of population (GNP per capita) in 1998 of above $9266, while for low-income states it was below $755. The great majority of the high-income or rich states are populated predominantly by white people of European origin, though this group also includes Taiwan and Singapore. The low-income or poor states are all predominantly populated by people of colour of non-European origin, and are almost all located in sub-Saharan Africa and in Asia. World Bank data for 1998 (World Bank 2000a) show that the under-five mortality rate in the rich states was six per 1000, compared to 107 per 1000 in the poor states; life expectancy at birth for men and women respectively was seventy-five and eighty-one in the rich states, and fifty-nine and sixty-one respectively in the poor states. The overwhelming majority of the estimated 1 billion people surviving on an income of less than 1 dollar a day were, of course, living in the poor countries. It is hardly surprising that the situation reflected in these figures has been described as 'global apartheid', the stratification of the world's population into rich and predominantly white countries and poor (and 'middle income') predominantly non-white countries (Alexander 1966; Booker and Minter 2001). This racialized stratification is maintained by a system of domestic immigration controls and economic protection, which prevents extensive migration from poor to rich countries, while at the same time limiting the extent to which poor economies can participate in world trade on fair terms. The poor countries are roughly equivalent to the homelands of the apartheid regime. Like apartheid this stratification is legitimated by assumptions in the rich states that it is somehow 'natural' for people to have different opportunities and expectations in life, assumptions sustained by centuries of European colonialism. Without going into historical explanations in terms of 'old' racisms, the contemporary existence of such enormous socio-economic differences with such a strong racialized dimension is in itself perhaps the most significant marker of the global dimension of racism. It is not that the people of the rich countries are necessarily consciously or actively racist, but they preside over and benefit from a world system which impoverishes and excludes non-white people on a mass, global scale. This is what is meant by 'structural racism', but it is by no means to suggest that racism is the sole 'explanation' for global poverty, simply a plausibly important explanatory factor.

A second global aspect of racism is, of course, the extent of racialized inequalities and injustices *within* nation-states. The *World*

Development Report (World Bank 2000a, 46) notes in passing that 'the life expectancy of African Americans is about the same as that in China and in some states in India.' There is no systematic global monitoring of racial inequalities and injustices within states. At any one time dozens of serious ethnic conflicts and confrontations between states and communities are taking place across the world in which racism often, perhaps always, plays a part. Wherever there are ethnically or racially based injustices, there are likely to be racist attitudes and beliefs to legitimate and normalize them. Here we offer two examples of international monitoring of individual states, the first by Amnesty International and the second by the Council of Europe.

Amnesty International (2001) has produced a detailed dossier on racism and the administration of justice. It is therefore not dealing with structural, socio-economic aspects of racialized injustice, but with more immediate and direct forms of discrimination and oppression perpetrated by states on members of minority ethnic groups. The report does not claim to be a comprehensive, global survey but it documents instances of racism in the administration of justice from across the whole world, from rich, poor and middle-income states. At one extreme, in Burundi, 'discrimination in the criminal justice system is blatant' against Hutus, with the criminal justice apparatus dominated by the Tutsi ethnic group in the wake of the massacres of Tutsi civilians in the early 1990s. The report notes that, in the USA, 'extensive studies and analysis of relevant data have shown that racial discrimination is a significant feature of the administration of justice across the country.' Hence, for example, 'blacks and whites are the victims of murder in almost equal numbers, yet more than 80 per cent of prisoners executed between 1977 and 2001 were convicted of the murder of a white person' (see also Wacquant 2002). Brazil is a major 'middle income state' in which 'there have been frequent occurrences of assaults, massacres and targeted killings . . . of indigenous peoples and those who defend their rights.' Yet 'racism in the administration of justice leads to impunity for the perpetrators', with much of the activity funded and committed by agents of the state itself. The Amnesty International report documents briefly the long established and continuing oppression of minority ethnic groups by governments across the world, including, of course, the more populous states such as India, China, Russia and Indonesia.

The Council of Europe has established a European Commission against Racism and Intolerance (ECRI), which has produced a series of country-by-country reports on all its member states. The reports document examples of direct and institutional racism across organizations and agencies, both public and private, in twenty-six European states. In its second report on the UK, for example, particular concern was noted by ECRI about 'the xenophobic and intolerant coverage of [asylum seekers and refugees] in the media . . . [and] in the tone of the discourse resorted to by politicians', as well as 'racial prejudice in the police' (ECRI, 2001a, 4). Similar observations are made about most, if not all, European states in the other reports, though the particular features vary considerably, as, of course, do the particular racialized minority groups.

There are some unmistakably universal aspects of the development of racism across the continent of Europe in the past thirty years or so. European racisms are now more rooted in notions of cultural difference and the defence of 'European culture' rather than biological otherness and notions of white or Aryan 'superiority'. Of course cultural difference has always played a part in European racisms, not least in most forms of anti-Semitism and in anti-Roma sentiment. Equally too, it would be wrong to underestimate the continued virulence of direct racism against visible minorities. Nevertheless racism has found renewed respectability and support across Europe by embracing the cultural dimension which underpins the idea of a 'Fortress Europe', keeping out people of other continents on the basis of irreconcilable cultural differences. The parties of the far right have found considerable electoral success across the continent by combining this perspective with 'national populism'. This has been accompanied by the tendency of mainstream parties of both left and right 'to play to the same gallery, particularly through the construction of a "Fortress Europe" and the scapegoating of refugees' (MacMaster 2001, 192). MacMaster cites strong evidence for his conclusion that 'the most crucial factor in the reproduction of racism has been the role of mainstream political parties and governments' (ibid., 200). Reviewing the situation across Europe as a whole in 2000, ECRI (2001b, 8) reiterates the same point about 'democratic parties . . . entering into coalition with extremist, racist and xenophobic political parties' or 'xenophobic themes [creeping] . . . into the positions adopted by democratic political parties'. This seems to be the case virtually without exception across the whole continent, east and west, north and south. Electoral support for the racist far right has ebbed and flowed according to national and local contexts, but data such as that collated by ECRI leaves no doubt that racisms have a significant presence within mainstream European politics as well as within civil society, albeit taking different forms in different national and local contexts.

Globalization and the causation and incidence of racism

In a social scientific sense it is impossible to assess whether racism across the globe is increasing or decreasing. There have been and continue to be so many racisms and so many different levels at which they operate. However, if we narrow down the parameters somewhat, there is a widespread perception that economic globalization and 'liberalization', the increasing economic power of TNCs, and the developing post-colonial, post-communist domination of the world's economy and polity by the rich countries go alongside increasing global structural racism or global apartheid. The neo-liberal argument that free trade as interpreted by the North can benefit poorer producers of the South has not been upheld in practice; in fact the reverse is more often the case. Hence the increasing gap between rich and poor states can be understood as a racialized phenomenon linked to economic globalization. These global, racialized inequalities demand, of course, a critical questioning of the impact of economic globalization itself, for, as Halliday (2002 187) puts it, 'if most of those who live in the world do not have access to the goods of globalization, then it appears that we have an increasingly unequal, oligarchic system in which globalization reinforces, even as it concentrates, an elite' who are its most obvious beneficiaries. In similar vein Bauman (1998, 70) suggests that one of the social processes associated with economic globalization is a 'world-wide *restratification*, in the course of which a new socio-cultural hierarchy, on a world-wide scale, is put together.' Many strands of the anti-globalization movement oppose this global restratification, and therefore have potential and actual common cause with anti-racism.

Such perceptions are not confined to radicals and activists. In May 2000 Mary Robinson, the United Nations High Commissioner for Human Rights, said that 'globalization is leading to a rise in racism . . . poor countries are not benefiting from the consequences of globalization such as open markets and the information revolution. As long as that continues, the gap between rich and poor will widen and discontent will rise' (Doole 2000). In this context, the rise of fundamentalist Islamism, for example, has to be understood as 'a form of protest – political and discursive – against external domination' (Halliday 2002, 131) and against the increasing inequalities between rich and poor. The impact of economic globalization on structural racism can also be linked to state racism directed against minority ethnic groups. Sivanandan (2001a), for example, suggests that 'the nation state, particularly in the Third World and the eastern bloc, is the agent of global capital', operating through agencies such as the World Bank, the IMF and the WTO. This neo-colonial project is undermining indigenous economic activity, so that 'the nationalism which had cohered the [post-colonial] state from independence began to give way to ethnic and communal divisions' (ibid., 88). This perhaps lies at the root of the state persecution and repression of minority ethnic groups in so many post-colonial states.

Fortress Europe and the new Europeanized racism can also be linked to globalization in a wider sense. European integration is conceived as the means of strengthening the member states' economies to compete more effectively on a global scale, not least with the Chinese, Japanese and South-East Asian economies, which perhaps has something of an ethnic dimension. It can also be seen as a cultural and political reaction to globalization, a means of establishing a continent-wide bloc within which Europeans can insulate themselves from the aspects of globalization they fear, including migration but going well beyond it. Among such fears would be competition from farmers in poor countries producing food at much lower cost. The EU's agricultural regime is a mechanism designed to protect the livelihood and culture of Europe's farmers, while denying access to its food markets by the farmers of the poor countries. It can be argued that this is a form of structural racism at the supranational, regional level.

At the same time the new Europeanized racism may not be so new; it carries with it traces of white supremacy, but it is frequently referred to as 'xenophobia' because much of it is often directed towards Central and Eastern Europeans. Sivanandan (2001b) makes the important point that xenophobia is presented in the media and mainstream political discourse as the innocent and natural fear of strangers, whereas racism is culpable and unnatural. Sivanandan (2001b, 2) suggests that xenophobia is 'racism in substance but xeno in form – a racism that is meted out to impoverished strangers even if they are white', and he deploys the term 'xeno-racism' to describe the phenomenon. Xeno-racism has, of course, a long history in Europe, for example as experienced by Irish people in England (see Hickman 1998). The contemporary development of the European Union appears to have contributed to a strengthening of European xeno-racism within its boundaries without a notable diminution of xeno-racist attitudes towards its own minorities. The development of the EU can plausibly be seen as an aspect of the globalization of governance, so this is an aspect of globalization which may have contributed to the strengthening of xeno-racism.

Castles (2000, 164) sees racism as fundamental to the contemporary period of late modernity and economic globalization, involving 'the colonisation of the rest of the world, not only in the direct sense of political control, but also through the diffusion of Western cultural values'. Castles talks of the 'globalization of racism', albeit taking quite different forms across the world. Evidence such as that touched on briefly above certainly supports such a perspective. The argument is that economic globalization with its political and cultural consequences is sustaining and strengthening racism at structural and state levels, particularly in poorer countries. But there are other facets of globalization in its wider sense which, arguably, are contributing to undermining racisms. The first of these is the mobilization of racialized groups in the rich states, many of whom trace their origins to migration from poor states, one of the features of globalization. In the long term, migration is forcing the rich states to confront racism at structural, institutional and direct levels within their borders. Assimilation remains the officially preferred option, sometimes only whispered as such, but perhaps, as Brubaker (2001) suggests, making a comeback in the past decade in the rich states. Yet assimilation may not be sustainable given the strength of minority ethnic communities and the development of human rights discourse and the politics of identity. The struggle for authentic multicultural, multi-ethnic societies and for effective anti-racist measures continues apace not just in the rich states, but across the world (see Cornwell and Stoddard 2001). In this respect arguments implying an inevitable link between immigration and racism seem over-pessimistic, not to say defeatist, in linking globalization only to the development of racism. Hence we move on to consider global and regional responses to racism or, in other words, the contribution of globalization to anti-racism.

Global and regional responses

In considering anti-racism, it is important to note that racism and anti-racism are not simple opposites. Anti-racism involves the recognition, even the essentialization, of 'race', and anti-racist measures such as positive discrimination in favour of certain groups will involve negative discrimination against others. Anti-racism, like racism, is a highly complex phenomenon, as ably analysed by Bonnett (2000).

In many ways anti-racism has become a global orthodoxy in recent decades in and beyond the West, certainly as judged by the proclamations of governments and supranational agencies. The development of this orthodoxy has been shaped by three 'movements' in particular which have had a global impact – the defeat of Nazism in the 1940s, the civil rights movement in the United States in the 1960s, and the defeat of apartheid in South Africa in the 1980s. The example of Nazi Germany as a state which implemented racist measures to the ultimate, catastrophic extent continues to loom large in global consciousness. The civil rights movement swept away much of the formally institutionalized apparatus of racial segregation and injustice in the USA, demonstrating the apparent incompatibility between such measures and the development of the global economic superpower. The policy response, introducing such concepts as contract compliance and affirmative action, has also had a global impact – such ideas are now common currency as many governments across the world try to develop more effective anti-racist measures. The defeat of apartheid was achieved by the ANC, but was supported by a global anti-apartheid movement and demonstrated the unsustainability of such an explicitly racialized state within an increasingly globalized capitalist economy. As Bonnett (2000, 61) says, 'the willingness of Western nations to inaugurate and sustain an international consensus around anti-racism cannot be divorced from their desire to protect their own political interests . . . racism has continued to be viewed primarily in terms of its capacity to threaten the existing global order i.e. as a source of conflict, a disruptive factor.' Nevertheless the existence of an official global anti-racist orthodoxy does reflect the continued significance of the three 'global', historical movements above, alongside many other less celebrated ones of course. Here we will consider briefly the activity of the UN and the EU in developing anti-racist policy on a global and regional scale respectively.

The creation of the United Nations was an immediate and direct consequence of the defeat of Nazism, and its Charter (1945) and its Universal Declaration of Human Rights (1948) stand against 'distinction of any kind, such as race, colour'. In 1951 UNESCO declared that 'race is not so much a biological phenomenon as a social myth' (quoted by Bonnett 2000, 68). In 1965, spurred on by the anti-apartheid struggle and the emergence of the post-colonial states, the UN adopted its International Convention on the Elimination of All Forms of Racial Discrimination (ICERD). Signatories of ICERD are obliged to pursue anti-racist measures on a broad front, and to report back biannually to the Committee on the Elimination of Racial Discrimination (CERD). Banton (2002) shows that ICERD has developed into an important, global legal instrument for challenging racism within the increasingly universal discourse of human rights. For example, CERD has played an important role in advocating the rights of Aboriginal people in Australia in recent years, taking the government to task on the issues of land rights and treatment in police custody. After a protracted debate, the USA finally ratified ICERD in 1994, and by 2001 157 states had become parties to the convention (Banton 2002, 81). While it would be fair to say that ICERD mechanisms have not as yet formed a prominent part of anti-racist discourse in the states of the West, they are likely to become increasingly significant as the language of human rights and their legal enforcement become a central element of anti-racist strategy.

One recent UN event brought the global dimensions of racism into sharp focus, namely the World Conference against Racism, Racial Discrimination, Xenophobia and Related Intolerance, held in Durban in September 2001. This was intended as a vehicle for strengthening anti-racist measures across the world, in the manner of other UN world conferences on the environment and on women. The virtue of such events is that they contribute to keeping an issue 'hot', adding further pressure on governments to act and getting particular oppressions aired by the global media. The NGOs made a big impact on the event, much more so than the two previous world conferences on racism, both held in Geneva in 1978 and 1983. The headlines, however, focused on the immense opposition to particular anti-racist discourses which was mounted by powerful states. Hence the USA and European nations blocked effective reparations for slavery; Israel and the USA blocked the notion of Israeli aggression towards Palestinians as racist; and India blocked the notion of caste-based discrimination as racist. Banton (2002, 167) concludes that the conference was 'a calamity that has damaged the reputation of the UN and has set back the prospect for international co-operation in this field.' Yet it also demonstrated that anti-racist movements and NGOs have become more internationalized, more globalized even, focusing increasingly on the key issue of racialized inequalities between rich and poor nations. The conference aired and gave a global voice to a vast range of anti-racist movements and struggles. This was an act of global recognition contributing to global awareness and solidarity, which was not entirely diminished by political squabbles.

At the regional, European level the lead on anti-racist policy and legislation was taken by the Council of Europe when it adopted its

European Convention on Human Rights and Fundamental Freedoms (1950), which included a specific prohibition of racial discrimination. The European Court of Human Rights was established in 1958. The Council of Europe had ten founder member states, including the UK, and by 2001 there were forty-one member states. The first British case brought by individuals before the court in 1967 concerned an East African Asian family separated by racist immigration legislation. As reported by Webber (2001, 81), it was found that the legislation and its application 'was so blatant in its racial discrimination as to constitute degrading treatment of the applicants, contrary to the absolute prohibition of such treatment in the Convention.' The report on this case 'remained confidential at the request of the British government until 1994' (ibid.)! It was not until 2000 that the convention was adopted into British law – surely a vivid illustration of governments' reluctance to make even small steps towards effective anti-racist machinery. Webber concludes that the effects of adoption will be very modest, but it could have a positive impact on the treatment of people in detention, particularly deaths or injuries in custody. This is an issue which has sorely affected minority ethnic communities in Britain, as elsewhere.

The European Union has been very slow to develop policy and legislation addressing racism. While the Treaty of Rome explicitly outlawed gender discrimination in the workplace, there was no clear reference to other forms of discrimination. Until 1997 the EU had no formal legislation on 'race' and legislative competence remained firmly with the member states, as it still does today. However the EU has gradually and inevitably become involved in issues of race and ethnicity as the single market and the idea of Social Europe develop. The EU promotes a single market in goods and people, implying a single immigration and citizenship policy, and uniform human rights across the member states.

Anti-racist discourse in the EU goes back to the mid-1980s (see Lloyd 2000), when the Single European Act was passed amid growing understanding that the EU required a 'social dimension' in order to maintain social cohesion in the face of the increased unemployment and regional inequalities which economic integration would create, and which would be exploited by the political extremes. 1986 saw a Joint Declaration against Racism and Xenophobia by the European Commission, the Council of Ministers and the European Parliament. In 1994 the European Commission established the Kahn Commission, which advocated the development of EU anti-discrimination legislation. This took shape in the form of Article 13 of the 1997 Treaty of Amsterdam, which gave the commission powers to develop legislation against discrimination based on racial or ethnic origin, disability, age, sexual orientation, and religious belief. The commission has produced two important directives, the strongest legislative measure that the EU allows.

The Race Directive of June 2000 requires member states to make illegal discrimination on grounds of racial or ethnic origin (but *not* nationality) in employment and training, and to 'provide protection' against such discrimination in education, social security, cultural services and the provision of goods and services generally. Indirect discrimination is included, and monitoring bodies have to be established by member states along the lines of the UK's Commission for Racial Equality. The Employment Directive of October 2000 outlaws discrimination at work on grounds of racial or ethnic origin, religion or belief, disability, age or sexual orientation. The race equality agenda has thus proceeded quite swiftly by EU policy-making standards, and in some ways it parallels the progress made on the gender equality issue in the 1970s, using directives to try to enforce equal rights. Time will tell in terms of its impact.

The Kahn Commission also led to the establishment of the European Monitoring Centre on Racism and Xenophobia (EUMC), which has produced some important studies of racism across the EU. For example one recent document (EUMC 2002) reports on a study of racism, football and the internet. If the internet is one of the more positive features of globalization, this report certainly highlights the globalization of racism in the year of the World Cup. The report found thirty-two football sites in seven EU states which displayed 'latent racism' and nine sites in five states which displayed 'strong racism'; 32 per cent of Italian sites had racist content. The report advocates a wide range of measures to undermine racism in the sport. Another recent report from the EUMC (Allen and Nielsen 2002) documents the great increase in negative media stereotyping of Muslims and asylum seekers as terrorists in the months after September 11 across all the EU member states. The British media were identified as having particularly 'disproportionate' coverage of 'extremist Muslim groups and British Muslims who declared their willingness to join an Islamic war against the west', thereby reinforcing 'very basic Islamophobic stereotypes'. The EUMC's work thus promotes the anti-racist cause within Europe, and indeed globally, by the publication of its findings on the internet.

A problematic aspect of official European anti-racism is the multiplicity of institutions involved – the Council of Europe with its convention, court and ECRI; the EU with its court (the European Court of Justice), directives and the EUMC; and all supposedly working alongside the UN with its ICERD and CERD. To the outsider this looks like globalized bureaucratization. For NGO and grassroots anti-racist organizations the problems of pan-European mobilization are twofold. First larger, more 'respectable' organizations inevitably tend to become co-opted into the official bureaucratic structures, not least because they depend on the latter for their funding. Second, there are enormous differences in the political and cultural identities and mobilizations of minority ethnic groups across the continent. Nevertheless as Lloyd (2000, 402) discusses, 'informal co-operation has already given rise to spontaneous and joint demonstrations, as for instance in . . . opposing European meetings of the extreme right'. Lloyd (ibid., 404) proposes that such 'loose, perhaps ad hoc co-operation . . . may be most effective at the European level, and suggests forms which global civil society may take in the future.' Hence the European and global anti-racist 'movement' may take a similar form and indeed be loosely linked to anti-globalization movements.

Future trends

It would appear that, over the past two decades, there have been two distinct and perhaps contradictory processes at work across the rich states of the West in terms of policies and processes shaping racism and racial injustices. First, in all of them there has been a shift towards a deeper multiculturalism and away from stronger forms of assimilationism. This may have been more pronounced in those states more comfortable with inward migration, but it appears to be a universal and, hence, perhaps 'structural' shift. At the same time, and equally important, there has been a strengthening of racialized, exclusionary immigration and asylum policies, accompanied by worsening, or at best unchanging, socio-economic inequalities between minority ethnic communities and the majority, and the menacing activity of overtly racist political movements and the racist violence which they promote. In the states of the EU, for example, the 'successful' economic integration of states such as Ireland and Spain has been accompanied by an upsurge of racism directed against migrant workers (see Fanning 2002; Corkill 2001). Racism continues to be structurally endemic within the rich states of the West, whether the economy is booming or in recession, whether the government is to the left or the right of centre. As the peoples of these states become more multi-ethnic, so the importance of both multicultural and racist structural processes will increase. The development of more effective anti-racist measures, starting with the abandonment of Fortress Europe and newly racist national government policies, would self-evidently contribute to stemming the tide of European racism.

The predominant focus of this chapter has been on the 'white' racism or racisms of the rich Western nations. Looking at poor and middle-income states, there are such diverse and particularistic processes at work that considerations of the future are almost impossible to take an overview upon. For example, the question of whether the caste system in India is an example of racism and how its future might be linked with globalization is simply beyond our scope here. Nevertheless there are at least two prominent aspects of globalization which would seem to be playing a part in shaping ethnic divisions in poor and middle-income states. First, increasing income inequality *within* poor and middle-income states is plausibly linked to economic globalization; this is frequently inscribed on existing ethnic divisions with the effect of deepening ethnic inequalities, and hence extending what we have described as 'structural' racism within a particular society. Second, the post-Cold War period has seen a global transformation of authoritarian regimes, which has been accompanied by the re-emergence of suppressed ethnic divisions. The most obvious example is Yugoslavia, but Russia and Indonesia come quickly to mind. China has a very long tradition of racialized discourse (Dikötter 1992), which is resurfacing. In a rather simplistic sense it would appear that the globalization of 'Western' political pluralism is having a profound effect on the racialization or ethnicization of middle- and low-income states. It would be quite wrong to suggest that this process is simply fostering racism; it is more than possible that it can eventually lead to positive change. For example, Turkey's struggle to gain EU membership has seemingly prompted a less authoritarian approach to the Kurdish people.

In terms of the global future, both Scholte (2000) and George and Wilding (2002) map out a plausible framework for public policy which Scholte describes as 'thick reformism'. This is distinct from neo-liberalism and mild reformism, which advocate little or no global intervention to challenge socio-economic injustices and inequalities. Thick reformism is also distinct from the diversity of 'radical approaches', with their particularisms, utopianisms and sometime cynicisms. Scholte (2000, 291) describes thick reformism as aiming to 'shift the initiative to public management . . . [so that] state, sub-state and suprastate laws and institutions take firm hold of the steering wheel and harness the forces of globalization to explicit and democratically determined public policies.' Scholte's useful list of specific suprastate reforms outlines a comprehensive range of strengthened regulatory frameworks to bolster 'human security', reduce social injustices and enhance democracy.

Above all there can be no doubt that supranational measures to tackle world poverty effectively would have an enormous beneficial impact on global structural racism. Townsend and Gordon (2002b) have recently mapped out the kind of measures required to develop such a strategy, which include radical changes in the terms of trade between poor and rich states, legal enforcement of the right to an adequate living standard, a legally binding minimum level of overseas development assistance at 1 per cent of GNP, new international company law to limit super profits being made in poor states, and an international financial transactions tax to support the introduction of child benefit in poor states. The hope is that the emerging unease with and resistance to the increase in poverty across all the states of the world will generate sufficient momentum to 'moderate the international hierarchy of power' (Townsend and Gordon 2002a, 418), particularly as regards public finance.

Suprastate mechanisms for 'conflict management' should also play a decisive role in undermining state racism directed against oppressed minorities. More speculatively, Scholte suggests that suprastate institutions can also contribute to the development of multiculturalism or even interculturalism by advocating good practice in, for example, the development of school curricula which give appropriate recognition to minority cultures. More specific to institutional and direct racisms, the strengthening of the weak UN and EU mechanisms discussed above is clearly essential to the development of successful global governance. The difficulties of the UN Durban conference and the growth of far right racism in Europe suggest that the obstacles are formidable, and that the role of supranational policy and institutions is likely to be modest in the immediate future.

Thick reformism cannot be delivered by 'globalization from above', which is demonstrably only capable of promoting neo-liberalism and thin reformism, because it is nurtured and orchestrated by corporate, transnational capital. Thick reformism embracing anti-racism is developing out of 'globalization from below', increasingly sustained by labour, environmental and social movements within civil society and national states (Falk 2000). These latter movements have often been tainted by racism, xenophobia, nationalism and protectionism. Bonnett (2000, 170) notes that 'contemporary discussions of anti-racism are often marked by their parochialism . . . [around] various "national traditions" and "national debates".' However, there is also a growing awareness that economic globalization driven by neo-liberalism cannot be resisted by parochial, inward-looking movements or particularistic interests. The stumbling progress towards more effective global and pan-European anti-racist measures is the product of this realization.

Further reading

Banton, M. (2002). *The International Politics of Race*. Cambridge: Polity [reviews the development of official anti-racist and human rights discourse, focusing on Britain and the USA and the role of the UN].

Bonnett, A. (2000). *Anti-Racism*. London: Routledge [a thought-provoking deconstruction of anti-racism, using examples from across the world which demonstrate its particularity to context].

Castles, S. (2000). *Ethnicity and Globalization*. London: Sage [suggests that economic globalization fosters racism, but also shows that global migration has challenged the monocultural nation-state in the West].

Halliday, F. (2002). *Two Hours that Shook the World*. London: Saqi Books [lucidly reflects upon Islamism and anti-Islamism in the context of economic globalization, global governance and global inequality].

10

Globalization, Migration and Asylum

Stephen Castles and Sean Loughna

Introduction

For many people, migration is the crucial signifier of globalization. Other cross-border flows, such as movements of capital, commodities, cultural products and ideas, may be less visible. But the presence in northern cities of people of different physical appearance, religions and languages is a powerful symbol of change. All too often, the new-comers are stigmatized as threats to prosperity, welfare, culture and national identity. The ubiquitous fear that immigrants will 'take over the neighbourhood' is a way of trying to grasp the very real trans-formations brought about by globalization and economic restructur-ing. Such fears focus on undocumented migrants and asylum seekers. The outrage is greatest with regard to migrants who arrive by boat or clinging to Channel Tunnel trains. Such entries evoke archaic fears of invasion and loss of sovereignty – a dream theme for nationalist demagogues. Media campaigns and political mobilization focus on these groups, although they are only a minority of immigrants.

Such are the forces behind the idea of a 'migration crisis', which developed in the early 1990s. The fall of the Berlin Wall had appar-ently opened the way for floods of East–West migrants, while vio-lence and impoverishment in less developed countries were leading to growing inflows from the South. Politicians conjured up images of welfare states being swamped by the 'misery of the world'. The extreme right built its Europe-wide resurgence on anti-immigration campaigns. The 'migration crisis' was popularized by academics and other opinion leaders (Weiner 1995; Zolberg 2001) and became the label for a new global social problem: the uncontrollability of mobility between the impoverished areas of the South and East and the wealthy North and West. The clash of civilizations was happening not in some remote and exotic place, but daily in our cities.

The reactions of policy makers and officials to the perceived crisis were shaped by long-standing national discourses, for all nation-states are the result of historical processes of incorporation of migrants and minorities. But national responses, such as stricter border control and special police regimes for immigrants, proved ineffective under conditions of globalization and burgeoning transnational networks. Migration control became a key theme of international politics and supranational co-operation. Inevitably, social policy was called upon to play its part.

The genesis of modern social policy lay in the need to create, discipline and manage industrial working classes in emerging industrial economies. This ambivalent role goes back to the beginnings of modernity. The growth of market-oriented farming from the fifteenth century was accompanied by land enclosures and mass displacement, which led to the emergence of hordes of vagabonds and beggars all over Western Europe. To deal with this threat to order and safety, control regimes combining punishment and welfare were devised. The poor were classified as either 'deserving' or 'undeserving'. For instance, an Act of Henry VIII in 1530 introduced begging licences for beggars who were old and incapable of work. Healthy vagabonds, however, were to be whipped and sent back to their parish of birth. An Act of Elizabeth I introduced the parish-based poor law, which was to remain in force until 1834 (Marx 1976, chaps 26, 27). By the sixteenth century, asylums for the destitute were being turned into workhouses, which developed the labour discipline necessary for industry, as well as introducing mass-production manufacturing (Ruehle 1970). At the height of the Industrial Revolution in 1834, the workhouse system became the basis of welfare in Britain.

But discipline was not enough. The physical and moral degeneration of the working population in early industrial societies was a threat to the expansion and survival of industrial capitalism. Restrictions on child labour and measures to improve working conditions and safety were essential. They could only be imposed by the state, since individual employers were driven by market competition to exploit their workers to the utmost. Moreover, industry needed a mobile and flexible workforce. As long as poor law was parish-based, a modern industrial labour force was impossible. National welfare systems were vital. Bismarck's social policy in late nineteenth-century

Germany made the welfare state the guarantor not only of the physical well-being of the working class, but also of their loyalty to the state, and hence of political legitimacy. The carrot of welfare was linked to the stick of repression: Bismarck simultaneously banned the Social Democratic Party.

It is our argument that, in a similar way, contemporary social policy is concerned with the need to create, discipline and manage a global workforce suitable for the emerging global economy. Unlike earlier social policy regimes that were constituted essentially at the national level, today's social policy towards migrants has both national and transnational elements. This is the central theme of this chapter. We will start by describing current patterns of international migration – both economic and forced – and discuss why globalization has transformed the character of migration. Then we will look at national social policies for immigrants and asylum seekers – a rapidly growing sector in all Western European countries – before moving on to examine transnational social policies, which are mainly concerned with regulating North–South relationships and containing unwanted mobility in areas of origin.

Volume and types of international migration

Estimates by the United Nations Population Division for 2000 indicate that there were 175 million international migrants worldwide. (International migrants are defined as people who had lived outside their country of birth for at least twelve months.) This figure leaves out undocumented migrants. Their numbers are unknown. However, the 2000 US Census indicated that there could be 9 million illegal residents in the USA, and there are certainly millions in Western Europe too. Even so, migrants make up only 2 to 3 per cent of the world's population. If there is a 'migration crisis', it is clearly not one of absolute volume. The growth and distribution of migration is perhaps more significant. The global total has doubled since 1975, and 60 per cent of migrants now live in developed countries; there almost one in ten persons is a migrant, compared with one in seventy in developing countries (United Nations 2002). Since the 1980s, flows from less developed to developed countries have grown rapidly, despite restrictive policies. There have also been large flows of labour migrants to the newly industrializing countries (NICs), especially in East Asia. Within receiving countries there is further clustering, as immigrants settle mainly in large cities and industrial areas.

Governments divide international migrants into categories, to facilitate selection and control. One broad distinction is between *voluntary migrants* and *forced migrants*. The former are motivated mainly by economic considerations, and make up the majority of international migrants. The main categories of *voluntary migrants* are:

- temporary labour migrants (also known as guestworkers or overseas contract workers)
- highly skilled and business migrants
- permanent migrants or settlers
- undocumented migrants (also known as irregular or illegal migrants)
- family reunion migrants joining people who have already entered under another category
- return migrants: people who return to the their countries of origin after a period abroad

Temporary labour migration and family reunion are currently the largest categories. The global competition for Indian information technology professionals is a recent expression of the hunger for skilled migrants. Historically, the emphasis was often on permanent settlement: in the greatest migration of all, some 54 million people moved from Europe to the USA, mainly between 1820 and 1914. Today, easy transport and communications encourage a trend towards temporary and circulating migrations, in which many people move repeatedly between their home and other countries.

Forced migrants who cross international borders include:

- *refugees*: according to the 1951 United Nations Convention Relating to the Status of Refugees, a refugee is a person residing outside his or her country of nationality who is unable or unwilling to return because of a 'well-founded fear of persecution on account of race, religion, nationality, membership in a particular social group, or political opinion'
- *asylum seekers*: people who move across international borders in search of protection, but whose claims for refugee status have not yet been decided
- *people trafficked* across borders for purposes of exploitation.

The global refugee population grew from 2.4 million in 1975 to 14.9 million in 1990. A peak was reached after the end of the Cold War, with 18.2 million in 1993. By 2000, the global refugee population had declined to 12.1 million. Refugees came from countries hit by war, violence and chaos. The ten main places of origin were Afghanistan (with 2.6 million refugees in 1999), Iraq (572,000), Burundi (524,000), Sierra Leone (487,000), Sudan (468,000), Somalia (452,000), Bosnia (383,000), Angola (351,000), Eritrea (346,000) and Croatia (340,000) (UNHCR 2000).

Annual asylum applications in Western Europe, Australia, Canada and the USA combined rose from 90,400 in 1983 to 323,050 in 1988, and then surged again with the end of the Cold War to peak at 828,645 in 1992 (UNHCR 1995). Applications fell sharply to 480,000 in 1995, but began creeping up again to 534,500 in 2000 (OECD 2001). Nearly the whole of the decline can be explained by falls in asylum applications following changes in refugee law in Germany and Sweden. The UK had relatively few asylum seekers in the early 1990s, with 32,300 in 1992, but numbers increased at the end of the decade, to 55,000 in 1998 and 97,900 in 2000 (ibid., 280).

The trafficking of women and children for the sex industry occurs all over the world, while both male and female workers may end up in debt bondage to repay extortionate debts to smugglers and traffickers. There are no reliable figures on trafficked persons. The media and politicians sometimes imply that most illegal migration is dominated by organized crime. This is misleading, and it is important to distinguish between trafficking and smuggling (Gallagher 2002). Trafficking refers to people being forced or deceived into migration, so that they can be exploited. Smuggling is often a reaction to tighter border restrictions. People who want to migrate for economic reasons have to rely on smugglers to cross borders. Sometimes even genuine refugees have to pay smugglers, because it is no longer possible to enter possible countries of asylum to make a claim for protection under the 1951 convention.

How globalization transforms migration

Population movements in response to demographic growth, climatic change, economic needs and conflict have always been part of human history. However, it is important to understand the new forces driving migration. Since the 1970s, global economic and political transformations have led to increases in both economic and forced migration. Globalization may be characterized as the widening, deepening and speeding up of worldwide interconnectedness in all aspects of contemporary social life (Held et al. 1999, 2). The key indicator of globalization is the rapid increase in cross-border flows of all sorts: finance, trade, ideas, pollution, media products and people. The key organizing structure for these flows is the transnational network, which can take the form of transnational corporations, international organizations, global criminal syndicates or transnational communities. The key tools are modern information and communications technology and cheap air travel (Castells 1996). Those in power generally welcome trade and capital flows, but flows of people and ideas are often seen as threats to national sovereignty and identity.

The most obvious cause of migration is the disparity between areas in levels of income, social well-being and human rights. Globalization has exacerbated these disparities. Globalization is a process of differential inclusion and exclusion of different areas. The core areas of the global economy – the Western countries, Japan, the Asian Tigers and other NICs – interact mainly with each other with regard to trade, finance and migration. The South is a source of raw materials, natural products and cheap labour. These divisions are uneven: global restructuring has led to pockets of wealth among southern elites and pockets of social exclusion in deindustrialized areas of the North and of transition countries. Some areas of the South have become disconnected from the economies of the North. This is apparent in global trade rules, which permit northern governments to subsidize their own producers and cause impoverishment in the South. For instance, US subsidies to cotton farmers are greater than all US aid to Africa. These subsidies help ruin West African smallholders, leading some of them to give up and migrate to Europe (Wallis 2002). Similarly, the EU's Common Agricultural Policy is allowed to subsidize farmers and dump produce in the South in violation of liberal principles.

Violence is another major factor. Situations of conflict, generalized violence and mass flight emerged in the Third World from the 1960s, in the context of struggles over decolonization and state formation (Zolberg et al. 1989). Local conflicts became proxy wars in the East–West conflict, with the superpowers providing modern weapons to their protégés. Such conflicts escalated from the 1980s, due to the inability to achieve development and to build stable states in large areas of the South. International warfare was largely replaced by internal wars connected with ethnic divisions, problems of state formation and competition for economic assets. The means of warfare have also changed. The protagonists are not large standing armies but irregular forces. The aim is not control of territory, but political control of the population. Ninety per cent of those killed are civilians. Both government forces and insurgents use exemplary violence, including torture and sexual assault, as means of control. Mass population expulsion is often a strategic goal, which is why the 'new wars' have led to such an upsurge in forced migration (Kaldor 2001).

Northern economic interests (such as the trade in oil, diamonds or small arms) play an important part in starting or prolonging local wars. At a broader level, trade, investment and intellectual property regimes that favour the industrialized countries maintain under-development in the South. Conflict and forced migration thus form an integral part of the North–South division. This reveals the ambi-guity of efforts by the 'international community' to prevent forced migration. As will be discussed below, powerful states and interna-tional agencies seek to do this through both entry restrictions in the North and 'containment' measures in the South. At the same time, the North does more to cause forced migration than to stop it, through enforcing an international economic and political order that causes underdevelopment and conflict.

The South, however, reconnects with the North through the pro-liferation of transnational informal networks, which include interna-tional crime, the drug trade, and terrorist groups, as well as more benign types of social and cultural linkages (Duffield 2001). Thus underdevelopment and internal warfare are increasingly seen as threats to security in the North. Migration of undocumented migrants and asylum seekers is one of the unexpected ways in which the South is reconnecting with the North. While northern govern-ments work together to erect barriers against such mobility, global-ization actually creates the conditions that encourage and facilitate migration.

- The selective inclusion and exclusion of specific areas and groups in global economic networks undermine economies and states, leading to impoverishment and human rights abuse.
- Rapid improvements in transport and communications make it easier for people to move between countries and to live in new contexts.
- Transnational networks facilitate migration, by allowing migrants to maintain their social relationships and cultural identities in transnational social space. Because they follow the logic of glob-alization, they often prove more effective than official migration restrictions, which follow an earlier national logic.
- Global cultural industries beam the idealized cultural attractions of northern lifestyles into the most remote villages, motivating people to migrate.

- The high demand for labour in the North, combined with strong barriers to mobility, has created business opportunities for a new 'migration industry'. This includes legal participants, such as travel agents, shipping companies and banks, as well as illegal operators such as traffickers and smugglers.

These factors have been poorly understood by governments. Migration policies based on neo-classical notions of individual decision making and on national control models have often failed, because they ignore the dynamics of migration as a transnational social process. Moreover, the attempt to base migration control on a bureaucratic distinction between economic and forced migration ignores the reality that many migrants have mixed motivations: they are simultaneously fleeing failed states, collapsed economies and devastated environments; they are moving both in order to gain protection from violence and to improve the livelihoods of their families. The experience of the last ten years has shown that border restrictions alone are not sufficient. Just as Europeans were willing to endure danger and hardship to seek a better future in the New World a century ago, today's poor and oppressed are prepared to take enormous risks to reach the North.

The upsurge in international migration, especially from South to North, has led to strong public reactions in receiving countries. Migration and asylum have been lumped together with concerns about terrorism and security – especially since 11 September 2001. Restriction of migration and control of immigrants groups are high on the political agenda, both for national governments and such supranational organizations as the EU. Social policy and the differential treatment of various groups of entrants is a central part of such strategies.

European social policies towards immigrants and asylum seekers

Labour migration played a crucial role in Western Europe in the post-1945 boom. The growth of manufacturing industry was concentrated in the old industrial countries. As governments' and employers' internal labour reserves were used up, they recruited migrant workers from Southern Europe, North Africa and Turkey. Former imperial powers such as France, the Netherlands and Britain welcomed immigrants from ex-colonies. Typically, such workers were incorporated in the lower skilled jobs of industry, construction and the services, while many local workers were able to achieve upward mobility. The result was labour-market segmentation on the basis of ethnicity and gender. This type of migration ended with the 1973 oil crisis. New investment strategies emerged. North American and Western European capital flowed into manufacturing zones in low-wage countries. The petro-dollars of the oil boom provided cheap loans for industrialization in East Asian and Latin American NICs. Former labour-recruiting countries adopted zero immigration polices, yet family reunion continued. By the 1980s, new flows of asylum seekers and undocumented workers were emerging (Castles and Miller 2003, chap. 4).

Legal immigration into the EU during the 1990s averaged about 1.5 million persons per annum. Illegal immigration into the EU is estimated by Europol to be 500,000 per annum (Commission of the European Communities 2000). Such flows are occurring against the backdrop of major demographic changes. The working-age population is declining while the number of elderly people continues to rise (United Nations 2000a). At the same time, birth rates among immigrants are higher than among the native population of richer host countries, increasing the proportion of the population who are immigrants or children of immigrants (Boeri et al. 2002). With improving educational opportunities, the number of young people available to fill low-skilled or physically demanding jobs is falling dramatically. Although governments claim that asylum seekers and undocumented workers are unwelcome, they have come to play a crucial role in Western European economies – especially in informal sectors which are expanding due to neo-liberal policies of deregulation and privatization (Reyneri 2001).

In recent years, there has been increasing recognition of the need to import skilled and unskilled labour into EU member states, despite the unemployment of some 15 million existing residents. Global competition for highly skilled workers has meant a shortfall in sectors such as information technology and the health professions. Other shortages, such as the deficit of public-sector workers in the UK, are due to low pay and high housing costs. Low-skilled demand sectors include casual and seasonal work in agriculture, catering and tourism. In response to these pressures, economic migration to EU countries from outside the region has been redefined in more positive terms of flexibility, adaptability and efficiency, rather than a threat to wages and standards of welfare. Governments of some EU countries are therefore encouraging greater labour-market flexibility and more economic migration, especially of the highly skilled (Süssmuth 2001).

However, the movement of asylum seekers and undocumented migrant workers is seen as undesirable because it escapes state control. Consequently, although the skills profiles of asylum seekers and undocumented migrant workers are often similar to those recruited through official schemes, ever-stricter controls are applied to counter forced and spontaneous migration (Düvell 2002, 499). There is a popular presumption in many receiving countries that migrants provide cheap substitutes for native-born workers, thus depressing wage levels, displacing natives, causing unemployment and abusing the welfare system. Such beliefs have led to pressure on governments to tighten controls; frequent changes in government policy have been a direct response to these concerns. Since the early 1990s, there have been concerted efforts to prevent asylum seekers from working and limit their access to welfare. In some countries, detention of asylum seekers is being adopted as a deterrent.

The changing patterns of immigration have affected welfare systems. National responses have varied according to differing social policy models and ideas about the incorporation of immigrants. Up to the 1980s, the official strategy in 'guestworker' recruiting countries such as Germany was to prevent settlement and family reunion. Migrant workers had quite strong work-related welfare rights, but were not to be included in general educational and welfare systems. Instead separate provision was made through national or special needs classes in schools and subsidies to non-governmental (mainly church-based) welfare associations. In France, by contrast, the emphasis was on the republican model of integration, which emphasized equal treatment and rejected measures to respond to the special needs of immigrants (Weil 1991). Sweden sought to achieve equality both by including immigrants in general provisions and by providing special services to respond to linguistic and cultural needs. The UK moved from an initial ideal of assimilation to a policy of multiculturalism, based on recognition of cultural difference, and provision of a range of special services (Castles and Miller 2003, chaps 9, 10; Bommes and Halfmann 1998; Ireland 2000).

In the more recent immigration countries of Southern Europe, both the migration experience and the welfare model have differed. Migration has been mainly spontaneous and undocumented. States have lacked the capacity and will for effective control, and migrants have moved into growing informal economies. Welfare systems have historically been based mainly on the activities of the church and civil society, with the state playing a weaker role. To some extent, the informal economy can be seen as a substitute for welfare for asylum seekers and undocumented migrants, as indeed for poor people in the wider population. The ready availability of low-skilled jobs without any need for documents or bureaucratic procedures is a lifeline for the socially excluded. At the same time, this system forces down wages for unqualified work and exacerbates ethnic segmentation. Thus undocumented workers and asylum seekers can survive, but often at the cost of impoverishment and hostility from local people.

By contrast, in Germany, the UK and other Northern European states, immigrants are seen as competing for resources within a limited pot of tax-funded provisions, and hence their entitlements are restricted. It is interesting to note that some countries with generous welfare systems, such as the Netherlands and Sweden, ended up with the highest levels of immigrant segregation and unemployment (Entzinger 2002; Westin 2000). The reasons for this need more investigation, but it appears that special welfare provisions have sometimes had the effect of isolating and stigmatizing immigrants. Despite its openly exclusionary character, Germany's work-based welfare system seems to have produced better results in the long run (Doomernik 1998). Thus, although there are major differences in national approaches to migrant incorporation and welfare, the long-term result in European countries has been similar: labour-market segmentation has been matched by residential segregation of immigrants in disadvantaged housing areas.

Similarly, despite significant historical and cultural differences, asylum policies in EU countries have been reactive to external events, particularly conflict and consequent displacement. Beginning in the 1980s and accelerating in the 1990s, there was a significant convergence in practice in three key aspects: restricting access to the territory of states; discouraging asylum applications by restricting access to welfare benefits; and the replacement of permanent asylum with various forms of temporary protection. France, Germany, the Netherlands and the UK have all introduced an array of regulations and legislation aimed largely at restricting the numbers of people entering their territory to seek asylum. Some countries have also applied pressure upon, and provided assistance to, transit countries. For example, Germany has assisted the Czech Republic, Hungary and Poland to strengthen their borders. EU states tend to see the problem as one of numbers (although security concerns have also been cited recently). Yet, although there is little evidence available, existing data suggest that the type and level of welfare assistance provided has very little impact upon decisions to seek asylum, or upon the choice of country in which to apply for protection (Koser 1997; Koser and Pinkerton 2002).

New types of migration have led to unexpected challenges for national welfare systems. Undocumented workers and asylum seekers have special welfare profiles. In view of their origins in areas of impoverishment and conflict, and the stresses experienced in the actual process of migration, these groups are in great need of support when they arrive. Yet they are frequently either excluded from welfare altogether or subjected to isolating and stigmatizing special regimes. In a situation where most governments aim to exclude these groups from their countries through non-arrival measures (visa restrictions, carriers' liability) or border control, 'access to welfare has become the second line of defence in the fight to reduce the number of asylum seekers' (Schuster 2000, 123). European governments face a dilemma. Right-wing politicians and the media accuse asylum seekers of profiting from generous welfare systems, and demand their exclusion. Yet welfare states are based on universalistic principles. Denying health services, education and welfare to disadvantaged groups can endanger public health and safety, and may in the long run fuel racism.

The result, throughout Europe, has been policies which stop short of complete exclusion but which offer second-class and degrading provisions. Asylum seekers and undocumented workers are generally excluded from all mainstream benefits and services, and can only access emergency medical services at the risk of subsequent deportation. A seven-country study in 2000 found that asylum seekers were disadvantaged through such measures as benefit levels below the official subsistence minimum (UK), payments in kind (e.g. food vouchers) rather than cash (UK, the Netherlands, Germany), limited duration of benefits (France, Italy), or no benefits at all (Greece) (Schuster 2000). Since such welfare arrangements are often combined with a prohibition of working, many asylum seekers find themselves destitute. This is no coincidence: politicians see welfare restrictions as part of deterrent strategies. However, since the vast majority of asylum seekers come from countries to which they cannot return due to pervasive violence and human rights abuses (Castles et al. 2003), the result is not to deter their entry, but rather to turn them into an underclass who have no choice but to accept illegal jobs, however exploitative they may be. Discriminatory welfare regimes therefore help create the low-wage labour force, which even advanced capitalist countries cannot do without. Since many asylum seekers will remain permanently, the effects on social integration and cohesion are a matter of great concern.

All mainstream parties advocate exclusionary measures towards asylum seekers. From 1996 to 2000, there was a shift in political power from centre-right to centre-left parties in seven EU member states: France, Germany, Greece, Italy, the Netherlands, Sweden and the UK. However, there was no significant liberalization of asylum policy or practice in any of them, but rather an increased focus on restrictive policies. Schuster has identified and examined three factors which influenced these governments in taking an increasingly stringent approach: the constraints of a coalition government; a response to the rise in support of the far right; and similar perspectives on seeing asylum migration as a 'problem' and developing a shared view on tackling it. But, as Schuster argues, the issue of coalition governments did not apply to Greece, Sweden and the UK and thus does not appear very significant. As for the second factor, in all EU countries where violent attacks against asylum seekers have occurred, it has been simultaneous with the growth of the far right. This was the case even in Greece and Italy, which had no previous history of violent racism. Rather than challenge the position of the far right, the mainstream parties have engaged in the same rhetoric, assuming that most asylum seekers are 'bogus' and benefit fraudsters.

Indeed, some of the measures introduced in recent years – particularly prohibition of employment, dispersal of asylum seekers to regions with little experience of ethnic minorities and accommodation in special centres – have left them vulnerable to xenophobic attacks. Regardless of political ideology, the control of borders is seen as essential to state sovereignty. Indeed, the shift to more conservative governments in the last few years in Denmark, Austria, Italy, France and Spain has led to even stricter anti-immigrant measures. The few remaining centre-left governments, for instance in Sweden and the UK, have kept pace with their right-wing colleagues in introducing such measures. The difficulty of effective control and management is shown by the constant changes in legislation. The UK, for instance, adopts a new immigration law about every three years.

Under conditions of globalization, immigration cannot be fully controlled. The effect of anti-immigrant measures is thus not to prevent entries, but rather to differentiate the working population through a new division between the 'deserving' and the 'undeserving'. Social inclusion is increasingly afforded only to those in paid employment. Those who are unable to work legally are seen as 'undeserving', taking more out of the system than they put in. Asylum seekers are compelled to become part of this latter group because they are forbidden to work while their application is being processed. They are therefore denied the means to join the 'deserving' (Sales 2002). Their labour makes a valuable economic contribution, but this goes unrecognized because it is largely within the informal sector.

Welfare restrictions do not prevent entry, but lead to marginalization and criminalization of excluded groups.

International humanitarianism as global social policy

Today European governments claim to be seeking 'partnership with countries of origin' to address the root causes of forced migration, but often this really means working with governments of 'sending' countries to improve migration control. This became a key theme at the Seville European Council of June 2002. Proposals were made by the Spanish and the British prime ministers to link readmission agreements to aid and co-operation, making it possible to put economic pressure on countries unwilling to readmit failed asylum seekers. The conclusions adopted by the Seville Council stopped short of imposing economic sanctions, but did call for a 'systematic assessment of relations with third countries which do not cooperate in combating illegal immigration'. The council also adopted many of the measures suggested by the Spanish presidency on improved border control (Statewatch 2002). EC President Romano Prodi emphasized that 'our partners must understand that there has been a qualitative upgrading of the importance we attach to the migration component of our relations' (Commission of the European Communities 2002).

We have discussed EU migration policy in more detail elsewhere (Castles et al. 2003). Here we want to take a wider perspective, and examine international humanitarian action as a new form of global social policy. The international humanitarian regime consists of a set of legal norms, as well as a number of institutions. The legal core of the regime is a set of United Nations conventions and covenants, such as the 1951 United Nations Convention Relating to the Status of Refugees. The most important institutions are intergovernmental agencies such as the United Nations High Commissioner for Refugees (UNHCR), the International Committee of the Red Cross (ICRC), the World Food Programme (WFP) and the United Nations Children's Fund (UNICEF), as well as hundreds of non-governmental organizations (NGOs) such as Oxfam, Médecins sans Frontières (MSF) and the International Rescue Committee (IRC). The declared aim of such bodies is to protect and assist refugees and other victims of war and human rights abuse. However, it seems increasingly that humanitarian agencies are becoming part of a global system of control and containment of people who might otherwise migrate to the North.

Humanitarian action developed in the context of the Cold War. Offering asylum to those who 'voted with their feet' against communism was a powerful source of propaganda for the West. Refugee policy was 'used with the intent of frustrating the consolidation of communist revolutions and hopefully destabilizing nascent communist governments' (Keeley 2001, 307). Since the 'non-departure regime' of the Iron Curtain kept the numbers low, the West could afford to offer a warm welcome to those who managed to flee after events such as the 1956 Hungarian Revolution or the 1968 Prague Spring. However, the mass exoduses of people fleeing violence in the Third World evoked a very different response. Northern countries and international agencies claimed that such situations were qualitatively different from the individual persecution for which the 1951 convention was designed (Chimni 1998). The solution of permanent resettlement in developed countries was not seen as appropriate – except for Indo-Chinese and Cuban refugees, who did fit the Cold War mould. The 'durable solutions' proposed by the UNHCR for such refugees was either repatriation to the country of origin or integration in the country of first asylum (usually a poor neighbouring country).

In the post-Cold War period, human rights abuse, violence and mass flight has grown sharply, as a result of the 'new wars' described above. Many of the people who flee violence become refugees, but the majority remain within the borders of their home state as internally displaced persons (IDPs). It is estimated that the number of IDPs worldwide rose from 1.2 million in 1982 to 14 million by 1986, and to over 20 million by 1997 (Cohen and Deng 1998). IDPs are more numerous than refugees, yet are often without any effective protection or assistance. The key problem is sovereignty: in international law, IDPs are the responsibility of their own government, since they have not crossed international borders, yet it is often this very government that has persecuted and displaced them.

Internal conflicts, which generate large refugee and IDP populations in the South, present major problems for the North. They are seen as potential threats to global stability and security, as well as potential sources of asylum seekers and undocumented migrants. Trying to resolve and prevent conflicts can be seen as both a moral and a political imperative. However, such conflicts are closely linked to underdevelopment, which in turn is partly a result of the unequal global order. Often the underlying causes of conflict include inefficient administration, corruption and authoritarian rule. Such conditions both perpetuate underdevelopment and precipitate conflict. Western governments and international development agencies have become increasingly aware of the links between economic failure and internal conflict. Stability and security are seen as the precondition for development. Thus development assistance has been repackaged as a structural form of conflict prevention (Duffield 2001). The convergence between the notions of development and security leads to increasing interaction between military and security actors on the one hand, and the UN, civil society and NGOs on the other. Indeed, it has become increasingly difficult for NGOs to separate their own development and humanitarian activities from the influence of the North's new security regime (ibid.).

Global spending on humanitarian assistance has increased steadily over the past fifty years. It rose dramatically in the 1990s, peaking at US$5.7 billion in 1994 (UNHCR 2000). The proportion of overseas development assistance (ODA) allocated by governments to humanitarian assistance, as opposed to long-term development, also grew significantly. At its peak, also in 1994, it represented 10 per cent of ODA. During the 1990s, the UNHCR was the lead agency in many of the world's large humanitarian operations and the co-ordinator of much of the assistance provided to people displaced by conflict. The UNHCR's budget doubled between 1990 and 1993 from $564 to $1.3 billion. Expenditure subsequently dropped to $887 million in 1998 and then rose to just over $1 billion in 1999 in response to the Kosovo crisis. Since then, funding to the UNHCR and other humanitarian agencies has been considerably reduced, forcing the closure of offices and programmes around the world.

Most government funding for the UNHCR and other agencies comes from a small number of industrialized states. In 1999, for example, North America, Japan and Western European countries accounted for 97 per cent of all government contributions to the UNHCR. As well as providing fewer funds to the UNHCR, donor governments are tending to earmark their donations for particular countries, programmes or projects, based on their own national priorities. In 1999, the UNHCR received over 90 per cent of the funds requested for programmes in the former Yugoslavia, compared with only about 60 per cent of those it requested for some of its programmes in Africa.

Overall, it is possible to speak of a 'global humanitarian industry', which, like other neo-liberal institutions, is becoming increasingly privatized through the use of NGOs and private companies as sub-contractors. The 1990s saw the biggest increase in the number of NGOs, their size and their operational capabilities, as well as resources available to them. It has been estimated that the total funding channelled through NGOs worldwide to be in excess of $8.5

billion a year (Bennett and Gibbs 1996). In 1994, there were estimated to be over 100 NGOs operating in the camps of Rwandans in Zaire (now the Democratic Republic of Congo), 170 more in Rwanda itself, 150 in Mozambique, and some 250 in Bosnia and Herzegovina (UNHCR 2000). This increase in the numbers and capacity of NGOs is principally a result of donor policies. Public sector funding accounted for 1.5 per cent of NGOs in 1970, compared with 40 per cent by the mid-1990s (Ryder 1996). Since the late 1990s, governments have increasingly shifted their resources away from the UNHCR and other international governmental organizations and towards NGOs. Increasingly, too, private companies are hired to provide transport, logistics and security in emergency situations.

These developments have profound consequences for humanitarian action. In the past the key humanitarian principle has been to remain neutral and to help victims of violence on both sides of a conflict. However, the problem of this approach was that humanitarian assistance 'inevitably became part of the local political economy' (Duffield 2001, 79). The aid goods were used by the combatants as a way of sustaining the conflict and did little to protect victims of war or to stop mass exoduses. Increasingly, the international community turned to direct military intervention. In the course of the 1990s there were seven major military operations designed (at least in part) to prevent mass refugee flows. Six were under the auspices of the United Nations Security Council (in northern Iraq, Bosnia and Herzegovina, Somalia, Rwanda, Haiti and East Timor), while a seventh (in Kosovo) was carried out by NATO (Roberts 1998).

Such military interventions have had mixed results. In some cases (such as Iraq, Bosnia and Haiti) they have been successful in stopping conflicts and mass displacement, without necessarily bringing about long-term solutions to the underlying causes. In other cases, such as Kosovo and East Timor, military intervention has – at least initially – precipitated the very mass forced migrations it was designed to prevent. The intervention in Somalia was a disaster, while that in Rwanda was too late to stop genocide. In any case, the 'international community' is much less willing to intervene in conflict situations that do not lead to mass influxes to the North. There has been no such intervention in Myanmar, Sri Lanka, Azerbaijan, Sudan, Ethiopia or Angola – to name just a few recent major conflicts. This *selectivity* indicates that intervention is based not on lofty moral interests, but on the security and political interests of the rich countries.

In the early twenty-first century, the willingness to carry out military interventions and major humanitarian actions seems to have dropped – probably due to the high costs and considerable risks involved. In the wake of 11 September 2001, US and British leaders seem to have returned to traditional forms of great power politics in their own national interests. However, even in such cases as the military actions against Afghanistan and Iraq, the humanitarian industry has played an important role. In both cases, strategic planners anticipated that military action would lead to a mass outflow of refugees, as well as major IDP problems. The UNHCR, other UN agencies and major NGOs were thus included in planning, and were provided with special funding to pre-position aid goods and to prepare to assist the threatened populations. In the case of Afghanistan, a substantial return of refugees did take place, although international donors soon lost interest in post-conflict reconstruction, and failed to deliver much of the promised funding. At the time of writing, it is too early to assess the humanitarian response in the case of Iraq.

Possible contours of a fairer migration policy framework

Migration is one of the most visible, controversial and crucial facets of globalization. As the numbers of asylum seekers heading west rose sharply during the 1990s, so did the number of undocumented (often smuggled) migrants, as Western governments strengthened their borders to resist entry. But also during the 1990s, governments in the European Union and North America increasingly realized their need to import skilled and unskilled labour in order to compensate for ageing populations and to maintain key industries and services.

States wish to accept migrants on their own terms, distinguishing between those whose entry and residence it can control ('the wanted') and those it does not control ('the unwanted'), notably asylum seekers and undocumented migrant workers. The upsurge in international migration, especially from South to North, has led to strong public reactions in receiving countries and has contributed to the growth of far-right political parties. European governments have responded to this by taking a more hardline approach to asylum seekers and undocumented migrants. There has been an increasing tendency to criminalize these migrants by associating them with smugglers and traffickers, and to impoverish and marginalize them by withdrawing welfare benefits while denying them the right to work. The result is labour-market segmentation, residential segregation and increasing conflict.

We have argued that social policy is a central part of strategies to manage and control immigrant populations. On the national level, differential welfare provisions and entitlements for varying groups help to structure an increasingly transnational labour force, and particularly to ensure its availability for low-skilled work. Systematic use of the labour of undocumented workers and asylum seekers fits in with neo-liberal strategies of deregulation, privatization and casualization. The failure to provide for legal recruitment of low-skilled migrant workers in Britain's new immigration legislation in 2002 seems to parallel the experience of the USA, where the widespread use of undocumented Mexican workers has been central to the profitability of agriculture, construction and certain service industries for nearly half a century.

On the international level, control of migration has become a key aspect of inter-state co-operation. Regional bodies, especially the EU, are seeking to increase their role in migration management. Recent attempts by the EU to use aid and trade policy to influence migration policies of countries of origin are possible harbingers of future international control regimes. At the global level, legal norms and institutions originally set up to help refugees and other victims of violence and human rights abuse are increasingly being used to contain unwanted migration. This is blurring the boundaries between humanitarian action, military intervention and high politics. Such contradictions throw up new challenges for everybody working in the social policy field, whether as social workers at the national level or humanitarian workers at the international level.

We will now attempt to outline some of key concepts that might make up a fairer and more joined set of policies that address the movement of asylum seekers and other migrants to Western states, focusing on the policies of the EU and its member states. In this way we can address the policies of an important group of states that have jointly made a commitment to make progress in this matter and where a basis to build upon already exists.

The primarily economic perspective of policy makers has apparently misled them into thinking that migration was something that could be turned on and off like a tap. But migration is a self-sustaining social process with its own dynamics. Once established, migration networks and ethnic communities around Europe have helped sustain later flows of new types. The absence of effective and fair policies to allow full participation of immigrants in society has led to serious social divisions. Right-wing groups exploited such problems and organized campaigns of racist violence.

Efforts at co-operation on migration policy within the European Community did not develop until the late 1980s. The 1997 Treaty of Amsterdam established community competence in the areas of migration and asylum. Principles for European Union common policy were laid down by the European Council meeting in Tampere in October 1999. The policy includes four main elements, each of which we shall address in turn. These four main elements are:

- the more efficient management of migration flows
- a common European asylum system
- partnership with countries of origin
- fair treatment of third-country nationals.

The more efficient management of migration flows

A whole range of measures has been taken to separate 'wanted' from 'unwanted' migration. 'Wanted' migrants include highly skilled migrants such as the Indian IT professionals that Germany tried to attract through a 'green card' system, and the African and Asian doctors and nurses that are vital to the British National Health Service. Among the 'unwanted' are asylum seekers and undocumented workers, as well as their family members. The paradox is that demographic and economic factors have led to an urgent need for low-skilled workers. Deregulation and privatization have resulted in the emergence of informal sectors – at first in Southern Europe but now in countries such as the UK, France and Germany as well. These act as powerful magnets for undocumented migrants.

Instead of denying the need for low-skilled labour, fair and effective policies need to assess real needs and set up a system that allows recruitment for the industries and services in question. We also need to recognize the human right of migrants to live with their families. This means that family reunion should be a right for those who want it. In view of Europe's current demographic decline, some level of settlement could only be beneficial.

A common European asylum system

At present we are still a long way from a common European asylum system, and member states interpret their obligations to provide protection to refugees under the 1951 Geneva Refugee Convention in different ways. The main emphasis has been on closing borders. Claims by some politicians and sectors of the media that many asylum seekers are 'bogus' and really economic migrants appear to have created a hostile climate. Yet the great majority of asylum seekers come from countries experiencing civil wars and ethnic conflicts. Of course, war and internal violence does lead to economic disruption too, so many asylum seekers have 'mixed motivations': they seek both protection and the chance of a new livelihood for themselves and their families. Immigration policies need to recognize this 'migration asylum nexus'.

A fair asylum policy should therefore have the following components:

* recognition of the right of protection under the Geneva Refugee Convention for all those who have to flee persecution or violence
* active information activities by governments and civil society organizations to combat misleading campaigns about bogus asylum seekers
* policies to support integration of asylum seekers and refugees into local communities
* recognition of the important role of ethnic communities in assisting integration
* policies to address the root causes of refugee movements (see below).

Partnership with countries of origin

In 1998, the European Commission (EC) set up a High Level Working Group (HLWG) on Immigration and Asylum. The aim was to link EC and member state authorities responsible for immigration with authorities responsible for external affairs, trade and international development. The action plans contained a mix of measures concerning migration control, conflict resolution, protection of human rights, development and poverty reduction. The plans do not appear to have had a great deal of effect – not surprisingly in view of the conflicts in some of these places – but they have at least set a precedent for future action in this area.

It is important to realize that it is above all the inequality between North and South which drives migration. This inequality is the result of a form of globalization which allows economic domination by powerful industrial nations and multinational corporations. Large areas of the South have become disconnected from the world economy and have experienced impoverishment, social decline and conflict as a result. The EU does attempt to reduce this inequality through aid policy. But the policies of the EU and its member states in the areas of external affairs, trade, investment and intellectual property actually do much to perpetuate the North–South split. Examples include the Common Agricultural Policy, which leads to impoverishment of many farmers in less developed countries, and the international arms trade, in which many European companies participate (often with government support).

Thus the most important contribution the EU could make to a fair migration policy actually lies outside the realm of migration policy, as it is normally understood. There needs to be a co-ordinated effort by those responsible for policies on border control, external affairs, trade and international co-operation to address the root causes of migration – and that means working for a less unequal world.

Fair treatment of third-country nationals

The Treaty of Amsterdam paved the way for anti-discrimination rules which mandate equal treatment irrespective of race or ethnic origin, and lay down a framework for equal treatment in employment. These are important reforms, but anti-discrimination measures stop a long way short of equal citizenship rights. Fair treatment of third-country nationals implies that long-standing immigrants should get the same rights as nationals of member states, such as the right to work and live in other member states, and to vote and stand for office in local and European Parliament elections. This extension of rights was proposed by the European Union Migrants Forum prior to the Treaty of Amsterdam in 1997, but rejected on the grounds that it would impinge on national sovereignty.

A fair migration policy cannot just be about entry to the EU. It must also ensure that those migrants who decide to settle enjoy full rights of participation in every social area. Substantial progress has been made in many member states, but it is now time for more comprehensive harmonization at the EU level. This means:

- European standards on integration policy, including measures to ensure fair access to services, housing and education
- full implementation of anti-discrimination policy, with a strong role for the European Court of Justice

- harmonization of citizenship policy, so that immigrants and their descendants can become full citizens if they wish
- the extension of European citizenship rights to long-standing residents of third-country origin. Many of these do not wish to become naturalized due to legal and social ties in their home countries. European citizenship can provide a basis for full participation in the host country.

Further Reading

Castles, S., and Miller, M. J. (2003). *The Age of Migration: International Population Movements in the Modern World.* 3rd edn, Basingstoke: Palgrave; New York: Guilford.

Cohen, R. (1997). *Global Diasporas: An Introduction.* London. UCL Press.

Critical Social Policy (2002). Special issue: *Asylum and Welfare* No. 72, 3 August.

Faist, T. (2000). *The Volume and Dynamics of International Migration and Transnational Social Spaces.* Oxford: Oxford University Press.

Van Hear, N. (1998). *New Diasporas: The Mass Exodus, Dispersal and Regrouping of Migrant Communities.* London: UCL Press.

Zolberg, A. R., and Benda, P. M. (eds) (2001). *Global Migrants, Global Refugees: Problems and Solutions.* New York and Oxford: Berghahn Books.

Epilogue: Global Social Problems and Global Social Policy: Future Prospects

As the contributors to this volume have demonstrated, what were once regarded as territorially bounded social problems now have a global dimension. There is an increased realization that tackling issues such as crime or the illegal supply of drugs necessitates a greater degree of international co-operation. Moreover, increased information flows have served to highlight both the acute levels of need in many developing countries and the ways in which the actions of their more prosperous neighbours can ameliorate or exacerbate this situation.

   Increased recognition of the global aspects of social problems does not mean, though, that historic disputes about both the cause and resolution of such phenomena will become any less intense. There may, for example, be a growing consensus about the need to tackle poverty in some of the poorest nations in the world. However, there is unlikely to be unanimity concerning the underlying cause of such disadvantage. Some will contend that the problem is caused by the pursuit of inappropriate economic policies by corrupt governments. Others, in contrast, are likely to point to unfair trading agreements and subsidies or the unwillingness of richer nations to provide appropriate forms of aid. Such divisions will be reflected in the remedies put forward. Those in the former category are likely to call for a rapid expansion of free trade and inward investment, while their 'opponents' will favour more egalitarian trade agreements and debt relief programmes. Importantly, nation-states tend to favour explanations and solutions that reflect their own perceived economic and social interests. It should be noted, though, that it is becoming more difficult for nation-states to decide what is in the 'national interest'. For example, government may be asked to protect manufacturing jobs in an indigenous industry by curbing the inflow of cheap imports. Equally, a domestic retailer may ask the government to abolish unnecessary tariffs on such imports on the grounds that the sale of these goods will increase profitability and local job opportunities.

Similarly, while most nation-states acknowledge that 'domestic' social problems now have a global dimension, there is likely to be a difference of opinion about the best way to respond to this development. Those who believe that globalization should be embraced, or, at least, not resisted may be prepared to accept that their response to existing or emerging social problems will need to alter quite radically. This may involve working more closely with other nations in regional or transnational forums, such as the European Union and the United Nations. It may even lead in some circumstances to a willingness to cede authority to such institutions.

In contrast, those nations that adopt a more global 'sceptic' approach may be more inclined to resist what they regard as the largely negative influence of globalization by means of economic protectionism and the adoption of domestic policies that attempt to bolster their distinctive cultural traditions. Certainly, those nations who believe that globalization amounts to little more than 'the creation of a global free market and the consolidation of Anglo-American capitalism within the world's major economic regions' (Held and McGrew 2002, 4) are likely to favour a 'resistance' strategy of this kind. Social democratic nations have been particularly concerned at the way in which the neo-liberal underpinning of contemporary globalization has served to encourage the notion that comprehensive forms of state welfare act as a fetter on future economic prosperity.

Those believing that globalization provides an opportunity for creating a fairer world in which social problems can be tackled more effectively have begun to map out the way in which this could be achieved. For example, Monbiot believes that it is not necessary to oppose globalization but rather 'to capture it, and to use it as a vehicle for humanity's first global democratic revolution' (2003, 23). He suggests that the creation of a World Parliament, a Fair Trade Organization and an International Clearing Union would be important first steps on the road to the creation of greater global fairness. The key question, though, is whether there is a public appetite for a movement of this kind? Held and McGrew (2002) are convinced that we are seeing the emergence of a 'cosmopolitan social democracy'. This movement is characterized by:

the promotion of the impartial administration of law at the international level; greater transparency, accountability and democracy in global governance; a deeper commitment to social justice in the pursuit of a more equitable distribution of the world's resources and human security; the protection and reinvention of community at diverse levels (from the local to the global); and the regulation of the global economy through the public management of global financial and trade flows, the provision of global public goods, and the engagement of leading stakeholders in corporate governance (Held and McGrew 2002, 131)

For Held and McGrew, a cohesive transnational movement of this kind will be in a position to 'overcome fierce opposition from well-entrenched geopolitical and geoeconomic interests' (ibid., 136).

While one can admire the sentiments of these commentators, doubts remain both about the possibility of 'taming globalization' (Held and Koenig-Archibugi 2003) and of the emergence of a more progressive global ideology. Although there has undoubtedly been a rapid growth in transnational governmental and non-governmental organizations and policy forums, these fall far short of any form of global governance. Furthermore, it is clearly premature to suggest that we are witnessing a 'reconfiguration of political power' (see Held and McGrew 2002, 9–24). In particular, there is limited evidence to suggest that the so-called Washington consensus based on neo-liberal principles is currently in retreat. If anything, its tentacles appear to be stretching still further. It is, of course, possible that this neo-liberal variant of globalization will eventually be replaced by a more 'progressive' ideology. Certainly, globalization and 'welfarism' have 'co-existed' in earlier periods. However, the assault upon collectivism in this current stage of globalization may prove more effective, thereby making the re-establishment of a pro-welfare climate less likely in the near future.

Those seeking to re-establish such a climate will need to acknowledge that this is likely to be a long, incremental process. Given that it took a century or more for the dream of a national welfare state to be achieved, it will surely take far longer for a more progressive world order to emerge.

It is also important to consider whether we might witness a greater degree of convergence in the way in which developed nations respond to social problems as a consequence of globalization. While there is likely to be increased international and transnational co-operation, particularly in those areas where territorial boundaries have become less significant, this will not necessarily give rise to more uniform policy responses. While globalization may have changed the parameters in which governments must now operate, there is no reason to think that diverse policy responses based on the historic institutional patterns and processes of individual nation-states will diminish in importance in the foreseeable future (Taylor-Gooby 2001; Rothstein and Steinmo 2002).

References

Abbott, P., and Wallace, C. 1992: *The Family and the New Right*. London: Pluto.

Abel-Smith, B., and Townsend, P. 1965: *The Poor and the Poorest*. London: Bell.

Aguilera Ribeaux, D. 2001: *La violencia intrafamiliar: tratamiento jurídico en Cuba*. Havana [mimeo].

Alexander, B. K., 2000: The globalization of addiction. *Addiction Research*, 8, 501–26.

Alexander, T. 1996: *Unravelling Global Apartheid*. Cambridge: Polity.

Allen, C., and Nielsen, J. 2002: *Summary Report on Islamophobia in the EU After September 11*. Vienna: European Monitoring Centre on Racism and Xenophobia [www.eumc.eu.int].

Alvarez Suarez, M. 1998: Mujer y poder en Cuba. *Temas*, 14, 13–25.

Amnesty International 2001: *Racism and the Administration of Justice*. Oxford: Alden Press [www.amnesty.org].

Annan, K. 2000: Foreword. *World Drug Report 2000*. Oxford: Oxford University Press.

Anon. 1909: Nations uniting to stamp out the use of opium and many other drugs. *New York Times*, 1 July, 25.

Anon. 1913: We gain in China and Great Britain loses. *New York Times*, 3 May.

Anon. 1923: Ask world control of drug production: delegates to National Anti-Narcotics Conference favor an international agreement. *New York Times*, 1 June, 13.

Anon. 1926a: Foes of drug evil call a world meeting: conference on narcotic education at Philadelphia next month will be first of its kind. *New York Times*, 1 June, 13.

Anon. 1926b: Says opium critics exaggerate evils. *New York Times*, 4 November, 7.

Anon. 1928: Opens world drive on drug traffic: Anti-Narcotic Union plans active warfare in all states and countries. *New York Times*, 1 March, 8.

Atkinson, A. 2002: Is rising income inequality inevitable? A critique of the 'transatlantic consensus'. In P. Townsend and D. Gordon (eds), *World Poverty*. Bristol: Policy Press, 25–51.

Axford, B. 1995: *The Global System: Economics, Politics and Culture*. Cambridge: Polity.

Banton, M. 2002: *The International Politics of Race*. Cambridge: Polity.

Basail Rodríguez, A. 1999: *Legitimidad y eficacia del sistema político Cubano: ensayo sobre las políticas públicas en los '9*. Havana [mimeo].

Bauman, Z. 1998: *Globalization: The Human Consequences*. Cambridge: Polity.

Bayne, N. 2000: Why did Seattle fail? Globalization and the politics of trade. *Government and Opposition*, 35, 131–52.

Beck, U. 1992: *Risk Society*. London: Sage.

Beck, U. 1996: World risk society as cosmopolitan society? *Theory, Culture & Society*, 13, 1–32.

Beer, G. 1958: *The Old Colonial System, 1660–1754*. Gloucester, MA: Smith.

Beneria, L. 1991: Structural adjustment, the labour market and the household: the case of Mexico. In G. Standing and V. Tokman (eds), *Towards Social Adjustment*. Geneva: ILO.

Bennett, J., and Gibbs, S. 1996: *NGO Funding Strategies*. Oxford: INTRAC/ICVA.

Berridge, V. 1999: *Opium and the People*. London: Free Association Books.

Birdsall, N., and Haggard, S. 2002: After the crisis: the social contract and the middle class in East Asia. In E. B. Kapstein and B. Milanovic (eds), *When Markets Fail*. New York: Russell Sage Foundation, 58–101.

Blanc, A., Wolff, B., Gage, A., Ezeh, A., Neema, S., and Ssekamatte-Sebulia, J. 1997: *Negotiating Reproductive Outcomes in Uganda*. Kampala, Uganda: Institute of Statistics and Applied Economics; Calverton, MD, Macro International.

Boeri, T., Hanson, G., and McCormick, B. 2002: *Immigration Policy and the Welfare System*. Oxford: Oxford University Press.

Bommes, M., and Halfmann, J. 1998: *Migration in nationalen Wohlfahrtstaaten: theoretische und vegleichende Untersuchungen*. Osnabrück: Universitätsverlag Rasch.

Bonnett, A. 2000: *Anti-Racism*. London: Routledge.

Bonoli, G., George, V., and Taylor-Gooby, P. 2000: *European Welfare Futures*. Cambridge: Polity.

Booker, S., and Minter, W. 2001: Global apartheid. *The Nation*, 9 July [www.thecriticalvoice.com/global_apartheid.html].

Brubaker, R. 2001: The return of assimilation? Changing perspectives on immigration and its sequels in France, Germany and the United States. *Ethnic and Racial Studies*, 24, 531–48.

Bruun, L., Pan, L., and Rexed, I. 1975: *The Gentleman's Club: International Control of Drugs and Alcohol*. Chicago: University of Chicago Press.

Brysk, A. (ed.) 2002: *Globalization and Human Rights*. Berkeley and Los Angeles: University of California Press.

Burkitt, I. 1990: *Bodies of Thought: Embodiment, Identity and Modernity*. London: Sage.

Bush, G. 2001: President Bush discusses global climate change. June. <http://www.whitehouse.gov/news/releases/2001/06/20010611-2.html>, accessed 28 October 2002.

Butler, D., and Kavanagh, D. 2002: *The British General Election of 2001*. Basingstoke: Palgrave.

Buttel, F. H. 2000: Ending hunger in developing countries. *Contemporary Sociology*, 29, 1, 13–27.

Camdessus, M. 2001: A trade round for development. *OECD Observer*, 226/227, 36–8.

Caño Secade, M. del C. 1997: *Mujer: transformaciones sociales e internacionales de género*. Paper presented at Latin American Studies Association [mimeo].

Carter, N. 2001: *The Politics of the Environment: Ideas, Activism, Policy*. Cambridge: Cambridge University Press.

Castells, M. 1996: *The Rise of the Network Society*. Oxford: Blackwell.

Castles, S. 2000: *Ethnicity and Globalization*. London: Sage.

Castles, S., and Miller, M. J. 2003: *The Age of Migration: International Population Movements in the Modern World*. 3rd edn, Basingstoke: Palgrave; New York: Guilford.

Castles, S., Crawley, H., and Loughna, S. 2003: *Forced Migration, Conflict and Development: Patterns of Mobility to the European Union, Causes and Policy Options*. London: Institute of Public Policy Research.

Chambaz, C. 2001: Lone parents in Europe. *Social Policy & Administration*, 35, 658–72.

Chimni, B. S. 1998: The geo-politics of refugee studies: a view from the South. *Journal of Refugee Studies*, 11, 350–74.

Clarke, J. 2001: Social problems: sociological perspectives. In M. May, R. Page and E. Brunsdon (eds), *Understanding Social Problems*. Oxford: Blackwell, 3–15.

Cohen, R., and Deng, F. M. 1998: *Masses in Flight: The Global Crisis of Internal Displacement*. Washington, DC: Brookings Institution Press.

Commission of the European Communities 2000: *Communication from the European Commission to the Council and European Parliament on a Community Immigration Policy*. Brussels: Commission of the European Communities, COM 757/2000.

Commission of the European Communities 2001: *On an Open Method of Coordination for the Community Immigration Policy*. Brussels: Commission of the European Communities, 11 July, COM (2001) 387.

Commission of the European Communities 2002. *Press Release: Romano Prodi Speech, 21 June*. <http://europe.eu.int/rapid/start/cgi>.

Commonwealth Secretariat 1992: *Confronting Violence: A Manual for Commonwealth Action*. London: Women and Development Programme, Commonwealth Secretariat.

Corkery, J. M. 1997: *Statistics of Drug Addicts Notified to the Home Office, United Kingdom, 1996*. London: Home Office.

Corkill, D. 2001: Economic migrants and the labour market in Spain and Portugal. *Ethnic and Racial Studies*, 24, 828–44.

Cornia, G., Jolly, R., and Stewart, F. (eds) 1987: *Adjustment with a Human Face*. Oxford: Clarendon Press.

Cornwell, G., and Stoddard, E. (eds) 2001: *Global Multiculturalism: Comparative Perspectives on Ethnicity, Race and Nation*. Oxford: Rowman & Littlefield.

Dauvergne, P. (ed.) 1998: *Weak and Strong States in Asia-Pacific Societies*. Sydney: Allen & Unwin.

Deacon, B. 1998: Social policy in a shrinking world. In P. Alcock, A. Erskine and M. May (eds), *The Student's Companion to Social Policy*. Oxford: Blackwell, 128–35.

Deacon, B. 2000: Globalisation: a threat to equitable provision? In H. Dean, R. Sykes and R. Woods (eds), *Social Policy Review 12*. London: Social Policy Association.

Deacon, B. 2001: International organisations, the EU and global social policy. In R. Sykes, B. Palier and P. Prior (eds), *Globalisation and European Welfare States*. Basingstoke: Palgrave, 59–76.

Department of Health 2000: *Domestic Violence: A Resource Manual for Health Care Professionals*. London: Department of Health.

DHS III 1995: *Colombia Demographic Health Surveys*. Colombia: Profamilia; Calverton, MD: Macro International.

Dieter, H. 2002: World economy – structures and trends. In P. Kennedy, D. Messner and F. Nuscheler (eds), *Global Trends and Global Governance*. London: Pluto Press, 65–96.

Dietz, F. 1964: *English Public Finance, 1558–1641*. London: Cass.

Dikötter, F. 1992: *The Discourse of Race in Modern China*. London: Hurst.

Dobash, R. E., and Dobash, R. P. 1980: *Violence against Wives: A Case Against the Patriarchy*. Shepton Mallet: Open Books.

Dobash, R. E., Dobash, R. P., Cavanagh, K., and Lewis, R. 2000: *Changing Violent Men*. London: Sage.

Donnan, E. 1932: Eighteenth century merchants: Micajah Perry. *Journal of Economic and Business History*, 4, 94–5.

Donnison, D. 2001: The changing face of poverty. In M. May, R. Page and E. Brunsdon (eds), *Understanding Social Problems*. Oxford: Blackwell, 87–106.

Doole, C. (2000) UN links globalisation to racism. <http://www.globalpolicy.org>.

Doomernik, J. 1998: *The Effectiveness of Integration Policies towards Immigrants and their Descendants in France, Germany and the Netherlands*. Geneva: International Labour Organization.

Douglas, M. (ed.) 1987a: *Constructive Drinking: Perspectives on Drink from Anthropology*. Cambridge: Cambridge University Press.

Douglas, M. 1987b: A distinctive anthropological perspective. In M. Douglas (ed.), *Constructive Drinking*. Cambridge: Cambridge University Press, 3–15.

Duffield, M. 2001: *Global Governance and the New Wars: The Merging of Development and Security*. London and New York: Zed Books.

Düvell, F. B. J. 2002: Immigration, asylum and welfare: the European context. *Critical Social Policy*, 22, 498–517.

ECRI (European Commission against Racism and Intolerance) 2001a: *Second Report on the United Kingdom*. Strasbourg: Council of Europe [www.coe.int/ecri].

ECRI (European Commission against Racism and Intolerance) 2001b: *Annual Report 2000*. Strasbourg: Council of Europe [www.coe.int/ecri].

Elliott, L. 2002: An EU cow is given $2.20 daily – the world's poor live on $1 a day. *The Guardian*, 30 October.

Ellsberg, M., Rena, H., Herrara, A., Liljestrand, J., and Winlarist, A. 1996: *Confites en el infierno: prevalencia y características de la violencia conyugal hacia las mujeres en Nicaragua*. Managua: Asociación de Mujeres Profesionales por la Democracia en el Desarrollo.

El-Zanaty, F., Hussein, E., Shawley, G., Way, A., and Kishsor, S. 1995: *Egypt Demographic and Health Surveys III*. Cairo: National Population Council; Calverton, MD: Macro International.

Entzinger, H. 2002: The rise and fall of multiculturalism: the case of the Netherlands. In C. Joppke and E. Morawaska (eds), *Towards Assimilation and Citizenship: Immigration in Liberal Nation-States*. London: Palgrave.

Environmental News Network 1999: Small island states meet over rising sea levels. <http://www.enn.com/enn-news-archive/1999/07/071499/smallislands_4336.asp>, accessed 23 October 2002.

EUMC (European Union Monitoring Centre) 2001: *Attitudes Towards Minority Groups in the European Union*. Vienna: European Monitoring Centre on Racism and Xenophobia [www.eumc.eu.int].

EUMC (European Union Monitoring Centre) 2002: *Racism, Football and the Internet*. Vienna: European Monitoring Centre on Racism and Xenophobia [www.eumc.eu.int].

European Commission 1997: *Racism and Xenophobia in Europe*. Euro-barometer Opinion Poll 47, 1. Brussels: European Commission.

European Commission 2000: *Breaking the Silence*. Luxembourg: Office for Official Publications of the European Commission.

Falk, R. 2000: Resisting globalization-from-above through globalization-from-below. In B. Gills (ed.), *Globalization and the Politics of Resistance*. Basingstoke: Macmillan, 47–56.

Fanning, B. 2002: *Racism and Social Change in the Republic of Ireland*. Manchester: Manchester University Press.

FAO (Food and Agriculture Organization) 1996: *The State of Food and Agriculture, 1996*. Rome: FAO.

FAO (Food and Agriculture Organization) 2000: *The State of Food and Agriculture, 2000*. Rome: FAO.

FAO (Food and Agriculture Organization) 2001: *The State of Food and Agriculture, 2001*. Rome: FAO.

Farrell, G. 1998: A global empirical review of drug crop eradication and United Nations' crop substitution and alternative development strategies. *Journal of Drug Issues*, 28, 395–436.

Featherstone, M. 1991: *Consumer Culture and Postmodernism*. London: Sage.

Findlay, M. 1997: Crime, community penalty and integration within legal formalism in the South Pacific. *Journal of Pacific Studies*, 45, 145–66.

Findlay, M. 1999: *The Globalisation of Crime*. Cambridge: Cambridge University Press.

Finlayson, A. 2003: *Understanding New Labour*. London: Lawrence & Wishart.

Fitzpatrick, T. 2001: *Welfare Theory: An Introduction*. Basingstoke: Palgrave.

Frey, B. S. 1997: Drugs, economics and policy. *Economic Policy*, 25, 387–9.

Fukuyama, F. 1992: *The End of History and the Last Man*. New York: Free Press.

Gallagher, A. 2002: Trafficking, smuggling and human rights: tricks and treaties. *Forced Migration Review*, 12, 25–8.

George, V. 1996: The future of the welfare state. In V. George and P. Taylor-Gooby (eds), *European Welfare Policy*. Basingstoke: Macmillan.

George, V., and Howards, I. 1991: *Poverty amidst Affluence: The UK and the USA*. Aldershot: Edward Elgar.

George, V., and Wilding, P. 2002: *Globalization and Human Welfare*. Basingstoke: Palgrave.

Giddens, A. 1990: *The Consequences of Modernity*. Cambridge: Polity.

Giddens, A. 1991: *Modernity and Self-Identity*. Cambridge: Polity.

Giddens, A. 1993: *Sociology*. Cambridge: Polity.

Giddens, A. 1996/1997: Anthony Giddens on globalization: excerpts from a keynote address at the UNRISD Conference on Globalization and

Citizenship. *UNRISD News (United Nations Research Institute for Social Development Bulletin)*, 15, 4–5.

Giddens, A. 1999: *Runaway World*. London: Profile Books.

Gillioz, L., de Puy, J., and Ducret, V. 1997: *Domination et violences envers les femmes dans la couple*. Lausanne: Editions Payot.

Gilpin, R. 1987: *The Political Economy of International Relations*. Princeton, NJ: Princeton University Press.

Goldblatt, D. 1997: Liberal democracy and the globalization of environmental risks. In A. McGrew (ed.), *The Transformation of Democracy?* Cambridge: Polity.

Gorringe, T. 1999: *Fair Shares: Ethics and the Global Economy*. London: Thames & Hudson.

Gould, A. 2001: *Developments in Swedish Social Policy: Swedish Welfare in Transition*. Basingstoke: Palgrave.

Grabosky, P., Smith, G., and Dempsey, G. 2001: *Electronic Theft: Unlawful Acquisition in Cyberspace*. Melbourne: Cambridge University Press.

Guan, X. 2001: Globalization, inequality and social policy. *Social Policy and Administration*, 35, 242–58.

Haemmig, R. B. 1995: Harm reduction in Bern: from outreach to heroin maintenance. *Bulletin of the New York Academy of Medicine*, 72, 371–9.

Hague, G. 1999: Domestic violence policy in the 1990s. In S. Watson and L. Doyle (eds), *Engendering Social Policy*. Buckingham: Open University Press.

Hague, G., and Malos, E. 1998: *Domestic Violence: Action for Change*. Cheltenham: New Clarion Press.

Haj-Yahia, M. 1996: Wife abuse in Arab society in Israel: challenges for future change. In J. Edleson and Z. Eisikovits (eds), *Future Interventions with Battered Women and their Families*. Thousand Oaks, CA: Sage.

Halliday, F. 2002: *Two Hours that Shook the World*. London: Saqi Books.

Hanmer, J., and Sutton, J. 1984: Writing our own history: the early days of Women's Aid. *Trouble and Strife*, winter, 55–60.

Harcourt, R. 1613: *A Relation of a Voyage to Guiana*. London: Hakluyt Society.

Harrington, M. 1962: *The Other America*. Harmondsworth: Penguin.

Harrison, L. 1986: Tobacco battered and the pipes shattered: a note on the fate of the first British campaign against tobacco smoking. *British Journal of Addiction*, 81, 553–8.

Harvey, D. 1989: *The Conditions of Postmodernity*. Oxford: Blackwell.

Hasanbegovic, C. 2001: *Violencia marital en Cuba: principios revolucionarios versus viejas creencias*. Canterbury: University of Kent. School of Social Policy, Sociology and Social Research.

Hasanbegovic, C. 2002a: *Love and the State: The Politics of Domestic Violence in Argentina and Cuba*. PhD thesis, University of Kent.

Hasanbegovic, C. 2002b: Public and social policy responses to wife abuse in Argentina and Cuba. *CESLA*, 3, 99–136.

Hay, C. 1999: *The Political Economy of New Labour*. Manchester: Manchester University Press.

Held, D. 2002: Globalization, corporate practice and cosmopolitan social standards. *Contemporary Political Theory*, 1, 1, 59–78.

Held, D., and Koenig-Archibugi, M. (eds) 2003: *Taming Globalization*. Cambridge: Polity.

Held, D., and McGrew, A. 2002: *Globalization/Anti-Globalization*. Cambridge: Polity.

Held, D., McGrew, A., Goldblatt, D., and Perraton, J. 1999: *Global Transformations: Politics, Economics and Culture*. Cambridge: Polity.

Hertz, N. 2002: *The Silent Takeover*. London: Arrow.

Hickman, M. 1998: Reconstructing deconstructing 'race': British political discourses about the Irish in Britain. *Ethnic and Racial Studies*, 21, 289–307.

Hillgenberg, H. 1999: A fresh look at soft law. *European Journal of International Law*, 10, 499.

Hirst, P., and Thompson, G. 1996: *Globalization in Question*. Cambridge: Polity.

Hirst, P., and Thompson, G. 1999: *Globalization in Question*. 2nd edn, Cambridge: Polity.

Hoffman, K., Demo, D., and Kaye, M. 1994: Physical wife abuse in a non-Western society: an integrated theoretical approach. *Journal of Marriage and the Family*, 56, 131–46.

House of Commons Select Committee on the Affairs of the East India Company 1970: *Report from the Select Committee on the Affairs of the East India Company*. Shannon: Irish University Press.

Hutton, W. 2002: *The World We're In*. London: Little, Brown.

ICASO (International Council of Aids Service Organization) 2002: *Update on the UNGASS Declaration of Commitment on HIV/AIDS*. Toronto: International Council of AIDS Service Organizations.

Ignatieff, M. 2001: What will victory look like? *The Guardian*, 19 October.

INCB (International Narcotics Control Board) 1997: *Report of the International Control Board for 1996*. New York: United Nations Publications.

INCB (International Narcotics Control Board) 2000: *Report of the International Control Board for 1999*. New York: United Nations Publications.

INCB (International Narcotics Control Board) 2002: *Report of the International Control Board for 2001*. New York: United Nations Publications.

Interdepartmental Committee on Drug Addiction 1961: *Drug Addiction: Report of the Interdepartmental Committee*. London: HMSO.

International Planned Parenthood Federation 2002: *Global Challenges in Ending Gender-Based Violence*. <www.ippf.org/resource/gbv/chogm99/global.htm>.

Ireland, P. 2000: Reaping what they sow: institutions and immigrant political participation in Western Europe. In R. Koopmans and P. Statham (eds), *Challenging Immigration and Ethnic Relations Politics*. Oxford: Oxford University Press, 233–82.

Jaffe, P., Wolfe, D., and Kaye, M. 1990: *Children of Battered Women*. London: Sage.

Jakobsson, U., Bergman, L., Braunerhjelm, P., Folster, S., and Henrekson, M. (eds) 1998: *Entrepreneurship in the Welfare State*, Stockholm: SNS Forlag.

Jakobsson, U., Bergman, L., Braunerhjelm, P., Folster, S., and Genberg, H. (eds) 1999: *The Road to Prosperity*. Stockholm: SNS Forlag.

James I, King of Great Britain and Ireland, 1604: Commission pro Tobacco. In T. Rymer (ed.) *Foedera*, London, 601–2.

Johnson, H. 1996: *Dangerous Domains: Violence against Women in Canada*. Toronto: Nelson.

Jones-Finer, C. (ed.) 1999: *Transnational Social Policy*. Oxford: Blackwell.

Kaldor, M. 2001: *New and Old Wars: Organized Violence in a Global Era*. Cambridge: Polity.

Kam, Y.-M., and Harrison, L. 2001: Globalisation, cultural change and the modern drug epidemics: the case of Hong Kong. *Health, Risk & Society*, 3, 39–57.

Kapstein, E. B., and Milanovic, B. (eds) 2002: *When Markets Fail*. New York: Russell Sage Foundation.

Keeley, C. B. 2001: The international refugee regime(s): the end of the Cold War matters. *International Migration Review*, 35, 1, 303–14.

Kendall, R. 2003: Cannabis condemned: the proscription of Indian 'hemp'. *Addiction*, 98, 143–51.

Kennedy, P. 2002: Global challenges at the beginning of the twenty-first century. In P. Kennedy, D. Messner and F. Nuscheler (eds), *Global Trends and Global Governance*. London: Pluto Press, 1–21.

Kim, K., and Cho, Y. 1992: Epidemiological survey of spousal abuse in Korea. In C. Viano (ed.), *Intimate Violence: Interdisciplinary Perspectives*. Washington, DC: Hemisphere Publishing Corporation.

Klein, N. 2002: *Fences and Windows*. London: Flamingo.

Klein, N. 2003: Cut the strings. *The Guardian*, 1 February.

Kleinman, M. 2002: *A European Welfare State?* Basingstoke: Palgrave.

Koser, K. 1997: Social networks and the asylum cycle: the case of Iranians in the Netherlands. *International Migration Review*, 31, 591–611.

Koser, K., and Pinkerton, C. 2002: The social networks of asylum seekers and the dissemination of information about countries of asylum. *Findings* no. 165. London: Home Office.

Kosonen, P. 2001: Globalization and the Nordic welfare states. In R. Sykes, B. Palier and P. Prior (eds), *Globalisation and European Welfare States*. Basingstoke: Palgrave, 153–72.

Kuenyehia, A. 1994: The impact of structural adjustment programs on women's international human rights: the example of Ghana. In R. Cook (ed.), *Human Rights of Women: National and International Perspectives*. Philadelphia: University of Pennsylvania Press.

LaFeber, W. 2002: *Michael Jordan and the New Global Capitalism*. New York: W. W. Norton.

Larguía, M., and Dumoulin, J. 1986: Women's equality and the Cuban revolution. In J. Nash and H. Safa (eds), *Women and Change in Latin America*. South Hadley, MA: Bergin & Garvey.

Larrain, S. 1993: *Estudio de frecuencia de la violencia intrafamiliar y la condición de la mujer en Chile*. Santiago: Pan American Health Organization.

Lee, E. 1998: *The Asian Financial Crisis*. Geneva: International Labour Office.

Legrain, P. 2002: *Open World: The Truth about Globalisation*. London: Abacus.

Levinson, D. 1989: *Family Violence in Cross-Cultural Perspective*. London: Sage.

Levitt, T. 1983: The globalization of markets. *Harvard Business Review*, 61, 92–102.

Lewis, D. 1999: Development NGOs and the challenge of partnership: changing relations between North and South. In C. Jones-Finer (ed.), *Transnational Social Policy*. Oxford: Blackwell, 49–60.

Lind, M. 2003: Free trade, fallacy. *Prospect*, January, 34–7.

Lloyd, C. 2000: Anti-racist responses to European integration. In R. Koopmans and P. Statham (eds), *Challenging Immigration and Ethnic Relations Politics: Comparative European Perspectives*. Oxford: Oxford University Press, 389–406.

Lupton, D. 1999: *Risk*. London: Routledge.

McAllister, W. B. 2000: *Drug Diplomacy in the Twentieth Century*. London: Routledge.

McAndrew, C., and Edgerton, R. 1969: *Drunken Comportment: A Social Explanation*. Chicago: Aldine.

McCusker, C., and Davies, M. 1996: Prescribing drug of choice to. illicit heroin users: the experience of UK community drug team. *Journal of Substance Abuse Treatment*, 13, 521–31.

McGiffen, S. P. 2002: *Globalisation*. Harpenden: Pocket Essentials.

McKibben, B. 1999: *The End of Nature*. New York: Anchor Books.

MacMaster, N. 2001: *Racism in Europe*. Basingstoke: Palgrave.

McRae, H. 1994: *The World in 2020: Power, Culture and Prosperity: A Vision of the Future*. London: Harper Collins.

Makinen, T. 1999: Structural pressures, social policy and poverty. *International Social Security Review*, 52, 4, 3–25.

Mann, M. 1986: *The Sources of Social Power*, Volume 1. Cambridge: Cambridge University Press.

Manski, C. F., Pepper, J. V., and Petrie, C. V. 2001: *Informing America's Policy on Illegal Drugs: What We Don't Know Keeps Hurting Us.* Washington, DC: National Academy of Sciences.

Marris, R. 1999: *Ending Poverty.* London: Thames & Hudson.

Marx, K. 1972: The opium trade. In K. Marx and F. Engels (eds), *On Colonialism.* New York: International Publishers, 217–20.

Marx, K. 1976: *Capital.* Harmondsworth: Penguin.

Marx, K., and Engels, F. 1934: *Manifesto of the Communist Party.* London: Lawrence & Wishart.

Marx, K., and Engels, F. (eds) 1972: *On Colonialism: Articles from the New York Herald Tribune and other Writings.* New York: International Publishers.

Masakazu, Y. 2001: Looking beyond Asia. *Japan Echo*, 28, 3, 59–64.

Matza, D. 1964: *Delinquency and Drift.* New York: John Wiley.

May, M., Page, R., and Brunsdon, E. (eds) 2001: *Understanding Social Problems: Issues in Social Policy.* Oxford: Blackwell.

Meadows, D. H., Meadows, D. L., Randers, J., and Behrens, W. W. 1974: *The Limits to Growth.* London: Pan.

Messner, D., and Nuscheler, F. 2002: World politics – structures and trends. In P. Kennedy., D. Messner and F. Nuscheler (eds), *Global Trends and Global Governance.* London: Pluto Press, 125–55.

Metrebian, N., Shanahan, W., Stimson, G. V., Small, C., Lee, M., Mtutu, V., and Wells, B. 1998: Prescribing drug of choice to opiate-dependent drug users: associated health gains and harm reductions. *Medical Journal of Australia*, 168, 596–600.

Miller, S. 1659: Epistle dedicatory. In S. Miller (ed.), *Panacea or the Universal Medicine*: London.

Milne, S. 2001: Terror & tyranny. *The Guardian*, 25 October.

Mintz, S. 1985: *Sweetness and Power: The Place of Sugar in Modern History.* Battleboro, VT: Viking.

Mishra, R. 1999: Beyond the nation state: social policy in an age of globalization. In C. Jones-Finer (ed.), *Transnational Social Policy.* Oxford: Blackwell, 29–48.

Moller, T. 2002: Sweden's Social Democrats consolidate their dominance. *Current Sweden*, 439, October.

Monbiot, G. 2000: *Captive State: The Corporate Takeover of Britain.* Basingstoke: Macmillan.

Monbiot, G. 2002: The rich world's veto on reform. *The Guardian*, 15 October.

Monbiot, G. 2003: *The Age of Consent.* London: Flamingo.

Mooney, J. 2000: *Gender, Violence and the Social Order.* Basingstoke: Macmillan.

Mullender, A., and Morley, R. 1994: *Children Living with Domestic Violence.* London: Whiting & Birch.

Munck, R. 2002: *Globalisation and Labour.* London: Zed Books.

Murphy, P. 2001: *Keeping Score: The Frailties of the Federal Drug Budget.* Santa Monica, CA: RAND Drug Policy Research Center.

NACO (National AIDS Control Organization, India) 2000: *Estimation of HIV Infection among the Adult Population.* New Delhi: NACO. [www.naco.nic.in].

Narayana, G. 1996: *Family Violence, Sex and Reproductive Health Behaviour among Men in Uttar Pradesh, India.* Paper presented at the Annual Meeting of the National Council on International Health, Arlington, Virginia.

Navarrete Calderon, C. 1999: *El estado de los estudios criminológicos de la violencia doméstica en Cuba: F. G. R. C informe de investigación.* Paper presented at the III International Workshop, Women at the Threshold of the New Millennium.

Negrete, J. 1983: The Andes: coca, the Incas and after. In G. Edwards, A. Arif and J. Jaffe (eds), *Drug Use and Misuse: Cultural Perspectives.* London: Croom Helm, 58–65.

Norberg, J. 2001: *In Defence of Global Capitalism.* Stockholm: Timbro.

O'Brien, R., Goetz, A. M., Scholte, J. A., and Williams, M. 2000: *Contesting Global Governance.* Cambridge: Cambridge University Press.

ODCCP 2002: *United Nations Office for Drug Control and Crime Prevention.* <http://www.undcp.org/about.html>, accessed 13 August 2002.

OECD 1996: *Trade, Employment, and Labor Standards: A Study of Core Workers' Rights and International Trade.* Paris: OECD.

OECD 2000: *OECD Economic Surveys: Russian Federation.* Paris: OECD.

OECD 2001: *Trends in International Migration: Annual Report 2001.* Paris: OECD.

Ohmae, K. 1990: *The Borderless World: Power and Strategy in the Interlinked Economy.* London: Collins.

Ohmae, K. 1995: Putting global logic first. *Harvard Business Review*, January–February, 119–25.

Oliva, C., Lauzan, Z., and Herrera, R. 1994: *La violencia antisocial contra las mujeres, los menores y los ancianos.* Havana: Minjus.

Owen, D. 1934: *British Opium Policy in China and India.* New Haven, CT: Yale University Press.

Page, R. 2001: The exploration of social problems. In M. May, R. Page and E. Brunsdon (eds), *Understanding Social Problems.* Oxford: Blackwell, 16–29.

Pahl, J. 1978: *A Refuge for Battered Women.* London: HMSO.

Pahl, J. 1985: *Private Violence and Public Policy.* Basingstoke: Macmillan.

Pahl, J. 1995: Health professionals and violence against women. In P. Kingston and B. Penhale (eds), *Family Violence and the Caring Professions.* Basingstoke: Macmillan.

Palier, B., and Sykes, R. 2001: Challenges and change: issues and perspectives in the analysis of globalization and the European welfare state.

In R. Sykes, B. Palier and P. Prior (eds), *Globalization and European Welfare States*. Basingstoke: Palgrave, 1–16.

Palme, J. 2002: How is the Swedish model faring? *Current Sweden*, 440, October.

Parker, H., Measham, F., and Aldridge, J. 1995: *Drug Futures: Changing Drug Use amongst English Youth*. London: Institute for the Study of Drug Dependence.

Patten, C. 2001: The challenge of globalisation. *Toynbee Journal*, summer, 1–4.

Pearson, R. 1997: Renegotiating the reproductive bargain: gender analysis of economic transition in Cuba in the 1990s. *Development and Change*, 28, 671–705.

Perneger, T. V., Giner, F., del Rio, M., and Mino, A. 1998: Randomised trial of heroin maintenance programme for addicts who fail in conventional drug treatments. *British Medical Journal*, 317, 13–17.

Pierson, C. 1996: *The Modern State*. London: Routledge.

Pierson, C. 2001: *Hard Choices: Social Democracy in the 21st Century*. Cambridge: Polity.

Pizzey, E. 1974: *Scream Quietly or the Neighbours will Hear*. Harmondsworth: Penguin.

Raikes, A. 1990: *Pregnancy, Birthing and Family Planning in Kenya: Changing Patterns of Behaviour*. Copenhagen: Centre for Development Research.

Ramsay, M., and Spiller, J. 1997: *Drug Misuse Declared in 1996: Latest Results from the British Crime Survey*. London: Home Office.

Randel, J., German, T., and Ewing D. (eds) 2000: *The Reality of Aid, 2000*. London: Earthscan.

Reinarman, C., and Levine, H. J. 1997: *Crack in America: Demon Drugs and Social Justice*. Berkeley: University of California Press.

Retallack, S. 2001: We've saved Kyoto! (Shame about the world's climate). *The Ecologist Report. Climate Change: Time to Act. The Ecologist*, 31, November.

Reuter, P. 2001: *The Limits of Supply-Side Drug Control*. Santa Monica, CA: RAND Drug Policy Research Center.

Reyneri, E. 2001: *Migrants' Involvement in Irregular Employment in the Mediterranean Countries of the European Union*. Geneva: International Labour Organization.

Rieger, E., and Liebfried, S. 1998: Welfare state limits to globalization. *Politics and Society*, 26, 363–90.

Roberts, A. 1998: More refugees, less asylum: a regime in transformation. *Journal of Refugee Studies*, 11, 375–95.

Robertson, R. 1992: *Globalization: Social Theory and Global Culture*. London: Sage.

Rodriguez, J., and Becerra, P. 1997: *Que tan serio en el problema de la violencia domestica contra la mujer? Algunos datos para la discusión*. VII Congreso Naciónal de Investigación en Salud Publica, 2–5 de Marzo.

Rothstein, B., and Steinmo, S. (eds) 2002: *Restructuring the Welfare State: Political Institutions and Policy Change.* Basingstoke: Palgrave.

Rowntree, J. 1905: *The Imperial Drug Trade.* London: Methuen.

Ruehle, O. 1970: *Illustrierte Kultur- und Sittengeschichte des Proletariats.* Frankfurt: Verlag Neue Kritik.

Ryder, P. 1996: *Funding Trends and Implications: Donors, NGOs and Emergencies.* Oxford: INTRAC.

Sales, R. 2002: The deserving and the undeserving? Refugees, asylum seekers and welfare in Britain. *Critical Social Policy,* 22, 456–78.

Schabas, W. 2001: *An Introduction to the International Criminal Court.* Cambridge: Cambridge University Press.

Scholte, J. A. 2000: *Globalization: A Critical Introduction.* London: Macmillan.

Schuster, L. 2000: A comparative analysis of the asylum policy of seven European countries. *Journal of Refugee Studies,* 13, 118–32.

Select Committee Report 1975: *Violence in Marriage.* London: HMSO.

Shen, C. 1997: *An Analysis of the Intergenerational Transmission of Marital Violence.* PhD thesis, National Chung-Hua University, Taiwan.

Shiva, V. 1998: The greening of global reach. In G. O. Thuatail, S. Dalby and P. Routledge (eds), *The Geopolitics Reader.* London: Routledge.

Sivanandan, A. 1999: Globalism and the left. *Race and Class,* 40, 5–19.

Sivanandan, A. 2001a: Refugees from globalism. *Race and Class,* 42, 3, 87–100.

Sivanandan, A. 2001b: Poverty is the new black. *Race and Class,* 43, 2, 1–5.

Sklair, L. 1995: *Sociology of the Global System,* 2nd edn, Hemel Hempstead: Harvester-Wheatsheaf.

Spicker, P. 2001: Cross-national comparisons of poverty: reconsidering methods. *International Journal of Social Welfare,* 10, 153–63.

Stark, E., and Flitcraft, A. 1996: *Women at Risk: Domestic Violence and Women's Health.* London: Sage.

Statewatch 2002: *EU Presidency Conclusion at the Seville European Council 21/22 June.* <http://www.statewatch.org/news/2002/june/14seville.htm>.

Straus, M., and Gelles, R. 1986: Societal change and change in family violence from 1975 to 1985 as revealed by two national surveys. *Journal of Marriage and the Family,* 48, 465–79.

Straus, M., Steinmetz, S., and Gelles, R. 1980: *Behind Closed Doors: Violence in the American Family.* Garden City, NY: Anchor Press.

Stewart, F., and Berry, A. 1999: Globalization, liberalization and inequality. In A. Hurrel and N. Woods (eds), *Inequality, Globalization and World Politics.* Oxford: Oxford University Press.

Stiglitz, J. 2002: *Globalisation and its Discontents.* London: Allen Lane.

Süssmuth, R. 2001: *Zuwanderung gestalten, Integration fördern: Bericht der unabhängigen Kommission 'Zuwanderung'.* Berlin: Bundsesminister des Innern.

Sykes, R., Palier, B., and Prior, P. (eds) 2001: *Globalization and European Welfare States.* Basingstoke: Palgrave.

Taylor-Gooby, P. (ed.) 2001: *Welfare States Under Pressure*. London: Sage.

Timonen, V. 2001: Earning welfare citizenship: welfare state reform in Finland and Sweden. In P. Taylor-Gooby (ed.), *Welfare States Under Pressure*. London: Sage, 29–51.

Tomlinson, J. 1999: *Globalization and Culture*. Cambridge: Polity.

Torres, R. 2001: *Towards a Socially Sustainable World Economy*. Geneva: ILO.

Townsend, P. 2000: Ending world poverty in the 21st century. In C. Pantazis and D. Gordon (eds), *Tackling Inequalities*. Bristol: Policy.

Townsend, P. 2002: Human rights, transnational corporations and the World Bank. In P. Townsend and D. Gordon (eds), *World Poverty*. Bristol: Policy Press, 351–76.

Townsend, P., and Gordon, D. 2002a: Conclusion: constructing an anti-poverty strategy. In P. Townsend and D. Gordon (eds), *World Poverty*. Bristol: Policy Press, 413–31.

Townsend, P., and Gordon, D. 2002b: Manifesto: international action to defeat poverty. In P. Townsend and D. Gordon (eds), *World Poverty*. Bristol: Policy Press, 433–6.

Townsend, P., and Gordon D. (eds) 2002c: *World Poverty: New Policies to Defeat an Old Enemy*. Bristol: Policy Press.

Trocki, C. A. 1999: *Opium, Empire and the Global Political Economy: A Study of the Asian Opium Trade, 1750–1950*. London: Routledge.

Turner, B. S. 2001: Risk, rights and regulation: an overview. *Health, Risk and Society*, 3, 9–19.

Twigger, R. 1999: *Inflation: The Value of the Pound 1750–1998*. London: House of Commons Library.

UNAIDS 2001: *Population Mobility and AIDS: Technical Update*. Geneva: UNAIDS.

UNAIDS 2002: *Report on the Global HIV/AIDS Epidemic*. Geneva: UNAIDS [www.unaids.org].

UNDP (United Nations Development Programme) 1997: *Human Development Report, 1997*. New York: Oxford University Press.

UNDP (United Nations Development Programme) 1998: *Overcoming Human Poverty*. New York: UNDP.

UNDP (United Nations Development Programme) 1999: *Development Report, 1999*. New York: Oxford University Press.

UNDP (United Nations Development Programme) 2002: *Human Development Report, 2002*. Oxford: Oxford University Press.

UNHCR 1995: *The State of the World's Refugees: In Search of Solutions*. Oxford: Oxford University Press.

UNHCR 2000: *The State of the World's Refugees: Fifty Years of Humanitarian Action*. Oxford: Oxford University Press.

UNICEF 1987: *The State of the World's Children*. Oxford: Oxford University Press.

UNICEF 1999: *The State of the World's Children 1999*. New York: UNICEF.

UNICEF 2001: *The State of the World's Children 2001*. New York: UNICEF.

United Nations 1980: *Report of the World Conference of the United Nations Decade for Women: Equality, Development and Peace*. New York: United Nations Publications, E.80.IV.3.

United Nations 1985: *Report of the World Conference to Review and Appraise the Achievements of the United Nations Decade for Women*. New York: United Nations Publications, E.85.IV.10.

United Nations 1989: *Violence against Women in the Family*. New York: United Nations Publications.

United Nations 1993: *Declaration on the Elimination of Violence against Women*. New York: United Nations [gopher://gopher.undp.org/00/undocs/gad/RES/48/104].

United Nations 1995: *The World Summit for Social Development*. New York: United Nations.

United Nations 1997: *Report of the Special Rapporteur on Violence against Women*. Economic and Social Council, Commission on Human Rights, E/CN.4/1997/47.

United Nations 2000a: *Replacement Migration: Is It a Solution to Declining and Ageing Populations?* New York: United Nations Population Division.

United Nations 2000b: *Report on the mission to Cuba. E/CN.4/2000/68/Add.2*. <www.hri.ca/fortherecord2000/documentation/commission/e-cn4-2000-68-add2.htm>.

United Nations 2000c: *Verbal Note dated 8 March 2000 from the Permanent Mission of Cuba to the United Nations Office at Geneva. E/CN.4/2000/131*. <www.hri.ca/fortherecord/2000/documentation/commission/e-cn4-2000-131.htm>.

United Nations 2000d: *World Economic and Social Survey*. New York: United Nations.

United Nations 2002: *Press Release POP/844: Number of World's Migrants Reaches 175 Million Mark*. New York: United Nations Population Division.

United Nations 2003a: *Statistics Division: Indicators on Income and Economic Activity*. <http://unstats.un.org/unsd/demographic/social/inc-eco.htm>, accessed 23 April 2003.

United Nations 2003b: *A Call to End Violence against Women*. New York: United Nations; available at <www.unifen.org/campaigns/november25/>.

United Nations Information Service 1999: *Concerns over Heroin Use for Addicts Remain after Swiss Project Evaluated INCB Says*. Vienna: United Nations.

United Nations Office for Drug Control and Crime Prevention 2000: *World Drug Report 2000*. Oxford: Oxford University Press.

United Nations Security Council 2000: *Resolution 1308* (17 July).

Van der Plas, A. 1987: *Revolution and Criminal Justice: The Cuban Experiment, 1959–1983*. Dordrecht: CEDLA, Foris Publications.

Victim Support 1992: *Domestic Violence*. London: Victim Support.

Wacquant, L. 2002: From slavery to mass incarceration. *New Left Review*, 13, 41–60.

Wakeman, F. 1978: The Canton trade and the opium war. In J. Fairbank (ed.), *Cambridge History of China*, Vol. 10: *Late Ch'ing 1800–1911*. Cambridge: Cambridge University Press.

Wallach, L., and Sforza, M. 1999: *The World Trade Organization*. New York: Seven Stories Press.

Wallis, W. 2002: West Africa unites for attack on subsidies. *Financial Times*, 28–9 September, 3.

Ward, P., and Dobinson, I. 1988: Heroin: a considered response. In M. Findlay and R. Hogg (eds), *Understanding Crime and Criminal Justice*. Sydney: Law Book Co.

Waters, M. 1995: *Globalization*. London: Routledge.

Watts, C., Ndlovu, M., and Keogh, E. 1996: *The Magnitude and Health Consequences of Violence against Women in Zimbabwe*. Musasa Project Report. Harare: Kubatana-net.

Webber, F. 2001: The Human Rights Act: a weapon against racism? *Race and Class*, 43, 2, 77–94.

Weil, P. 1991: *La France et ses étrangers*. Paris: Calmann-Levy.

Weiner, M. 1995: *The Global Migration Crisis: Challenges to States and Human Rights*. New York: Harper Collins.

Weiss, L. 1998: *The Myth of the Powerless State*. Cambridge: Polity.

Westin, C. 2000: *Settlement and Integration Policies towards Immigrants and their Descendants in Sweden*. Geneva: International Labour Office.

Women's Aid 2002a: *Domestic Violence Factsheet No. 3*. <www.womensaid.org.uk/dv/dvfactsh3.htm>.

Women's Aid 2002b: *About Women's Aid*. <www.womensaid.org.uk/about/index.htm>.

World Bank 1980: *World Development Report*. New York: Oxford University Press.

World Bank 1990: *World Development Report*. New York: Oxford University Press.

World Bank 1997: *World Development Report*. New York: Oxford University Press.

World Bank 1999: *World Development Report 1999/2000*. New York: Oxford University Press.

World Bank 2000a: *World Development Report: Attacking Poverty*. New York: Oxford University Press.

World Bank 2000b: *Economic Analysis of HIV/AIDS. African Development Forum 2000 Background Paper*. Washington, DC: World Bank.

World Health Organization 1996: *Trends in Substance Use and Associated Health Problems*. Geneva: WHO.

World Health Organization 2000: *World Health Report 2000*. Geneva: WHO.

World Health Organization 2001: *Commission on Macroeconomics and Health: Investing in Health for Economic Development*. Geneva: WHO.
World Health Organization 2002a: *World Report on Violence and Health*. Geneva: WHO.
World Health Organization 2002b: *Violence against Women Information Pack*. <www.who.int/frh-whd/VAW/English/VAW_infopack.htm>.
World Health Organization 2004: *Gender-Based Violence*. Geneva: WHO; available at <www.who.int/gender/violence/en/>.
Yeates, N. 2001: *Globalisation and Social Policy*. London: Sage.
Yeates, N. 2002: The 'anti-globalisation' movement and its implications for social policy. In R. Sykes, C. Bochel and N. Ellison (eds), *Social Policy Review* 14. Bristol: Policy, 127–50.
Yu, Mei-Kuei 2002: *A Comparative Study between Taiwan and England on Women's Experiences of Domestic Violence and of Service Delivery Systems*. PhD thesis, University of Kent.
Zolberg, A. R. 2001: Introduction: beyond the crisis. In A. R. Zolberg and P. M. Benda (eds), *Global Migrants, Global Refugees: Problems and Solutions*. New York and Oxford: Berghahn, 1–16.
Zolberg, A. R., Suhrke, A., and Aguayo, S. 1989: *Escape from Violence*. Oxford and New York: Oxford University Press.

Index